Generative Studies in Spanish Syntax

Studies in Generative Grammar

The goal of this series is to publish those texts that are representative of recent advances in the theory of formal grammar. Too many studies do not reach the public they deserve because of the depth and detail that make them unsuitable for publication in article form.

We hope that the present series will make these studies available to a wider audience than has hitherto been possible.

Editors:
Jan Koster
Henk van Riemsdijk

Ivonne Bordelois/
Heles Contreras/
Karen Zagona

Generative Studies in Spanish Syntax

1986
FORIS PUBLICATIONS
Dordrecht – Holland/Riverton – U.S.A.

Published by:
Foris Publications Holland
P.O. Box 509
3300 AM Dordrecht, The Netherlands

Sole distributor for the U.S.A. and Canada:
Foris Publications U.S.A.
P.O. Box C-50
Riverton N.J. 08077
U.S.A.

CIP-data

ISBN 90 6765 141 9 (Bound)
ISBN 90 6765 142 7 (Paper)

© 1985 Foris Publications - Dordrecht

Printed in the Netherlands by ICG Printing, Dordrecht.

pß
1-8-88

To Alfredo Hurtado
who knew how to make poetry
out of friendship
and friendship
out of linguistics

Contents

Preface

The studies contained in this volume were solicited by the editors from among the community of scholars actively engaged in the study of Spanish syntax within the generative framework. Although we regret that not everybody in our list of about twenty names could submit a contribution, we are extremely pleased with the selection presented here. These are all original articles written for this volume, representing the authors' current research.

The influence of Noam Chomsky's work in these studies is evident. Without his efforts to develop a scientific, psychologically relevant theory of language, these studies and this volume would not exist. We acknowledge our indebtedness.

We also thank the editors of the Foris series Studies in Generative Grammar for the readiness with which they accepted this volume.

Finally, we are grateful to Gail Moore, Barbara Powell, and Sibyl Banton of the Arts and Sciences Word Processing Center at the University of Virginia for their invaluable help in preparing this manuscript.

Introduction

The essays that comprise this volume deal with various aspects of Spanish syntax from the perspective of Chomsky's Government-Binding Theory.

Generative grammar, since its inception, has set for itself the goal of accounting for the speaker/hearer's knowledge of language. The enterprise, then, has been conceived as that of seeking an answer to the following question: What principles or rules must be posited in order to account for the speaker/hearer's "linguistic knowledge"? Even casual consideration of the facts that can pretheoretically be included under "linguistic knowledge" reveals that the principles and/or rules in question may be fairly abstract, and that some of them could not possibly have been learned, given the poverty and degeneracy of the data available to the learner. This leads to a distinction between language-specific and universal principles.

In early formalizations of these notions (e.g. Chomsky 1957, 1965), the grammar of a particular language was construed as a system of rules, and linguistic theory (or Universal Grammar) as a two-part system: *a*) a theory of the possible form of grammars; *b*) an evaluation metric, capable of selecting the highest valued grammar for a given body of data.

This view, while consistent with the goal of accounting for the speaker/hearer's linguistic knowledge, contained an unwarranted assumption, namely, that for any language L, there was a well-defined set of sentences of L that the grammar of L should generate. Thus there was an emphasis on what Chomsky (1984) has recently termed *external language*. One of the major developments of recent years has been a change of focus from external to internal language, and a concomitant change away from systems of rules and towards systems of principles. Thus, instead of assuming phrase structure rules, subject to a great deal of variation across languages, a general X-bar schema is assumed, with variations severely limited by a few parameters like Head First / Head Last; and instead of an unlimited supply of transformations, a single rule schema *Move alpha* is assumed, whose application is regulated by independent modules such as Binding Theory and Theta Theory (see Chomsky 1981).

As a consequence of this shift of focus, Universal Grammar is no longer assumed to provide an evaluation metric for grammars, but rather to constitute the initial state in the language acquisition process, whose final (or steady) state is determined by how a small number of parameters is set.

Within this perspective, where *language* is interpreted as a particular type of knowledge, in other words, as a particular state of the mind, the notion of *external language* as a set of sentences loses all significance. In Chomsky's (1984) words, "each I(nternal)-language assigns a status to every expression, indeed every physical event. Some are sentences with a definite meaning (literal, figurative, or whatever); others are intelligible with, perhaps, a definite meaning, but are ill-formed in one or another way ("the child seems sleeping", "what do you wonder who saw?"); others are well-formed but unintelligible; others are identified as possible sentences of some languages, but not mine; others are mere noise. Different I-languages will assign status differently in each of these and other categories. The notion of E(xternal)-language has no place in this picture. There is no issue of correctness with regard to E-languages, however characterized, since E-languages are artifacts, not real things in the world as I-languages are" (p. 9).

Chomsky sees this view as related to Jespersen's (1924) "notion of structure", which is responsible for guiding the speaker in framing sentences of his/her own, in particular what Jespersen calls "free expressions".

There are also echoes of Humboldt (1971) here, with his claim that languages are not to be viewed as *ergon* (product) but as *enérgeia* (activity). This view, of course, fails to make the crucial distinction between behavior and knowledge, performance and competence in modern parlance, but it does emphasize quite correctly the fact that a language is not to be identified with a set of sentences.

Recent research along the lines suggested above has led to a highly modular view of language. The extraordinary success that this approach has had in explaining an increasing body of complex data on the basis of the interaction of relatively simple principles constitutes very strong support for it.

A final fact that deserves comment is the following: In contrast with the early stages in the development of generative grammar, which could be characterized as heavily anglocentric, the last few years have seen a broadening of the language types being studied from a generative perspective. This in turn has resulted in significant improvements in the theory. The healthy and fruitful character of this development need hardly be emphasized.

Following is a brief description of the articles contained in this volume.

Bordelois discusses parasitic gaps, and argues that they are anaphoric variables, which constitutes a departure from the typology of Chomsky's Binding Theory. Noting that the presence of Tense, an overt subject, or lack of adjacency seem to prevent the occurrence of parasitic gaps, just as they block Clitic Climbing, Bordelois argues that restructuring is a prerequisite for the occurrence of parasitic gaps.

Contreras deals with Spanish bare NPs, and argues that they contain an empty QP, which must be properly governed. He argues in favor of K(ayne)-government, which allows government across one, but no more than one, maximal projection.

Demonte studies non-subcategorized small clauses in passive structures. She argues that passive morphology expresses the external argument of the verb. This explains why agent-oriented predicates can occur in passive sentences, while theme-oriented predicates cannot. She also argues that predicates of external arguments represent the core case, while predicates of internal arguments are more restricted.

The paper by Groos and Bok-Bennema argues in favor of Spanish as a verb-initial language, with an optional category-neutral preverbal position. They argue that this approach accounts for word order in Spanish in a more principled way than Torrego's (1984) Inversion rule.

Otero deals with Spanish constructions with *se*, especially the type represented by *Se trató de muchos temas* 'ARB dealt with many topics'. He argues that the clitic in such sentences has the function of "absorbing" the plus value of [+Definite] in a finite INFL. More generally, he argues that two classes of clitic structures must be recognized, structures with an "identifier-clitic" such as *Ana la vio EC* 'Ana saw her', and structures with "absorber-clitics" such as *El buque se movió* 'The ship moved', and that the clitic in *Se trató de muchos temas* belongs to the latter class.

Picallo argues in favor of the Visibility Hypothesis proposed by Aoun (1981) and Chomsky (1981, forthcoming), which claims that all governed categories which have argument status must bear Case features or be in a Case-marked chain. Her argument is supported by data from Catalan and Spanish.

Plann examines the class of words including *encima*, *debajo*, *cerca*, and argues that they belong to the class of "substantives", i.e. they are [+N] but they are unspecified for the feature [V]. This claim is supported by a careful examination of the behavior of these words with respect to Case Theory.

Rigau discusses the difference between overt and null (and clitic) pronouns in Catalan and Spanish. Based on the fact that Catalan, but not Spanish, has PP clitics, she suggests an explanation for the different behavior of these two languages with respect to Montalbetti's (1984) Overt Pronoun Constraint.

Rivero discusses binding in NPs. She suggests that NPs have no syntactic subject position, and that the thematic frame associated with the head of an NP defines the domain of application of the Binding Theory. This leads her to a redefinition of *governing category*, based on "complete thematic domain" for NP, and "complete propositional domain" for S.

Suñer deals with the referential properties of subjects of finite embedded clauses, both indicative and subjunctive. She argues against a reformulation of the Binding Theory, suggested by Meireles and Raposo (1984), and against an account based on the Avoid Pronoun Strategy, suggested by Bouchard (1982). Instead, she suggests that the coreference possibilities of such subjects depend on lexical/semantic properties of the matrix verbs.

We hope this book will be the first of a series of volumes aimed at broadening and publicizing qualified research on Spanish along the main lines of generative theory, helping to unfold its full potential.

As we were preparing this volume for publication, news of Alfredo Hurtado's death reached us, filling us with deep consternation. Among his many gifts, Alfredo's sense of generative linguistics as a communal enterprise has been a refreshing and inspiring example for all of us and for the whole linguistic field, often marred by sterile competition. It is to him, to his very Latin style of generosity and enthusiasm, to his passionate quest for an original form of knowledge where theories would never betray the complexity, beauty and simplicity of natural languages, that we would like to dedicate this volume.

Ivonne Bordelois
Heles Contreras
Karen Zagona

Parasitic gaps: Extensions of restructuring*

Ivonne Bordelois, *Rijksuniversiteit Utrecht*

Because of their intriguing properties, parasitic gaps have motivated in recent times an increasing volume of research in the field. It is worth noticing, however, that the ongoing discussion seems to have focused more on their status as silent symbols (see Chomsky 1982, Engdahl 1983, Cinque 1984 for different views on this problem) than on the specific contextual features they may share with other symbols to be found in similar environments.

This paper will adopt the reverse strategy, aiming at a diagnosis of the inherent properties of parasitic gaps by analyzing their syntactic environment and the features they share with other gaps linked to $\overline{A}$ positions in similar contexts. In fact, Spanish offers a rich array of syntactic structures which display with remarkable clarity some of the most striking properties of parasitic gaps and the conditions required for their occurrence.

Grounded on this evidence, our central claim will be that parasitic gaps are a special type of anaphoric variables, thus departing from the usual distinction between variables and anaphors postulated in Binding Theory, as stated in Chomsky (1981). This modification will not only permit us to clarify some peculiarities concerning parasitic gaps, but will also prove necessary in order to approach some recalcitrant problems concerning Subjacency.

In order to support our claim, we will proceed as follows. After a brief review of the problem, we will examine the type of restructuring contexts needed for parasitic gaps to appear, and the impact of restructuring for Binding Theory whenever pronouns are involved. In the following section, we will cover other gaps which share relevant properties with parasitic gaps. In particular, the comparison with gaps occurring in adverbial clauses will enable us to examine the inherent properties of both categories of symbols, against the repertory of symbols that the theory makes available to us. Finally, some of the implications and consquences of this analysis for the theory of Subjacency will be pointed out. The conclusion will sum up our views, and some suggestions for further research will be briefly delineated.

1.

Chomsky's (1982) original contention is that parasitic gaps are generated as basic pronouns; this is why they may be found in positions prohibited by Subjacency. They may be interpreted as variables, however, because of the presence of an operator linking the licensing gap in S-structure. A condition necessary for this analysis to go through is that the licensing gap and the parasitic gap should not c-command each other, since according to Principle C, variables–as R-expressions–ought to be free. Contreras (1984b) showed convincingly, however, that c-command conditions hold indeed between licensing gaps and parasitic gaps, which motivated in turn a new analysis (Chomsky's lectures, Fall 1983), where parasitic gaps would be variables linked to a vacuous operator, thus forming an $\bar{A}$ chain connected with and subjacent to the $\bar{A}$ chain headed by the matrix operator.

1.1.

Without entering into the details of this analysis, we would like to concentrate now on the specific context required for parasitic gaps to occur. Spanish is transparent in this respect: only tenseless adverbial clauses exhibiting an infinitival verb admit parasitic gaps.[1]

(1)   Leí el artículo antes de que Juan lo hubiera corregido
        'I read the article before John had corrected it'
(2)   Leí el artículo antes de corregirlo
        'I read the article before correcting it'
(3)   *El artículo que leí antes de que Juan hubiera corregido
(4)   El artículo que leí antes de corregir
        'The article that I read before correcting'

Sentences (1) and (2) indicate that *antes* clauses may introduce either a subjunctive or an infinitival complement in adverbial position. But (3) and (4) show that parasitic gaps are possible only within the uninflected environment.[2]

The following examples are meant to demonstrate that tenselessness is, although necessary, not sufficient to guarantee the legal presence of parasitic gaps under its scope. Overt lexical subjects do not allow for parasitic gaps under their domain, even in tenseless contexts. This can be seen in those adverbial infinitival clauses where the subject may be expressed either by a PRO or an NP; while (5) and (6) represent this alternation, (7)-(10) illustrate the contrast whenever parasitic gaps are involved.

(5)   All llegar PRO a la casa, Juan abrió la puerta
       'On arriving PRO, John opened the door'
(6)   Al llegar Juan a la casa, abrió la puerta
       On arriving John to the house, (he) opened the door'
(7)   Todos admiramos el poema al leerlo
       'We all admired the poem when PRO reading it'
(8)   Todos admiramos el poema al leerlo el autor'
       'We all admired the poem when the author read it'
(9)   El poema que todos admiramos al leer
       'The poem that we all admired when PRO reading'
(10)   *El poema que todos admiramos al leer el autor

This is an interesting and surprising contrast, not predictable from the perspective according to which parasitic gaps are variables, since variables are in principle immune to the restrictions valid for anaphors, and only anaphors are sensitive to the presence of an accessible subject. PRO does not count here as an accessible subject, as opposed to lexical NP: this is what the contrast (9)-(10) illustrates, a difference we are going to elaborate further on in this analysis.

Another relevant contextual property hardly described in the literature concerns the fact that complements that are not strictly subcategorized by the matrix verb are not allowed between the main verb and the adverbial clause where the parasitic gap originates.[3]

(11)   Envié la carta sin firmarla
       'I sent the letter without signing it'
(12)   Envié la carta con un mensajero sin firmarla
       'I sent the letter with a messenger without signing it'
(13)   La carta que envié sin firmar
       'The letter that I sent without signing'
(14)   *La carta que envié con un mensajero sin firmar

What seems to hold here is a condition on adjacency for [V′ V] chains (where V′ is a non-maximal projection) disallowing [V″ V] sequences. Thus, if the adverbial clause is beyond the domain of strict government of the main verb (that is, beyond a maximal VP and depending on a higher predicate) the sentence becomes ungrammatical. On the other hand, strictly subcategorized complements are permitted:

(15)   El artículo que puse en el fichero sin archivar
       'The article that I put in the filing cabinet without filing'
(16)   El ejemplo que inserté en el artículo sin numerar
       'The example that I inserted in the article without numbering'

This type of adjacency appears to be unexpected under an analysis postulating parasitic gaps as variables linked to a vacuous operator, since there seems to be no natural way to state conditions involving the interdependence between the type of frame the main verb exhibits and the legitimacy of the vacuous operator in the adverbial clause. The obvious question, however, concerns the possibility of relating these data to the requirement of structural government between the matrix predicate and the adverbial clause, a requirement that would be fulfilled if their g-projections meet according to connectedness. Such, in fact, is Longobardi's (1985) proposal, modifying Kayne (1983). Lexical government from the verb will be hindered if non-strictly subcategorized complements are present, and (14) will be excluded under this proviso.

Crucially, however, government by itself does not suffice to preclude sentences like (17):

(17)   *El libro que compré después de haber persuadido a Juan de leer
         'The book that I bought after having persuaded John to read'[4]

While lexical government obtains, adjacency is interrupted by the presence of *John* in the verbal chain. Thus, it takes more than lexical government if one is to state the relevant conditions for the acceptable licensing of parasitic gaps.

This brief review of the exceptional contextual features of parasitic gaps (as long as one interprets them as variables) leads us to explore the possibility of a different alternative. To begin with, let us remember that parasitic gaps are by no means the only null categories in the grammar requiring the specific bundle of conditions we have described above. Clitic Climbing in Romance languages (excluding French, where Causative constructions exhibit an exceptional pattern) appear to respond to the same requirements, although in the case of clitics, supplementary conditions are also required.[5] The following examples illustrate this point.

Tenselessness

(18)   Quería que lo leyeras
         'I wanted you to read (subjunctive) it'
(19)   *Lo quería que leyeras
(20)   Quería leerlo
         'I wanted to PRO read it'
(21)   Lo quería leer
         'It I wanted to PRO read'

Subjectlessness

Subjectlessness is understood here as the lack of a *lexical* subject in the infinitival clause. In a verb like *dejar*, which takes both AcI (Accusativus cum Infinitivo) and controlled complements with a Dative controller (see Bordelois 1983) the alternation between a lexical and a PRO subject yields opposite results for Clitic Climbing.[6]

(22)   Dejó a Juan hablarle
        'He let John speak to him'
(23)   *Le dejó a Juan hablar
(24)   Le$_1$ (Dat.) dejó leerlo a Juan$_1$ (dative doubling)
(25)   Se$_1$ (= le) lo dejó PRO$_1$ leer a Juan$_1$
        'Him$_1$ it (he) let PRO$_1$ read to John$_1$,'

Adjacency

(26)   Quería en aquel tiempo conocerlo
        'I wanted in those times to meet him'
(27)   *Lo quería en aquel tiempo conocer
(28)   Quería conocerlo
        'I wanted to PRO meet him'
(29)   Lo quería conocer
        'Him I wanted to PRO meet'

These examples show that the fundamental symmetry in contextual features between parasitic gaps and climbing clitics cannot be dismissed as a mere coincidence. In other words, tenselessness, subjectlessness, and adjacency are shared as necessary conditions both by climbing clitics and parasitic gaps. Climbing clitics require furthermore stricter grammatical and lexical conditions, as mentioned in note 5, while parasitic gaps must be linked to a case-marked trace in the matrix sentence. The intersection appears to be substantial enough, however, to pursue our search for parallelism in this direction.

Notice that in the current literature (for instance, Aoun 1981, following a suggestion from Huybregts) clitic traces are analyzed as related to an $\bar{A}$ position while undergoing an anaphoric local relationship that is submitted to Principle A of the Binding Theory. That is, while the target is an $\bar{A}$ position, the movement and the corresponding trace are essentially an anaphoric one. The obvious suggestion is to deal with parasitic gaps as a sort of long anaphor of the same type as climbing clitics.

An important point may now be raised as an objection to this analysis. It concerns the problem of considering parasitic gaps as anaphoric when their local antecedent in the matrix sentence obviously bears an independent theta role. This implies a departure from the usual description of anaphoric chains with empty elements, where only one element may bear an independent theta role. This objection can be adequately countered if we realize that parasitic gaps are not unique in this respect: there is another conspicuous case of anaphoric chains with double theta roles. Following Aoun (1981), Bouchard (1984), Koster (1984), and Wahl (1985), among others, I am assuming here that there are compelling reasons for postulating anaphoric PRO, which contrasts with the arbitrary, ungoverned PRO requiring no direct, obligatory control. While parasitic gaps cannot be identified with PROs because of their very different distribution (parasitic gaps are found in object positions while PROs represent subject positions), they share with them the basic property of exhibiting an independent theta role with respect to their antecedent.

If parasitic gaps have anaphoric properties, the contrasts we have examined above may find a natural explanation. Let us assume, for instance, that the notion of accessible subject, crucial for the delimitation of a governing category and therefore for the legitimacy of anaphors restricted to this specific domain, is interpreted so that it refers exclusively to the lexical head of a chain coindexed under control, and not to its PRO foot. Lexical NPs in tensed environments, arbitrary PROs, and lexical NPs in infinitival complements will thus be accessible subjects, enforcing Opacity, while controlled PRO, being essentially an anaphor, will not. In a way we are saying that the subject that determines Opacity must also be an autonomous subject, an extremely natural assumption in terms of the Binding Theory. This is all the more plausible if we consider that not only main and embedded subjects are coindexed in a control chain, but also main and embedded inflection, since infinitival complements are interpreted according to the lexical properties of the subordinating verb and the conjunctions linking it to the adverbial clause. If one assumes that INFL is the head of $\bar{S}$ and that SUBJECT is an essential feature in the definition of the governing category, then it is not surprising to observe that clauses where both an autonomous inflection and a lexical independent subject (or an arbitrary PRO) fail to appear become a transparent domain for anaphoric relations. That is, there is an extension of the governing category incorporating within its scope a tenseless, subjectless clause under anaphoric control. The adjacency or relative adjacency of the verbs may be interpreted as contributing to the emergence of a complex predicate, since adverbial clauses function in fact as predicates of predicates (i.e. as secondary predicates). This complex predicate differs from the notion proposed in Rouveret and Vergnaud (1980) in that no thematic rewriting rules are involved in the present analysis. The matrix verb would act in this construction as a governing head.

While details remain to be worked out (for instance, it is clear that conditions on adjacency are far stricter for climbing clitics than for parasitic gaps), there is no doubt that the basic mechanism–transparency (tense-lessness plus subjectlessness) and the availability of a complex predicate–remains the same. These are clear symptoms that the behavior of parasitic gaps cannot be adequately captured under the label of variables without further specifications, since "normal" variables are in no way constrained by the type of conditions we have studied above. In what follows, we will refer to the notion of extended governing category as restructuring, without attaching to this term any more than a notational value.[7]

1.2

There is independent evidence indicating that restructuring is indeed at work in contexts exhibiting parasitic gaps. Thus, Engdahl (1983) observes that there are some contexts where parasitic gaps are not only possible but also obligatory:

(30)   The curtain that I tore in rolling Ø/* it up

The ungrammaticality of the pronoun is hard to motivate in the current analysis. Invoking the need for a vacuous operator heading the adverbial clause just in this context (but not in others) appears to be a dubious move, if no independent motivation is offered for such an exceptional requirement. Spanish also offers evidence in this direction. Most dialects exhibit the following alternation:

(31)   Golpeé la puerta al cerrarla
         'I slammed the door in shutting it'
(32)   La puerta que golpeé al cerrar Ø/*la
         'The door that I slammed in closing Ø/*it'
(33)   Leyó el teorema sin comprenderlo
         'He read the theorem without understanding it'
(34)   El teorema que leyó sin entender Ø/*lo
         'The theorem that he read without understanding Ø/*it'

If we accept the proposed extension of the definition of governing category, the ungrammaticality of the pronoun in the previous examples finds a natural explanation. Principle B will automatically bar the presence of such pronouns, c-commanded as they are by a trace functioning as their antecedent within the same governing category. The alternative theory will have to claim that the presence of a vacuous operator is necessary just in these cases, probably through an ad hoc stipulation. From our perspective, on the other hand, the alternation between obligatory and optional gaps can be justified on independent grounds. One should notice that the prepositions introducing adverbial clauses where parasitic gaps are obligatory are monosyllabic, thus permitting a closer proximity between the adjacent verbs. *Al* and *sin* contrast with *antes* and *después* in requiring a parasitic gap almost obligatorily, while the choice remains open in the latter case, where a pronoun may always appear:

(35)   El vestido que perdí antes de haber(lo) usado
        'The dress that I lost before having worn (it)'
(36)   El libro que arrojé después de leer(lo)
        'The book that I threw away after reading (it)'

We may assume that restructuring, which is generally optional once the basic syntactic conditions obtain, appears to become obligatory when the verbal chain is interrupted by a minimal phonological string, which means in fact that strict adjacency enforces the emergence of a complex predicate. These considerations are certainly not farfetched if one takes into account, for instance, the role that phonological conditions play in reanalysis in English, as shown in Stowell (1981): only monosyllabic verbal stems may incorporate particles through reanalysis.

Once restructuring has taken place, there is only one extended governing category, and therefore a pronoun bound to the trace of an antecedent under the same domain becomes illegal, as Principle B predicts. Principle C, on the other hand, excludes the presence of a "normal" variable in this context, if we want to maintain both Binding Theory and the existence of an extended governing category. Notice that under the alternative analysis it would certainly be implausible to postulate that vacuous operators must be present when a monosyllabic preposition heads the adverbial clause. In fact, the analysis positing a vacuous operator implies that at least a double bracketing intervenes between the main clause and the parasitic gap, and it offers no explanation for illicit overt pronouns whenever the vacuous operator fails to appear.

1.3.

In this section, evidence showing that restructuring is relevant in environments other than the one offered in parasitic gaps will be briefly explored in order to illustrate the interdependence of restructuring and Principle B. Let us examine the following sentences:

(37)   Pedro ordenó a Juan salir
(38)   Pedro ordenó salir a Juan
        'Peter ordered John to leave'
(39)   Pedro$_1$ ordenó a Juan seguirlo$_1$

(40)   *Pedro₁ ordenó seguirlo₁ a Juan
         'Peter₁ ordered John to follow him₁'

Ordenar, a verb taking dative controller, may appear in surface optionally as
V S PP or V PP S, as shown in the first sentences. Given the proverbial
syntactic freedom of the Spanish verbal system, there is nothing particularly
striking about these examples. Furthermore, there may well be a correlation
between the fact that object controllers may precede or follow the clauses
they relate to in those languages where subjects in general may precede or
follow the predicates they are linked to. What is interesting, however, is the
ungrammaticality of (40). The corresponding tree does not motivate any
expectation in this direction as long as we do not modify our assumptions
about the nature of the bracketing around the infinitival complement.

(41)

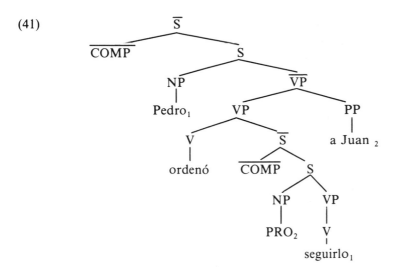

Notice that whenever *lo* is understood as referring to someone other than the
matrix subject, *Pedro*, the sentence becomes perfectly acceptable, which
means that nothing is wrong per se with structure (41). What is happening
here is that restructuring has applied, since all the conditions are present:
tenselessness, subjectlessness, and adjacency of the two verbs. It is evident
that if there is only one governing category and one accessible subject (*Pedro*),
the pronoun will be ruled out under the same grounds that exclude a sentence
like (42) under Principle B:

(42)   *John₁ loves him₁

One of the consequences of this analysis is that the status of the embedded PRO as accessible subject is severely jeopardized, as well as the protecting sentential bracketings that ought to confirm its ungoverned position. Besides confirming the reality of restructuring, this analysis converges with current views in the field concerning the anaphoric status of PRO, as mentioned above. It is only natural to verify that those domains where anaphoric relations are possible exclude pronominal relations, since anaphors and pronouns are in general in complementary distribution. The consistency of this approach is further evidence of its plausibility.

Notice, by the way, that *ordenar* does not allow for Clitic Climbing, although there may be some dialectal variation in this respect. This is exactly what we expect: Principle B is general enough to be enforced whenever restructuring is at work, while Clitic Climbing requires in addition a number of lexical conditions contingent upon specific variations.

Although space does not permit us to elaborate on this example,[8] it is perhaps interesting to point out that such phenomena are by no means restricted to Spanish. Thus, in English we have cases (brought to our attention by E. Engdahl) where restructuring rules out the presence of pronouns which ought to be legal under standard assumptions:

(43)   You promised the kid to take him to the movies
(44)   *Which kid did you promise *t* [PRO to take him to the movies?]
(45)   Which kid did you promise to take to the movies?

Again, the intriguing ungrammaticality of (44), given the naturalness of its source (43), is hard to predict if the complement of *promise* retains the rank of a governing category. If we assume that the movement of the wh-word permits the adjacency of both verbs across the trace, the obligatoriness of the parasitic gap in the embedded sentence, as shown in (45), is to be expected under restructuring. On the other hand, the trace of the variable is too close, as an antecedent, for the pronoun to be legal in (44): PRO does not count as an accessible subject, and Principle B rules out the pronoun, bound as it is in its extended governing category. Another example, quoted in the literature relating to *too* sentences, is the following:

(46)   *Senator Foghorn is too nice to like him

The strict adjacency between the matrix predicate and its complement enforces restructuring, i.e. the emergence of an extended governing category where Principle B will preclude the presence of a pronoun bound to its matrix antecedent. The sentence improves if a lexical accessible subject is inserted:

(47)   Senator Foghorn is too nice [for us to like him]

Again, these contrasts are hard to account for in case the complement of *too* is uniformly analyzed as an independent sentence, in which case we might expect (46) to be grammatical under current assumptions. The fact that it isn't lends support to our hypothesis and corroborates the relevance of restructuring beyond the domain of parasitic gaps.

2.

We should now ask whether the curious properties displayed by parasitic gaps represent an isolated phenomenon. The answer is negative. There are several instances of anaphoric gaps connected with $\overline{A}$ positions which exhibit quite striking parallelisms with parasitic gaps. This section will be devoted to the study of such silent categories.

2.1.

Adverbial clauses are, in general, islands in terms of Subjacency (see Belletti and Rizzi 1981). There seems to be, however, an interesting exception in this respect:

(46) *El libro que me fui sin haber leído
'The book that I left without having read'

The same conditions appear to hold here as the ones we have established for parasitic gaps. Thus, one may observe the following contrasts:

(49) *El libro que me fui sin que Juan hubiera leído
'The book that I left without John having read'
(50) *El libro que me fui a Inglaterra sin haber leído
'The book that I went to England without having read'

In (49) the adverbial clause exhibits both a lexical subject and an inflected verb in the subjunctive mood; in (50) adjacency fails to obtain. In neither case are the conditions for restructuring present, while in (48) the opposite is the case.[9]

The gap we are studying (which we will call from now on the adverbial gap) has been treated as a silent resumptive pronoun in Chomsky (1982). One of the reasons for considering it a pronoun and not a variable is that it appears in positions inaccessible to movement, if movement is to be regulated by Subjacency. But under the view supported in the present analysis, Subjacency loses its relevance, since the notion of extended standard category, based on restructuring, allows for direct anaphoric linking between the adverbial gap and the antecedent operator.

2.2.

Given the evident parallelism exhibited by adverbial gaps and parasitic gaps, both requiring restructured environments, we may now ask whether the hypothesis that they are anaphoric in nature will yield further positive results. This indeed appears to be the case. Thus, as noticed by Belletti (mentioned in Chomsky 1982), prepositional phrases are incompatible with adverbial gaps:

(51)   *To whom did you leave for England without speaking?

The same is true for Spanish:

(52)   *Con quién te fuiste sin hablar?
        'To whom did you leave without speaking?'

If the prepositional phrase originates in the matrix sentence, (52) of course becomes acceptable; but this is not the intended reading here. Cinque (1984) also notices that the same holds true for parasitic gaps, and this is illustrated in the following examples:

(53)   Se olvidó de la muchacha al desilusionarse de ella
        'He forgot the girl once he got disappointed in her'
(54)   *De quién se olvidó al desilusionarse?
        'Who did he forget about when he got disappointed in?'

Notice that the prepositions are homogeneous in Spanish, so that one may not claim that conditions on identity of deletion preclude (54). If *desilusionarse* is interpreted as objectless, (54) is well formed; otherwise the parasitic gap does not find an appropriate configuration. If parasitic gaps are variables and adverbial gaps resumptive pronouns, the parallelism in behavior is hard to account for; particularly in the case of parasitic gaps, one does not know why prepositional phrases ought to be ruled out as in (54), because variables cover NPs as well as PPs. On the other hand, if parasitic gaps and adverbial gaps are anaphoric, the answer is quite simple, since there are no anaphoric prepositional phrases (for instance, there are no PP traces comparable to NP traces under NP movement, an interesting exception being *en, y* in French). But if there are no anaphoric prepositional phrases, obviously anaphoric gaps, either parasitic or adverbial, will never stand for prepositional phrases. Hence the ungrammaticality of the examples we have analyzed.

As noticed in Engdahl (1983), this type of gap is compatible with questions. This is an important point, for it makes it implausible to analyze both parasitic gaps and adverbial gaps as silent resumptive pronouns, a proposal found in Cinque (1984). As is well known, resumptive pronouns are found in relative clauses, but never in questions. The following examples show how parasitic gaps and adverbial gaps co-occur with questions:

(55) Qué libros te fuiste sin pagar?
'Which books did you leave without paying?'
(56) Qué libro te llevaste sin pagar?
'Which book did you take away without paying?'

This implies that the hypothesis that parasitic gaps and adverbial gaps are instances of silent resumptive pronouns has to be discarded. Nothing in the grammar, on the other hand, precludes the compatibility of anaphors with questions, which reinforces our claim.

There is a further advantage to be derived if the anaphoric nature of parasitic gaps is accepted. In the literature (see Chomsky 1982 and Kayne 1983 for discussion) the following contrast has been noticed:

(57) *Someone who John expected would be successful though believing
is incompetent
(58) Someone who John expected would be succesful though believing to
be incompetent

The ungrammaticality of (57) might be ascribed to a violation of the ECP, since the parasitic gap fails to exhibit a proper governor: no trace of movement appears in the embedded complementizer. Such is not the case in (58), where the tenseless clause dominated by *believing* allows for deletion of sentential boundaries, thus yielding a subject in a properly governed position. The explanation is acceptable if we confine ourselves only to this type of contrast between subject positions. It becomes less plausible, though, once we realize that parasitic gaps in object position (i.e. properly governed) also result in ungrammaticality as long as their clauses exhibit an independent inflection and agreement:

(59) *El libro que me robó antes de que Juan fotocopiara
'The book that he stole from me before John might xerox'

Clearly, if parasitic gaps are anaphoric, they will always be precluded in tensed contexts, whether in subject or object positions, as long as they are linked to an antecedent beyond the clausal boundaries. While ECP may rule out (57), an independent explanation has to be provided for (59). This ignores the crucial fact that in both cases Opacity (i.e. Principle A) is the relevant factor, thus making a unified analysis impossible.

On the other hand, in an analysis where parasitic gaps and adverbial gaps are treated as variables linked to a vacuous operator, it is not altogether clear how to state the interdependence of the vacuous operator and the transparent context, nor is it feasible to provide for the adjacency conditions we have studied, except perhaps in an ad hoc way. Notice also that the distribution of vacuous operators appears to be quite restrictive. It is not obvious, for instance, what will prevent the following:

(60)   *Who_1 t_1 forced $John_2$ [O_1 [PRO_2 to kiss t_1]]

There is a natural source for this sentence, namely:

(61)   She forced John to kiss her

Since there is a licensing gap in the matrix sentence, and the antecedent has the same position as subjects in *too* sentences, which are analyzed as having vacuous operators under strong c-command, some stipulation appears to be required in order to exclude (60). Under our analysis, since anaphoric gaps require local antecedents as anaphors usually do, the rightmost trace cannot be connected with the leftmost one and the sentence is excluded.

Notice that it would be far from easy to argue that vacuous operators are restricted to adverbial clauses, since they are also supposed to be present in the complement frame of *easy* sentences. The question of restricting the overgeneration of vacuous operators is an important one, and as long as it is not clearly solved, examples like (60) will remain problematic. In a theory where vacuous operators are excluded, on the other hand, such difficulties need not be dealt with.

Let us now sum up our arguments. The anaphoric nature of parasitic gaps and adverbial gaps has been validated through the analysis of numerous examples:

They appear in tenseless contexts

They appear in subjectless contexts

They require adjacency of main and embedded verbs

They share the above-mentioned properties with climbing clitics

Whenever restructuring becomes obligatory, adjacency being maximal, they become incompatible with pronouns, as expected

They are compatible with questions, unlike resumptive pronouns

Notice that in an analysis where adverbial gaps and parasitic gaps are considered variables without qualification, it would become extremely difficult to state all these conditions separately without appealing to a remarkably unnatural listing, otherwise unmotivated. There is a fundamental property, however, that parasitic gaps and adverbial gaps undoubtedly share with variables, and which distinguishes them from pure anaphors: they must be linked to an operator, whether directly, in the case of adverbial gaps, or indirectly, via an A antecedent, in the case of parasitic gaps. Thus, from the point of view of their basic dependence, they are variables, while from the point of view of the environment they require, they are anaphors. This apparent paradox can be resolved if we consider variables as a category cutting across pronouns and anaphors, instead of being parallel to them, as the Binding Theory with its trichotomy claims. This move is by no means a radical innovation. As mentioned before, there appears to be increasing evidence in the field about the double status of PRO as anaphor or pronoun, where the two characterizations are mutually exclusive, although some common features remain to identify the symbol as such. In a sense, the claim we are making is equivalent: there are pronominal variables, subject to Subjacency, and there are anaphoric variables, subject to Opacity (i.e. Principle A of the Binding Theory). Parasitic gaps and adverbial gaps illustrate the second type, as we have shown above. But they do not exhaust the class, if we are willing to examine a new area, the one concerning wh-movement in general. Notice that our claim implies two complementary predictions: while "normal" (i.e. pronominal) variables obey Subjacency and ignore Opacity, anaphoric variables in turn obey Opacity and ignore Subjacency. In those contexts where both Subjacency and Transparency are satisfied, a minimal overlapping may occur, as for instance in the case of parasitic gaps under *promise* (cf. (44)). But in general, although the two types of variables respond to different obstacles, they both share a basic dependence on a higher operator.

Interestingly enough, the evidence we are going to examine in the next section confirms these predictions, corroborating not only the need for recognizing the anaphoric status of some variables but also the positive results this recognition may yield with respect to some puzzling problems concerning Subjacency.

3.

As a preliminary caveat, let us point out that the contrasts we are examining indicate a relative rather than an absolute difference in grammaticality between the sentences that are starred and those that are not, a difference that may vary from dialect to dialect. The relevant point, however, is that no dialect fails to make a distinction between tenseless and tensed clauses, whereby the first are felt to be definitely better: they are, systematically, more fully grammatical than the others. This will be enough for us to make our point. Let us consider the following examples:

(62)   *El libro que no sé a quién preguntaste adónde había publicado Juan
'The book that I don't know to whom you asked where John had
published'

(63)   El libro que no sé a quién preguntar dónde publicar
'The book that I don't know who to ask where to publish'

The ungrammaticality of (62) is straightforward, considering that the trace of
the object in the most embedded clause is separated from its antecedent by
two filled complementizers, thus violating the wh-island constraint as subsumed in Subjacency. Even if Spanish, like Italian (see Rizzi 1982), allows for
a parameter where one $\bar{S}$ may be bypassed by the trace of a variable, two $\bar{S}$s
represent an absolute obstacle and therefore the sentence will be generally
considered unacceptable, or at least awkward.

   Given this analysis, the grammaticality of (63) becomes enigmatic, since
clearly the sentential bracketing appears to be the same. In particular, the
inner complementizers exhibit a wh-word (representing an indirect question)
which should not allow for a bridge connecting successively the wh-trace with
the main operator. The compatibility of infinitival complements with wh-
movement across indirect questions was first noticed by Rizzi (1982) while
studying the following examples:

(64)   *Quest'uomo, che non so se ritieni che Mario conosca abbastanza
bene, ci pottrebbe essere utile
'This man, that I don't know whether you believe that Mario knows
well enough, could be very useful for us'

(65)   ?Quest'uomo, che non so se ritieni di conoscere abbastanza, ci pottrebbe essere utile
'This man, that I don't know whether you believe to know well
enough, could be very useful to us'

(66)   Mario, che non immagino perchè tu non voglia rincontrare, è una
brava persona
'Mario, that I don't know why you don't want to meet, is a nice
person'

While restructuring is possible in (66) and partially in (65) –di disallows strict
adjacency here, apparently– it has to be discarded in (64), which explains the
different status of these sentences. But Rizzi only stated the facts, indicating
that examples like (65) and (66) might lead us to the "non-trivial conclusion
that infinitival complements are not dominated by a bounding node" (p. 66).
In his opinion, however, this could not be the case if the infinitivals were

embedded under indirect questions, which would then protect the sentential boundaries. His most illustrative example is the following:

(67)   *La sola questione che non so ancora a chi chiedere quando affrontare è la più delicata
'The only question that I do not yet know who to ask when to face is the most delicate'

At this point judgments may vary. If awkward, the sentence does not seem completely unacceptable even in English, and its Spanish equivalent is certainly beyond rejection:

(68)   El único problema que aun no sé a quién preguntar cuándo afrontar es el más delicado

One thing is true beyond any doubt, and this is the fact that whenever an inflected clause intervenes, the result is definitely worse, as shown in (64).

It is interesting to notice that in English also, violations to the wh-island constraint are to be found in infinitival contexts. Thus this example from Kayne (1981a):

(69)   John I don't know when I can arrange for you to see

Notice that in approaches like Bouchard (1984) or Kayne (1981a) one might not be able to account for contrasts like:

(70)   *The woman that I don't know when he saw

(71)   The woman that I don't know when to see

It is clear that the g-projection percolating system or the chain of coindexed verbs will disallow both sentences or allow for them both, contrary to evidence. This has also been noticed by Cinque (1984).

In what follows we will proceed to a brief review of similar contrasts in Spanish, where invariably a tensed context obstructs the linking of a variable with its operator, while the infinitival complement acts as a bridge. As we have stated above, the contrast between tensed and tenseless contexts varies in sharpness across different dialects, but a systematic tendency to favor uninflected environments is always present.

3.1. Relative clauses

These are typical islands for Subjacency, since the double bracketing of an

NP dominating $\bar{S}$ ought to be a barrier for wh-traces under the classical definition of Subjacency (Chomsky 1977). However, we can find exceptions in this respect. Notice the following contrast:

(72)   *Este es un poema sobre el cual he encontrado varias cosas que Borges ha dicho
'This is a poem over which I have found several things that Borges has said'

(73)   Este es un poema sobre el cual he encontrado varias cosas que decir
This is a poem over which I have found several things to say

3.2. Complex NPs

(74)   *El premio que perdimos la esperanza de que María ganara
The prize that we lost hope for Mary to win (subjunctive)

(75)   El premio que perdimos la esperanza de ganar
The prize that we lost hope of winning

3.3. PPs

As is well known, prepositional phrases are islands in Spanish as well as in the other Romance languages. What has not been noticed yet, however, is that prepositions heading an infinitival clause become transparent, that is, they function as bridges, while they block extraction whenever they introduce an inflected clause. So while verbs which directly introduce their clausal complements, like *querer*, allow in general for extraction as they fulfill the appropriate bridge conditions, verbs which require a preposition heading their complements, like *contar con*, allow for extraction only from the uninflected complement:

(76)   El libro que quiero que termines a tiempo
'The book that I want you to finish on time'

(77)   El libro que quiero terminar a tiempo
'The book that I want to finish on time'

(78)   *El libro que contaba con que Juan terminaría a tiempo
'The book that I counted on John's finishing on time'

(79)   El libro que contaba con terminar a tiempo
'The book that I was counting on finishing on time'

Since *querer* governs its complement, the contrast subjunctive vs. infinitival is not relevant in (76)-(77). But in (78) the conditional *terminaría* precludes extraction, while in (79) the infinitival allows it.

A similar effect can be observed among the class of verbs taking object controllers, when these alternate inflected and uninflected clauses under control:

(80)   Acusaron a Juan de que había robado una manzana
         'They accused John of having stolen an apple (indicative)'

(81)   Acusaron a Juan de haber robado una manzana (infinitival)

(82)   *La manzana que acusaron a Juan de que había robado
         'The apple that they accused John of having stolen'

(83)   La manzana que acusaron a Juan de haber robado

(84)   Obligaron a Juan a que devolviera el libro
         'They obliged John to give back the book (subjunctive)'

(85)   Obligaron a Juan a devolver el libro (infinitival)

(86)   *El libro que obligaron a Juan a que devolviera
         'The book that they obliged John to give back'

(87)   El libro que obligaron a Juan a devolver

The reader may notice here that in an analysis like Kayne's (1981a) the heading prepositions could be analyzed as complementizers when they introduce infinitival clauses, thus allowing for a g-projection onto the main verb, assuring therefore percolation and a licit extraction. Similar proposals have been worked out in Rizzi (1982) and Cinque (1984). The ungrammatical sentences do not permit the reanalysis of the preposition as complementizer, since *que* is present, and the characteristic prepositional islandhood is necessarily present. This analysis is plausible, particularly if we consider that these prepositions are selected by the main verb, while this is not the case with adverbial clauses.[10] But government is not the exclusive answer to this problem in case we want to relate (80)-(87) to (62), (63), (68), (73) –i.e. the cases of extraction from embedded questions or relatives– where although the structural environments are the same in terms of complementizers, still the uninflected environments are consistently more grammatical when compared to the corresponding uninflected ones.

Since we want to reach a unified generalization which will cover all of these examples, the natural suggestion is that besides structural government, requiring percolation projections, there is also another type of government, consisting of the projection of features of the c-commanding inflection onto the embedded one and resulting in a bridge which supersedes the intervening structural obstacles which would normally be operative under Subjacency. Pronominal variables may be linked to an operator across a subject and an autonomous inflection in case no structural obstacles prevent their incorporation in a percolation projection. Anaphoric variables, on the other hand, may ignore obstacles that might enforce Subjacency as long as feature percolation obtains through coindexing of the higher and embedded inflection; they are free to be linked to a matrix operator whenever Transparency obtains, implying also, of course, the absence of a lexical subject. These are then the two major strategies for linking operators and gaps across complex contexts, and it is only natural to learn that they require different conditions in each case.

4.

Notice that the analysis we are offering here is by no means restricted to Spanish. Thus, in Pesetsky (1982) we find illustrations of what he calls the Condition on Paths, illustrated in the following examples:

(88)   *What subjects* do you know *who* to talk to *t* about *t*?

(89)   **Which sonatas* are *these violins* easy to play *t* on *t*?

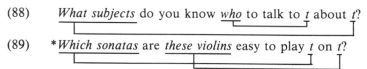

The contrast shows that crossing configurations do not allow for extraction, while embedded structures do, as seen in (88). Notice, however, that (88) appears to violate Subjacency, since extraction takes place from within an indirect question. Results are remarkably worse if the embedding pattern includes a tensed clause:

(90)   **Who* do you know *which books* John gave *t* to *t*?

What is missing here is the notion of anaphoric variables, which may violate Subjacency and may be subject furthermore to conditions excluding crossing. But an embedding pattern may yield felicitous extraction only in tenseless contexts (as noticed in Bordelois 1974), and only tenseless contexts allow for anaphoric variables.[11]

Although this analysis does not pretend to be exhaustive, the main lines have been clearly motivated. Besides the g-projections, depending on structural governors, there are f-projections, depending on the features of a higher inflection being cosuperscripted onto the embedded inflection. If INFL is the head of $\bar{S}$, it is not surprising that this type of bridge between INFL and the clause containing anaphoric variables may be blind to the presence and contents of a given complementizer along the intervening path. Thus the exceptional behavior of anaphoric variables with respect to Subjacency finds a natural explanation.[12]

5.

Notice that the idea that variables may be sensitive to Opacity is hardly original in the field. In Chomsky (1977) the Specified Subject Condition is invoked as the source of ungrammaticality for the following sentence:

(91)   *Who did he see Bill's picture of?

While Opacity was then supposed to be valid for all rules without exception, Subjacency constrained the scope of movement rules. It was in Lasnik and Freidin (1981) that this perspective was reversed and a sharp distinction drawn between anaphors (submitted to Opacity) and variables (submitted to other principles like Subjacency and Crossover). This distinction was definitely incorporated in Chomsky (1981), particularly in the Binding Theory, where anaphors and variables appear to be entirely different symbols with no common properties. Interestingly enough, the modular system proposed in LGB gave rise to a series of counterproposals that had in common the attempt to reduce some of the subsystems of the theory one to another. Thus in Aoun (1981), Bouchard (1984), Koster (1978) the proposal of a more generalized notion of Binding was explored from different angles. Our work shares the spirit of this enterprise, our central claim being that the necessary distinction between anaphoric variables and pronominal variables does in fact result in a clearer and simpler image of the theory. A further implication of our claim, one which we are not going to develop here, is that the primitive system of syntactic features is, like the phonological one, a binary structure: [± Anaphor], [± Pronoun]. Variables, as PROs, qualify along these discrete dimensions.

While many questions remain to be answered, the material we have analyzed does allow us to reach a positive conclusion. The enigmatic nature of parasitic gaps has led us to question the validity of a strict distinction between anaphors and variables, and this hypothesis has been confirmed in the context of adverbial gaps across restructured contexts.[13]

The relevance of restructuring in the emergence of an extended governing category was independently corroborated by the ungrammaticality of pronouns with local antecedents within the restructured contexts. Finally, the presence of variables that violate Subjacency in environments where Transparency obtains has confirmed the need for a principled distinction between pronominal variables and anaphoric variables.[14]

Paradoxical as this result may seem, it appears to us to be necessary, and it seems also to answer the deepest question posited by the rich, enigmatic nature of parasitic gaps. If so, we may have gone one step further in the task of deciphering what Chomsky has so persuasively named "the fascination of the silent symbols".

NOTES

*This paper represents a part of research being conducted under a grant offered by the Guggenheim Foundation in 1983. Among the many people to whom I'm grateful for comments and insight, I would like to thank in particular R. Bok-Bennema, H. Contreras, P. Coopmans, A. Groos, R. Huybregts, M. Luján, D. Lightfoot, J. Schroten, M. Suñer and J.-R. Vergnaud.
1. Gerundive adverbial clauses, on the other hand, never allow for extraction of parasitic gaps:

(i)   Corría mirando las nubes
        'She ran looking at the clouds'
(ii)   *Las nubes que corría mirando
        'The clouds that she ran looking at'

Notice that gerundive adverbial clauses are also islands for Clitic Climbing:

(iii)   *Las corría mirando
        'Them she ran after looking at'

For an analysis of Gerundives in Spanish, see Emonds (1982). In this article we will limit ourselves to parasitic gaps in adverbial clauses, exhibiting a licensing gap preceding them and being, in general, optional. As pointed out in Cinque (1984), there appear to be good reasons to consider these as a class apart from the obligatory gaps found in sentences like (iv):

(iv)   This is the man who everybody who meets likes

2. An interesting exception was pointed out to me by H. Contreras:

(i)   El libro que traje para que veas
        'The book that I brought for you to see'

In general, however, conjunctions introducing inflected clauses do not follow this pattern:

(ii)   *El libro que compré después que recomendaste
        'The book that I bought after you recommended'

Para sentences seem to depart from the normal conditions. We leave the question open at this point.
3. Predicates and manner adverbs are admitted, the same as strictly subcategorized complements, as mentioned below. An example of the first case appears in Engdahl (1983):

(i)   Which Caesar did Brutus imply was no good while ostensibly praising?

4. A similar example is mentioned in Bouchard (1982), where he observes that such constructions "do not seem to tolerate successive cyclicity" (p. 249):

(i)   *John found a book to convince Mary to read

If we assume that an anaphoric element is also present in these cases, there is a clear motivation for the ungrammaticality of (i), since the locality of the antecedent fails to obtain, the anaphoric chain being interrupted by *Mary*.

5. For an analysis on this subject, see Napoli (1981).

6. Similar facts have been studied by Quicoli (1976) for Portuguese.

7. Rather than postulating a readjustment of nodes, one may say that coindexing between the main and the embedded inflection brings about restructuring, with an inflection chain and a subject chain acting as discontinuous constituents ensuring cohesion via superscripting.

8. An interesting contrast is the following:

(i)   El artículo que Juan$_1$ acusó a Pedro de haberle$_1$ plagiado
           'The article that John$_1$ accused Peter of having plagiarized to him$_1$'
(ii)   *El artículo que Juan$_1$ acusó de haberle$_1$ plagiado a Pedro

The ungrammaticality of (ii) might be blamed on the fact that *le* is bound to *Juan* within the same extended restructuring category, while in (i) *Pedro* interrupts the required adjacency. It is worth noticing that restructuring will not bar coindexing between antecedents and pronouns in case the former are in a weak c-commanding position–as expected:

(iii)   El libro que le regalé a Juan$_1$ sin dedicarle$_1$
           'The book that I gave to John without dedicating to him'

9. As noticed by R. Bok-Bennema (p.c.), adverbial gaps appear to require stricter conditions than parasitic gaps in order to form natural complex predicates, as shown in (i):

(i)   *El documento que renunciaste antes de firmar
           'The document that you resigned before signing'

Probably, it is not a coincidence that most examples with adverbial gaps studied in the literature involve verbs of movement, which are also a natural input for constructions allowing for Clitic Climbing.

10. There is also a lexical complementarity between prepositions heading verbal complements–*a*, *de*, *en*– and prepositions heading adverbial clauses –*sin*, *después*– and such complementarity, although not always perfect (*por* may play both roles), indicates that adverbial clauses are potentially more independent, a point corroborated by their ability to prepose:

(i)   Por haber robado la fruta, lo acusaron
           'For having stolen the fruit, they accused him'
(ii)   *De haber robado la fruta, lo acusaron
           'Of having stolen the fruit they accused him'

11. Bridge conditions may play a role in the acceptability of these constructions. There is thus a contrast between (i) (pointed out to me by N. Chomsky) and (ii), where lexical and indefiniteness effects contribute to grammaticality:

(i)   *This is the man for whom I bought many presents to give
(ii)   There was one man for whom I found no presents to give

12. We are aware, in particular, of the fact that restructuring conditions appear to be stronger for parasitic gaps and adverbial gaps than for the anaphoric variables studied in this section. The crucial problem appears to be the notion of adjacency, which requires in these cases some relaxation; pending further research on this subject, I leave the question open at this point.

13. Among the questions that remain open, one of the more intriguing ones concerns what the unmarked value of variables should be in universal grammar. Since languages like Czech, as reported by J. Toman (p.c.), permit extraction only from tenseless contexts in complex sentences, one might argue that anaphoric variables are in fact the "primitive" ones. Strikingly enough, in Czech Clitic Climbing becomes obligatory when extraction from a tenseless context has taken place. An answer to this question, although necessary, would be premature at this point.

14. It is worth noticing that in Engdahl (1983) the fact that tenseless clauses are preferential contexts for parasitic gaps was observed, but no suggestion as to their possible anaphoric status was developed on such grounds.

Spanish bare NPs and the ECP*

Heles Contreras, *University of Washington at Seattle*

1. INTRODUCTION

This paper provides an account of the data in (1-3) based on the Empty Category Principle (ECP).

(1)   a.   Quiero *café*
             'I want coffee'
       b.   Falta *café*
            lacks coffee
            'Coffee is needed'
       c. *Me gusta *café*
            me pleases coffee
            'I like coffee'

(2)   a.   Quiero *tortillas*
            'I want tortillas'
       b.   Faltan *tortillas*
            lack tortillas
            'Tortillas are needed'
       c. *Me gustan *tortillas*
            me please tortillas
            'I like tortillas'

(3)   a.   No creo que haya probado *gota de vino*
            'I don't think (s)he has tasted a (single) drop of wine'
       b.   No creo que quede *gota de vino*
            'I don't think there is a (single) drop of wine left'

* I am indebted to A. Hurtado for stimulating conversations regarding the topic of this paper, and to M. Suñer and K. Zagona for helpful comments on a previous draft. Oral versions were presented in the summer of 1983 at the Universidad Autónoma de Madrid, the Universidad de Vitoria, the Sitges Colloquium on Romance Languages, and at the University of Washington Romance Languages Colloquium in April 1984. I am grateful to those audiences, whose comments were responsible for considerable improvement in the final product.

    E. Torrego in an oral presentation at the University of Washington Linguistics Colloquium, June 1984, suggested a Case-theory analysis of the material discussed here. I have not seen a written version of her proposal, so I am unable to contrast it with mine.

      c. *No creo que se acabe *gota de vino*
         'I don't think a drop of wine will be finished'[1]

It is hypothesized that the structure of the italicized phrases is $[_{NP} [_{QP} e] N']$, and that their distribution is sensitive to proper government of the empty QP. I assume Kayne's (1981a,b) notion of government, which allows a lexical category to govern across one, but no more than one, maximal projection.

    This account is superior to previous proposals in empirical coverage as well as in explanatory force. Suñer's (1982a) Naked Noun Constraint, for example, given in (4),

(4) $*[_{NP} Nu]$ V . . . unless Nu is a contrastive focus

rules out a preverbal-subject version of the *c* examples above but fails to distinguish between the *b* and the *c* examples. My proposal (Contreras 1984a) that topical subjects must be "referential" also fails to explain the difference between the *b* and the *c* examples.

    The ECP account proposed here provides evidence for a class of ergatives (in Perlmutter's (1978) and Burzio's (1981) sense) in Spanish. The facts in (1-3) suggest that *faltar* 'to lack' and *quedar* 'to remain' are ergative verbs (i.e. their subject is in object position), but *gustar* 'to like' and *acabarse* 'to finish' are not.

    The facts in (1-3) also support the analysis of Spanish as a VOS language. Suppose that Spanish were SVO, as normally assumed. Then the subject position in (5) would be governed by INFL.

(5)   El café me gusta
        the coffee me pleases
        'I like (the) coffee'

But if that position were governed, INFL would also govern, under Kayne's (1981a) assumptions, a QP inside the subject NP. Under these assumptions, (6) would be wrongly predicted to be grammatical:

(6) $*[_S [_{NP} [_{QP} e café] INFL [_{VP} me gusta]]$
        'I like coffee'

If we assume, on the other hand, that Spanish preverbal subjects are adjoined to S in S-structure, the ungrammaticality of (6) is explained since the subject is ungoverned. More about this later.

    The difference between ergative and passive verbs, illustrated in (7), is also explained under this analysis.

(7)   a.   Falta café
             'Coffee is needed'
        b. *Fue enviado café
             'Coffee was sent'

The corresponding S-structures are as in (8).

(8)   a. INFL $[_{VP}$ $[_{V'}$ falta $[_{NP}$ $[_{QP}$ $e]$ café$]^i]$ $[_{NP}$ *pro*$]^i]$
        b. INFL $[_{VP}$ $[_{V'}$ fue enviado $t_i]$ $[_{NP}$ $[_{QP}$ $e]$ café$]_i]$

An ergative subject does not move (to the postverbal subject position) at
S-structure; it receives Case by cosuperscripting with the (postverbal) subject
position (Chomsky 1981, 259ff). Consequently the empty QP in (8a) is
properly governed by the verb *falta*. A passive subject, on the other hand,
must move from object to subject position in order to receive Case. This
results in $[_{QP}$ $e]$ being ungoverned, but only under the VOS hypothesis, as
shown above. This is discussed in detail below.

   Finally, a proposal is advanced here to explain the different distribution of
topics and preverbal subjects:

(9)   a. *Café me gusta
             coffee me pleases
             'Coffee I like'
        b.   Café no creo que haya
             'Coffee I don't think there is (any)'

(9b), which contains a topic, is allowed under the assumption that topics do
not obey ECP. The question, then, is why (9a) can't be acceptable as a topic
construction. I suggest that topics must match the structure of the category
they are coindexed with (at LF'). This means that if (9a) were to be interpreted
as a topic construction, the "comment" sentence would have to be (10),
which is parallel to (1c), thus violating the ECP.

(10)   INFL $[_{VP}$ $[_{V'}$ me gusta$]$ $[_{NP}$ $[_{QP}$ $e]$ $e]]$

2. THE INTERNAL STRUCTURE OF BARE NPs

The Empty Category Principle (ECP)[2] proposed in Chomsky 1981 has been
the subject of extensive investigation in recent years.[3] Most of the discussion,
however, has centered on NP empty categories. Notable exceptions are
Kayne 1981a, Zagona 1982, and Torrego 1984, where it is shown that the
ECP is relevant to categories other than NP.

In this paper I want to provide additional evidence for the position advocated in the studies just mentioned.[4] In particular, I want to defend the hypothesis that the italicized NPs in (1-3) above contain an empty Quantifier Phrase (QP), and that the ungrammaticality of the *c* examples is due to the fact that this empty category is not properly governed.[5]

I will first provide evidence for the existence of an empty QP in the italicized NPs in (1-3). Then I will proceed to show that this empty category is properly governed in the *a* and *b* examples but not in the *c* examples. Finally, I will discuss various consequences of this analysis, as well as some outstanding problems.

There are at least two pieces of evidence in favor of the idea that the italicized NPs in (1-3) contain empty QPs. First, the interpretation of sentences like (1a) and (2a), for example, is similar to that of (11a) and (11b), respectively.

(11)　　a. Quiero algo de café
　　　　　　'I want some coffee'
　　　　b. Quiero algunas tortillas
　　　　　　'I want some tortillas'

The Spanish bare NPs cannot be interpreted generically, as is the case with English bare NPs in sentences like (12).

(12)　　Coffee is expensive

The other piece of evidence in favor of the analysis proposed is relevant only to mass nouns such as *café*.[6] Notice that there are certain verbs, like transitive *terminar* 'to finish', which are incompatible with quantified direct objects headed by mass nouns:[7]

(13)　　*Terminé mucho café
　　　　　'I finished much coffee'
　　　　　(cf.Terminé el café
　　　　　　　'I finished the coffee')

Under the empty-QP analysis of bare NPs, one would expect these verbs to be incompatible with bare objects as well, and in fact that is the case:

(14)　　*Terminé café
　　　　　'I finished coffee'

There are, then, both interpretive and syntactic reasons for supporting the presence of an empty QP in Spanish bare Noun Phrases.

3. THE DISTRIBUTION OF BARE NPs

Let us now consider the distribution of Spanish bare NPs. In (1-3) we see that they can occur as direct objects (*a* cases) and as postverbal subjects of ergative verbs (*b* cases), but not as postverbal subjects of nonergative verbs (*c* cases). The following examples show that bare NPs can also occur as objects of prepositions:

(15)   a. Quiero café con *leche*
          'I want coffee with milk'
    b. Hablamos con *amigos*
          'We talk(ed) with friends'

As for preverbal subjects, one must be careful not to confuse them with topics on the one hand, and on the other, to distinguish focused from nonfocused subjects.[8] Although the topic and focused preverbal subject positions may be filled by bare NPs, the nonfocused preverbal position may not, as shown by the following examples:

(16)   a. *Café* no creo que tengan
          'Coffee I don't think they have'   (Topic)
    b. *ESCLAVOS* construyeron las pirámides
          'SLAVES built the pyramids'[9]   (Focused preverbal subject)
    c. *Esclavos construyen pirámides
          'Slaves build pyramids'   (Nonfocused preverbal subject)

So, disregarding topics and focused arguments, and restricting our attention to nonfocused argument positions, we find the following distribution for Spanish bare NPs:

(17)   Examples

a.	Object of a verb	Yes	1a, 2a
b.	Object of a preposition	Yes	8a,b
c.	Ergative subject	Yes	1b, 2b
d.	Nonergative postverbal subject	No	1c, 2c
e.	Nonergative preverbal subject	No	16c

In order for this range of data to follow from the ECP, it must be the case that the empty QP in Spanish bare NPs is properly governed by X in the following configuration, where X = V or P,

(18) $[_{X'}$ X $[_{NP} [_{QP}$ *e*$]$ N'$]]$

on the assumption that ergative subjects occupy the same structural position as direct objects (see Burzio 1981). On the other hand, it must be the case that an empty QP contained in a nonergative subject is not properly governed. More precisely, I must establish the facts in (19) and (20).

(19) $[_{QP}\ e]$ is not internally governed in (18).
(20)   X properly governs $[_{QP}\ e]$ in (18).

(19) must be established because if $[_{QP}\ e]$ were internally governed, the difference between (17a,b,c) and (17d,e) could not follow from the ECP.
     I will now argue for (19).

4. ON THE DEFINITION OF GOVERNMENT

Consider the following definition of government, due to Aoun and Sportiche (1983) (henceforth AS-government):

(21) α governs β in the structure $[_{\gamma}\ldots\beta\ldots\alpha\ldots\beta\ldots]$ where
        (i) $\alpha = X^0$
        (ii) where δ is a maximal projection, δ dominates α if and only if δ dominates β.

Under this definition, a lexical head governs every category within its maximal projection which is not protected by another maximal projection. In particular, under this definition $[_{QP}\ e]$ in (18) is governed by the head N in its NP regardless of where that NP occurs. It is clear that this notion of government will not produce the partition sketched in (17).[10]
     Compare AS-government with the following definition suggested in Chomsky 1980 (henceforth OB-government):

(22) α is governed by β if α is c-commanded by β and no major category or major category boundary appears between α and β.

The crucial difference is the following: according to OB-government, a lexical head governs an adjacent sister but not the sister's "specifier"; according to AS-government, it governs both (in addition to nonadjacent sisters). Since OB-government offers the possibility of explaining the data in (11), it would be worthwhile examining the motivation for liberalizing the notion of government from the OB-version to the AS-version. If we can demonstrate that the liberalization is unmotivated, we will be in a better position to explain the distribution of Spanish bare NPs.
     The main argument presented in Chomsky (1981, 165) in favor of AS-go-

vernment has to do with the difference between gerunds and NPs illustrated in (23) and (24).

(23)   a. I like [$_{NP}$ PRO reading books]
       b. I like [$_{NP}$ his reading books]
(24)   a. *I like [$_{NP}$ PRO book]
       b. I like [$_{NP}$ his book]

Chomsky assumes the following structure for the NP objects in (23) and (24), respectively:

(25)   a. [$_{NP}$ NP* VP]
       b. [$_{NP}$ NP* N']

Under the AS-notion of government, the head of VP in (25a) does not govern NP*, and consequently PRO is allowed, whereas the head of N' in (25b) does govern NP*, so no PRO is allowed. This accounts for the difference in grammaticality between (23a) and (24a).

   The force of this argument is considerably diminished, however, by the fact that there is a different, better motivated way of deriving the same results.

   Consider the following rules of Case assignment from Chomsky (1981, 170):

(26)   (i) NP is nominative if governed by AGR.
        (ii) NP is objective if governed by V with the subcategorization feature: [__NP] (i.e. transitive).
       (iii) NP is oblique if governed by P.
        (iv) NP is genitive in [$_{NP}$ __ X'].
         (v) NP is inherently Case-marked as determined by properties of its

What strikes one in this set of rules is the anomaly of (26iv). In all other instances, Case is assigned by a governor. Since, at least in "configurational" languages, this seems to be the norm, one would need strong reasons to maintain that genitive Case assignment in English is different. But the conditions for genitive Case assignment can be quite naturally conceived as parallel to *of*-Insertion, as in (27).

(27)   the defeat of Germany

What is generally assumed in this case is that the preposition *of* is inserted to provide a Case-assigning governor for an NP which would otherwise not receive Case. If one thinks of *'s* as a postposition with the same function as *of*,

(26iv) can be reformulated as also involving a governor. But if this is the proper formulation of genitive Case assignment, the nonoccurrence of PRO in (24a) need not (in fact *can*not) be derived by AS-government. PRO is out in (24a) because it occurs in the environment which triggers the insertion of the postposition *'s*, which governs it. As for the occurrence of PRO in (23a), a full discussion would take us too far afield. Suffice it to say, however, that treating the complements in (23a) and (23b) as members of the same category (NP for Chomsky) seems incorrect, in view of the following differences:

a) Subcategorization:
    (i)   a.   We admired John's driving in the snow
             b. *We admired PRO driving in the snow
    (ii)   a.   We tried PRO reading the book
             b. *We tried our reading the book

b) Extractability:
(iii)   a.   Who$_i$ do you remember PRO kissing t_i?
            b. *What$_i$ did you admire John's driving t_i?

If the objects in (23) are categorically distinct, a reasonable assumption in view of (i-iii), then the insertion of an *'s* governor can be made sensitive to that difference, and thus the possible occurrence of PRO explained. See Wasow and Roeper 1972, Horn 1975, Williams 1975, and Reuland 1983 for relevant discussion.

Summing up, since there is a plausible explanation for the ungrammaticality of (24a) which does not rely on AS-government, (24a) can no longer be considered supporting evidence for this notion of government.

But there is also positive evidence that AS-government cannot be correct. Stowell (1981) has argued convincingly for analyzing small clauses as maximal projections of lexical categories. Under this analysis, the small clause in (28) has structure (29).

(28)   We consider *John proud of himself*
(29)   [$_{AP}$ [$_{NP}$ John] [$_{A'}$ proud of himself]]

Given this analysis, AS-government predicts incorrectly that the subject position of a small clause can never be filled by PRO. This is contradicted by examples like the following:

(30)   Proud of himself, John delivered a stirring speech

Small clauses are governing categories for the purposes of the Binding Theory, as indicated by the ungrammaticality of (31).

(32)   *Mary considers John proud of herself

This implies that the small clause *proud of himself* in (30) must have a subject binding the anaphor *himself*. That subject can only be PRO. (See Safir 1983 for related discussion.) All of this suggests that AS-government is not correct.

Let us now consider (20). In order for (20) to hold, it must be the case that maximal projections are not always boundaries to government, contrary to both OB- and AS-government. Kayne (1981b) has suggested a different version of government according to which a lexical category can govern across one but not two S-type boundaries.

I will consider Kayne's evidence briefly. First, let us look at government across S'. Consider the following facts:

(32)   *Je crois [Jean être intelligent]
        'I believe John to be intelligent'
(33)   Quel garçon$_i$ crois-tu [t_i être intelligent]?
        'Which boy do you believe to be intelligent?'

The standard account of the difference between (32) and its English counterpart is that *believe*, but not *croire*, is an S'-deletion verb. Thus, the former can govern the subject of the embedded clause, but not the latter. Within this theory, however, the grammaticality of (33) is unexpected.

Kayne's explanation is the following: Assume S-structures (34) and (35) for (32) and (33), respectively.

(34)   Je crois [$_{S'}$ *0* [$_S$ Jean etre intelligent]]
(35)   Quel garçon$_i$ crois-tu [$_{S'}$ t_i *0* [$_S$ t_i' être intelligent]]

If government can cross one, but not two, S-type boundaries, the difference in grammaticality follows. In (34) *crois* does not govern the subject *Jean*, which then fails to be assigned Case. In (35), however, the matrix verb governs t_i in Comp, which transmits its Case to *quel garçon*. There is then no violation of the Case Filter. The English counterpart to (34) is grammatical because the complementizer *0*, which is prepositional, can govern and assign Case in English, although not in French. From this parametric difference between English and French, Kayne derives not only the contrast between (34) and its English counterpart but also the presence versus absence of preposition stranding which distinguishes these two languages.

Kayne (1981a) has also suggested that government across one NP boundary should be allowed. His examples are quite similar to the data being discussed here. Consider the contrast in (36).

(36)   a.   Elle a trop lu [$_{NP}$ [$_{QP}$ *e*] de romans]
              she has too many read of novels
              'She has read too many novels'
        b.   *[$_{NP}$ [$_{QP}$ *e*] d'amis] son trop venus
              (of) friends have too many come
              'Too many friends have come'

This difference follows from the ECP if government is possible in the following configuration:

(37) X^0 [$_{NP}$ [$_{QP}$ *e*] N']

We can now define government in a way that accounts for both Kayne's examples and the Spanish data discussed here. I will refer to this notion of government as K(ayne)-government.

(38)   *K-government*
        A lexical category governs its sisters and the categories immediately dominated by its sisters.[11]

A welcome result of adopting this definition of government is that it solves a problem concerning small clauses. It is well known (Chomsky 1981, Stowell 1981) that the subject of a small clause can be externally governed, as shown in (39).

(39)   a.   Bill considers [$_{XP}$ Mary intelligent]
        b.   *Bill considers [$_{XP}$ PRO intelligent]

The only way to make this fact compatible with AS- and OB-government is to stipulate that XP is not a maximal projection. This is what Chomsky does in LGB (1981, 169). However, this is an anomaly within X-bar theory: a maximal projection–the small clause minus the subject–is contained within a larger projection of the same lexical category–the small clause with its subject–which is nonmaximal. This anomaly disappears if one adopts K-government. The structure for (39) can be assumed to be (40), as argued in Stowell 1981,

(40)   a.   Bill considers [$_{AP}$ [$_{NP}$ Mary] [$_{A'}$ intelligent]]
        b.   *Bill considers [$_{AP}$ [$_{NP}$ PRO] [$_{A'}$ intelligent]]

and the difference between (40a) and (40b) is then correctly predicted, since the subject of the maximal projection AP *is* K-governed.

A further argument in favor of K-government comes from facts related to the extractability of PPs from inside NPs, discussed by Cinque (1979) for Italian and by Zubizarreta (1979) for French, based on data first presented by Milner (1975). According to these authors, only "subject" PPs can be extracted out of NPs. I illustrate with Spanish data:

(41) a. La persona [$_{S'}$ de quien$_i$ [$_S$ apreciamos [$_{NP}$ la [$_{N'}$
          generosidad] [$_{PP}$ t_i]]]]   es Jorge
          the person   of whom   we-appreciate   the
          generosity   is George
          'The person whose generosity we appreciate is George'
      b. *La materia [$_{S'}$ de la que$_i$ [$_S$ conocemos [$_{NP}$ al [$_{N'}$
          The matter   of the which   we-know   to-the
          estudiante [$_{PP}$ t_i]]]]]   es la física
          student   is physics
          'The subject matter the student of which we know is physics'

It should be clear that these facts follow from K-government, given the structures shown in (41). In (41a), t_i is K-governed by the verb *apreciamos*, since its dominating PP is directly dominated by NP, which is a sister of the V dominating *apreciamos*. In (41b), on the other hand, the PP dominating t_i is more deeply embedded within its NP: it is a constituent of N'. K-government, consequently, does not allow the verb *conocemos* to govern it.

An obvious question at this point is why the N *estudiante* does not properly govern t_i in (41b). Although differences between the governing properties of N and V have been repeatedly noted in the literature, no satisfactory solution has been proposed. Kayne (1981a, 109) suggests that "V can sometimes govern across a maximal boundary of the type S, but N never can". This stipulation accounts for the well-known contrast in (42) versus (43), noted by Chomsky (1970):

(42)   John$_i$ appears t_i to be happy
(43)   *John$_i$ appearance t_i to be happy

But Kayne's stipulation does nothing to explain the ungrammaticality of (41b). What this example suggests is a strengthening of Kayne's stipulation to (44):

(44)   N is not a proper governor.

I will adopt this stipulation, noting its ad hoc character.

Notice that other attempts to distinguish between N and V in terms of government properties, although applicable to (42) and (43), fail to make the right predictions for (41b). Consider first Williams' (1982) account of the difference between (42) and (43). He relies on two principles, given here as (45) and (46).

(45) NP_i/NP_i
       No NP may be coindexed with an NP it contains.
(46)   *Strict Opacity Condition (SOC)*
       X cannot be free in Y, for any Y.

The term *free* in (46) is defined as follows:

(47)   X is free in Y if X is neither coindexed with a c-commanding NP in Y
       nor coindexed with Y itself.

Williams assumes three kinds of coindexing:

(48)   a. A phrase is coindexed with all its heads.
       b. Subjects and predicates are coindexed.
       c. Traces are coindexed with antecedents.

Given these assumptions, an NP like (49) is ill-formed:

(49) $[_{NPk}$ John$_i$'s $[_{N'}$ appearance $[_S$ t_i to be happy]]]

If $k \neq i$, t_i violates the SOC; if $k = i$, (49) violates the NP_i/NP_i principle. On the other hand, (50) is well-formed:

(50) $[_S$ John$_i$ $[_{VP}$ appears $[_S$ t_i to be happy]]]

By (48b), VP is assigned the same index as *John*; consequently t_i is not free in VP, and since t_i is not contained in an NP, there is no violation of NP_i/NP_i.

As Higginbotham (1983) points out, Williams' proposal works only by collapsing three different kinds of relation: the head/phrase relation, the subject/predicate relation, and the antecedent/trace relation. In the absence of independent arguments for using the same notation for these three different relations, Williams' account must be viewed with suspicion. Besides, nothing in Williams' account explains the contrast between (41a) and (41b), so even if his account were correct, a separate stipulation like (44) would be needed.

Higginbotham's (1983) account of (42) and (43) does not extend to (41) either. He explains the ungrammaticality of (43) as a violation of the Theta Criterion, on the assumption that the "subject of NP" position is a theta position. Thus, the chain [*John$_i$*, t_i] receives Case twice, once by the VP *to be happy* and once by the N *appearance*. Since neither example in (41) involves movement into a theta position, Higginbotham's account says nothing about these cases. I conclude, then, that stipulation (44) must be maintained, until it can be shown to derive from some more general principle.

I will now counter a possible objection to K-government. It has been proposed (Chomsky 1981, 168) that Ross's Left Branch Condition (Ross 1967) can be subsumed under the ECP. Under this proposal, (51) is ungrammatical because the trace of *whose* is not properly governed.

(52)   *Whose$_i$ did you read [$_{NP}$ t_i books]?

Clearly, if one adopts K-government this explanation must be given up, since t_i is K-governed by *read*. But in fact, given Chomsky's (1981) assumptions regarding government and the level of application of ECP, the LBC is not subsumed under ECP. First recall that Chomsky adopts AS-government (in fact a somewhat more liberal version which allows an X^0 to govern phrases which are adjoined to its maximal projection). Under AS-government, t_i is lexically governed by *book*. Now although Chomsky (1981, 168) states informally that t_i is governed *but not properly governed* (emphasis mine), this does not follow from his definition of proper government, which includes lexical government and local coindexing (Chomsky 1981, 168). Under this definition of proper government, any category which is lexically governed is automatically properly governed.

Suppose, then, that we give up AS-government in favor of OB-government. Now t_i is not properly governed in (51). However, now there is a conflict with Chomsky's (1981, 233ff) assumption that the ECP applies at LF. One would expect, for example, that no quantified NP could occur in the position occupied by t_i in (51). But this is surely false, as shown by (52).

(52)   John read [$_{NP}$ everybody's books]

If the ill-formedness of (51) is due to the ECP, and the ECP applies at LF, (52) should also be ungrammatical, since the trace left by *everybody* after the application of Quantifier Raising would not be properly governed. (This is also pointed out in Huang 1982, 499.)

I have argued elsewhere (Contreras 1983) that the ECP applies only at S-structure. If this is correct, it would be possible to acount for the ungrammaticality of (51) in terms of the ECP, but only by giving up K-government in favor of OB-government. Since I have shown that K-government is independently supported, there must be a different explanation for the ungrammaticality of (51). I do not know what the explanation is, but there are independent reasons to believe that it is not the ECP. Thus, French and Spanish allow structures somewhat similar to (51):

(53)   Combien$_i$ est-ce qu'elle a [$_{NP}$ t_i d'argent]?
how much is it that she has of money
'How much money does she have?'   (from Kayne 1981a, 97)

(54)   ¿Cuánto$_i$ quieres [$_{NP}$ t_i de café]?
how much   you want   of coffee
'How much coffee do you want?'[12]

Given these facts, it seems unlikely that the LBC can be subsumed under the ECP, and cases like (51) cannot be taken as counterexamples to K-government.[13]

5. SPANISH AS A VOS LANGUAGE

It has been argued (Zagona 1982, among others) that Spanish is a VOS language. The facts discussed in this paper provide further support for that position.

Suppose Spanish is SVO, as commonly assumed. Then we have structures like (6), repeated here:

(6)   *[$_S$ [$_{NP}$ [$_{QP}$ e] café] INFL [$_{VP}$ me gusta]]
'I like coffee'

INFL governs NP, and it K-governs the empty QP. The structure is then incorrectly predicted to be grammatical.

If we assume, on the other hand, that Spanish is VOS, (6) must be replaced by S-structure (55), with *café* adjoined to S, as argued in Contreras 1982.

(55)   [$_S$ [$_{NPi}$ [$_{QP}$ e] [$_{N'}$ café]] [$_S$ INFL [$_{VP}$ [$_{V'}$ me gusta] [$_{NP}$ t_i]]]]

QP is now ungoverned, and the structure is correctly ruled out by the ECP.[14]

Under the VOS hypothesis, there is no rule of V-Fronting in Spanish, contrary to the claim in Schwartz (1975), most recently argued for by Torrego (1984). Consider the effects of V-Fronting in a structure like (56).

(56)   [$_{S'}$ [$_S$ [$_{NP}$ e café] [$_{VP}$ [$_V$ se acabó] [$_{PP}$ cuándo]]]]]
coffee   finished   when

According to Torrego (1984), (56) would become (57) at S-structure.

(57)   [$_{S'}$ [$_{PP}$ cuándo$_i$] [$_S$ [$_V$ se acabó]$_j$ [$_S$ [$_{NP}$ e café] [$_{VP}$ t_j t_i]]]]
'When was the coffee finished?'

In this structure the preposed V governs the subject, and by our assumptions, it should K-govern *e*. This structure should, consequently, be grammatical, but it is not. So either K-government or V-Fronting is wrong. Before arguing for the latter, let me show how the ungrammaticality of (56-57) is predicted under the VOS hypothesis.

Disregarding INFL, the D-structure is (58), and the S-structure is (59).

(58) $[_S [_{VP} [_{VP} [_{V'} [_V$ se acabó$]]$ $[_{NP}$ *e* café$]]$ $[_{PP}$ cuándo$]]]^{15}$

(59) $[_S [_{PP}$ cuandó$]_i$ $[_S [_{VP} [_{VP} [_{V'} [_V$ se acabó$]]$ $[_{NP}$ *e* café$]]$ $[_{PP}$ $t_i]]]]^{16}$

Crucially, the structural relationship between the V and the postverbal subject is not altered by Wh-Movement. We then predict correctly that *¿Cuándo se acabó café?* 'When was coffee finished?' is ungrammatical for the same reason that *Se acabó café* 'Coffee was finished' is ungrammatical: namely, they both violate the ECP.

Let me now argue against V-Fronting in Spanish. This rule, according to Torrego (1984), moves to the left of the subject some projection of V. A crucial assumption of her analysis is that the trace of V is not a proper governor. Given this assumption, the ungrammaticality of (60)

(60)   *¿Cuánto no sabes quién pesa?
       'How much don't you know who weighs?'

is accounted for as follows: Wh-Fronting of the embedded subject *quién* 'who' triggers V-Fronting of *pesa* 'weighs'. Since the trace of *pesa*, by assumption, is not a proper governor, the trace of *cuánto* 'how much' is not properly governed, and the ECP is violated.

There are both empirical and theoretical problems with this approach. I have already shown how this account conflicts with the facts concerning the distribution of bare NPs under the assumptions defended here. Another empirical problem (pointed out in Contreras 1984) is the following. Consider structure (61).

(61)   *¿Cuánto no sabes quién está ganando?
       'How much don't you know who is earning?'

This is just as ungrammatical as (60). However, by Torrego's (1984) account it should have a perfectly well-formed S-structure. Under the option of applying V-Fronting only to *está* 'is', which is explicitly allowed in her treatment since *estar* is considered a main verb, the remaining verb *ganando* 'earning' should serve as a proper governor for the trace of *cuánto* 'how much'. Thus the ungrammaticality of (61) is unexplained under Torrego's approach.

On the theoretical side, the rule of V-Fronting presents the following problems. First, notice that this rule is unusual in that it allows a head constituent to move, leaving its complements and specifiers behind. Under X-bar theory, we expect other lexical categories to behave in the same way, but apparently they do not. This asymmetry is thus unaccounted for.

Second, notice that the formalization of this rule would require a much richer structural description than is currently assumed for movement rules. This rule cannot simply be subsumed under Move α, which is optional and has no structural description. Instead, it must apply obligatorily when a subcategorized [+wh] phrase has been preposed, as shown in (62), but only optionally when a [–wh] has been preposed, as shown in (63).

(62)   a.   ¿Qué vende Juan?
         b.   *¿Qué Juan vende?
               'What does John sell?'
(63)   a.   los libros que Juan vende
         b.   los libros que vende Juan
               'the books that John sells'

This calls for a highly specific structural description. A theory which does not allow rules of this type is clearly more constrained than one that does, and it must be preferred, other things being equal.

Another theoretical problem raised by V-Fronting is the fact that there is no explanation for the rule's inability to apply successive-cyclically. Rules that move categories to the left are successive-cyclic, for example, Wh-Movement and Adverb Preposing:

(64)   a.   ¿Qué$_i$ crees t_i' que vende t_i Juan?
               'What do you think that John sells?'
         b.   Ayer$_i$ creo t_i' que Juan fue a la tienda t_i
               'Yesterday I think John went to the store'

However, this is not the case with V-Fronting:

(65)   a.   ¿Qué$_i$ vende$_j$ Juan t_j t_i?
               'What does John sell?'
         b.   *¿Qué$_i$ vende$_j$ crees [t_i' t_j' Juan t_j t_i]?
               'What do you think John sells?'

There is no obvious explanation for the ungrammaticality of (65) within a theory with V-Fronting.

Considering these facts, I am inclined to believe that V-Fronting does not exist. If this is correct, there is no problem explaining the ungrammaticality of (57).

6. ERGATIVES AND PASSIVES

The distribution of bare NPs is helpful in deciding what the appropriate S-structures for passives and ergatives are.

Within the VOS hypothesis, the Passive subcase of NP-Movement must be interpreted as in (66).

(66)

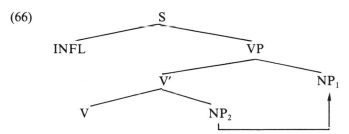

Given K-government, as we have seen, INFL governs NP_1, so our account of Passive is equivalent to the standard approach as far as Case assignment goes: the derived subject is assigned nominative Case by a governing INFL. Recall, however, that constituents of NP_1 are not K-governed by INFL or by any other category in configuration (66). The prediction, then, is that passives with postverbal subjects will not allow these subjects to be bare NPs. This is correct, as shown by (67).

(67)   a. *Fue comprado café
          'Coffee was bought'
    b. Fue comprado el café
          'The coffee was bought'
    c. *Fueron examinados estudiantes
          'Students were examined'
    d. Fueron examinados los estudiantes
          'The students were examined'

Passives thus contrast with ergatives, since the latter do allow bare NPs in postverbal subject position. We can account for this by assuming that ergative subjects undergo no movement. They originate in object position, as proposed by Burzio (1981), and they get Case by being cosuperscripted with the subject position. Thus, the S-structure for (1b) is (68).

(68)

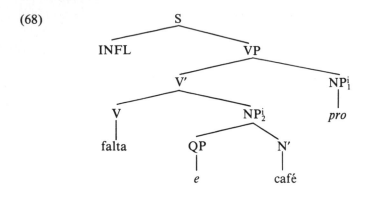

7. BARE NPs AS SUBJECTS OF SMALL CLAUSES

It is well known that the subject of a small clause can be externally governed, as indicated in (69).

(69)   a. We consider [$_{AP}$ John intelligent]
        b. John$_i$ is considered [$_{AP}$ t_i intelligent]

Positing final subjects for Spanish should not alter this fact, since government does not require adjacency. Thus in (70) we find the same relation as in (69).

(70)   a. Consideramos [$_{AP}$ inteligente [a Juan]]
        b. Juan$_i$ es considerado [$_{AP}$ inteligente t_i]

As for Case assignment, there is no problem either, since the adjacency requirements for Case assignment in Spanish are laxer than those in English (see Stowell 1981 and Zagona 1982 for discussion).
    The question that arises now is whether bare NPs can occur as subjects of small clauses. The following examples indicate that they cannot:

(71)   a. *Consideramos [$_{AP}$ caro café]
                'We consider coffee expensive'
        b. *Consideramos [$_{AP}$ inteligentes (a) estudiantes]
                'We consider students intelligent'[17]

This is precisely what we predict under K-government. Consider the S-structure of (71a):

(72)   Consideramos [$_{AP}$ [$_{A'}$ caro] [$_{NP}$ [$_{QP}$ e] café]]

The NP *e café* is K-governed by the verb *consideramos*, but *e* is not. The structure thus violates the ECP, and is disallowed.[18]

8. BARE NPs AS TOPICS

I begin by distinguishing *external* from *internal* topics, illustrated in (73) and (74), respectively.

(73)   a. En cuanto a los estudiantes, Marta es mi mejor alumna
           'As for the students, Martha is my best pupil'
        b. En cuanto al desayuno, quiero café con leche
           'As for breakfast, I want coffee with milk'
(74)   a. (En cuanto a) estudiantes, no creo que vengan
           '(As for) students, I don't think they will come'
        b. (En cuanto a) café, no creo que haya
           '(As for) coffee, I don't think there is (any)'

It is reasonable to assume that there is no coindexing for external topics in the grammar, and that their interpretation depends on pragmatic considerations. For internal topics, which have open sentences as "predicates", I will assume with Chomsky (1982) that coindexing between them and the variable in the open sentence takes place at LF′ (see also Hurtado 1983). In what follows, I will restrict my attention to internal topics.

    The sentences in (74) show that bare NPs can occur in topic position. I assume, following Chomsky 1977, that topics are base-generated. This means that the D-structure for (74a) is as follows:

(75)

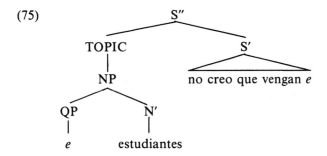

Quite clearly, $[_{QP}\ e]$ is ungoverned. This indicates that the ECP does not apply to topics, a reasonable assumption. However, bare NPs are not always acceptable in topic position, and this requires explanation. Consider (76).

(76)   a. *Estudiantes, no creo que hayan leído este libro
            'Students I don't think have read this book'
        b. *Café no creo que sea caro
            'Coffee I don't think it's expensive'

The difference between (74) and (76) is that in the former the topic is coindexed with a bare NP in a position where its $[_{QP} e]$ is governed, whereas in the latter that is not the case. How can we capture this difference formally? It will not do just to coindex the topic with an NP variable, since the variable in (74) would be indistinguishable from that in (76), as shown in (77).

(77)   a. $[_{NP} e \text{ café}]_i [_{S'} \text{ no creo que [INFL haya } e_i]]$
        b. $[_{NP} e \text{ café}]_i [_{S'} \text{ no creo que [INFL sea caro } e_i]]$

In (77a), e_i is governed by the verb *haya*, and in (77b) by INFL. There is no violation of ECP, so both structures should be good. What we need, in order to capture the difference between these two structures, is a parallelism condition holding between the topic and its coindexed variable, requiring the latter to have the same internal structure as the former. I will formulate this condition as follows:

(78)   *Parallelism Condition*
        In the structure X ... Y where X is a topic, and Y is its coindexed **variable, X and Y must have the same categorial structure.**

The intended effect of (78) is to break up e_i into an empty QP and an empty N', to match the structure of the topic in (74) and (76):

(79) $[_{NP} [_{QP} e] \text{ café}]_i \ldots . . [_{NP} [_{QP} e] e]_i$

Now the difference between (77a) and (77b) can be captured, since the rightmost $[_{QP} e]$ is properly governed only in the former.[19]

    In summary, even though the ECP does not apply to topics, the parallelism condition (78) has the effect of ruling out sentences where bare NP topics are coindexed with variables in positions which are not permissible for bare NPs.

9. BARE NPs AS PSEUDO-TOPICS

In this section, I will examine preverbal NPs which are adjoined to S, as in (80).

(80) $[_S [_{NP} \text{ los estudiantes}]_i [_S \text{ INFL } [_{VP} [_{V'} \text{ estudian}] t_i]]]$
        'The students study'

Since Spanish is assumed here to be VOS, preverbal subjects must be the result of movement. I assume this movement to be adjunction to S. These preverbal NPs, which need not be subjects, will be referred to as "pseudo-topics". The question I will address is why bare NPs cannot occur as pseudo-topics, as shown in (81).

(81)   *$[_S [_{NP} e$ café$]_i [_S$ INFL $[_{VP} [_{V'}$ es caro$] t_i]]$

Pseudo-topics, unlike topics, are the result of movement. It would be unreasonable to require syntactic movement to leave complex traces, like the ones that can be forced by condition (78). Consequently, we cannot explain the ungrammaticality of (81) by breaking t_i up into constituents, as we did in the case of real topics. But all we need to assume is that adjoined phrases, unlike topics, are subject to the ECP. Under this uncontroversial assumption, the ungrammaticality of (81) follows, since e is ungoverned.[20] This implies that sentences like the following must be interpreted as having real topics,

(82)   a. Café no queda
          'Coffee there isn't any left'
       b. Café no hay
          'Coffee there isn't any'

since as pseudo-topic constructions they would be ruled out just like (81).

10. SUMMARY

I have accounted for the distribution of bare NPs in Spanish by assuming that they contain an empty QP, and that the ECP is not restricted to empty NPs. The facts were shown to follow from K-government, which was argued to be superior to both OB- and AS-government. Our analysis of topics suggested the need for a parallelism constraint (78) to be applied as a filter at LF'. Some secondary results of these assumptions are: *a*) support for Spanish as a VOS language; *b*) elimination of the V-Fronting rule, which was argued to be empirically and theoretically inadequate; *c*) support for the existence of a class of ergative verbs in Spanish.[21]

11. PROBLEMS

There are a couple of problematic constructions which our analysis does not account for. First, as noted by traditional grammarians (see Bello 1847, #883), plural bare NPs may appear in nonergative subject position if they are conjoined:

(83)   Viejos y niños escuchaban con atención sus palabras
         'Old people and children listened attentively to his/her words'
                                                      (from Bello 1847)

This possibility does not extend to singular NPs, however:

(84)   *Café y leche son caros
         'Coffee and milk are expensive'

I have no explanation for this contrast. It should be noted, however, that
these facts do not invalidate the analysis proposed here. What they indicate is
that there is some factor, peculiar to conjoined plurals, which allows sentences like (83) to overcome an ECP violation.

   The other case that remains unexplained is that of focused NPs in nonergative position:

(85)   a. La cosecha la destruyeron LANGOSTAS
            'The crop was destroyed by GRASSHOPPERS'
                                                 (from Suñer 1982a, 213)
         b. LANGOSTAS destruyeron las cosechas
            'GRASSHOPPERS destroyed the crop'

Notice again that this possibility does not extend to singular NPs:

(86)   a. *Esas manchas las produce *CAFE*
            'Those stains are caused by COFFEE'
         b. *CAFE produce esas manchas
            'COFFEE causes those stains'

In fact, not even every plural bare NP is acceptable in these contexts:

(87)   a. ?*A Juan lo arruinaron CIGARRILLOS
            'John was ruined by CIGARETTES'
         b. ?*CIGARILLOS arruinaron a Juan
            'CIGARETTES ruined John'

Given these facts, all we can conclude is that there are some additional
factors, probably very specific in nature, which play a role in allowing certain
focused NPs to occur in positions which are banned by the ECP.

NOTES

1. The examples in (3) were first discussed within a generative framework by M.L. Rivero (1970).
2. The ECP is formulated as follows (Chomsky 1981):

(i)   An empty category must be properly governed.

An element is said to be properly governed if either: a) it is lexically governed, or b) it has a "local" antecedent.
   The notion of lexical government is discussed in section 4.
3. See, among others, Chomsky 1981, 1982, Kayne 1981a, Jaeggli 1982, Aoun 1982, and references therein.
4. For the opposite view, see Chomsky 1981, 278,280 fn. 23, and Jaeggli 1982.
5. Henceforth, I will refer to these NPs as *bare NPs*, and assume that their defining property is lack of a surface determiner. The presence or absence of a complement seems to be irrelevant, as shown by the fact that (i), with a complement to N', and (ii), with a complement to N, are just as ungrammatical as (1c) and (2c).

(i)   *Me gusta café con leche
        'I like coffee with milk'
(ii)   *Me gustan estudiantes de física
        'I like students of physics'

Suñer (1982a) assumes that there is something unique about "naked Ns", that is, Ns without determiner or complement. All the examples where she assumes that a complement makes the NP acceptable, such as (ii), must be reinterpreted, however, as cases of contrastive NP. These, as discussed in section 11, have peculiar properties.

(iii)   Hombres de calidad estudian el asunto
        'Men of quality study the matter'

6. This argument was suggested by an observation made by Luis Sáinz.
7. Not all quantified phrases are unacceptable in this environment. M. Suñer points out that (i), with a universal quantifier, is grammatical.

(i)   Terminé todo el café
        'I finished all the coffee'

The restriction in question, then, seems to be that *terminar* cannot take as a direct object a mass noun preceded by a nonuniversal quantifier. Since bare mass NPs are semantically equivalent to nonuniversally quantified phrases, the grammaticality of (i) does not undermine the argument presented in the text.
8. See Suñer (1982a, ch. 4) for an extensive discussion of bare NPs which emphasizes the difference between focused and nonfocused preverbal subjects.
9. The distribution of bare mass NPs seems to be more restricted than that of bare plurals. Thus, the former cannot occur in "true" subject position (pre- or post-verbal), that is, as nonergative subjects, even when they are focused:

(i)   *CAFE me gusta
(ii)   *Me gusta CAFE
        'I like COFFEE'

I comment on this difference in section 11.

10. Chomsky (1981, 168) suggests that the determiner position is governed but not properly governed by its head. Because it is governed, PRO cannot occur there (so you do not get *Bill likes* [*PRO book*]), and because it is not properly governed, a trace cannot occur there either (*Whose$_i$ do you like* [t_i book]?). The intent is to subsume Ross's Left Branch Condition (LBC) under the ECP. However, since Chomsky (1981, 164ff) basically adopts AS-government, he in fact fails to do so. As I will show later, it seems correct not to derive the LBC from ECP.

11. Further support for K-government can be found in Hendrick's (1983) convincing demonstration that the distribution of French *en* follows from the ECP under K-government.

12. It is true that only extraction out of a partitive is allowed. Thus (i) is ungrammatical.

(i)   *¿Cuánto$_i$ quieres [$_{NP}$ t_i café]?
       how much you want coffee
       'How much coffee do you want?'

I have no explanation for this fact.

13. Huang (1982a, 509) offers the following explanation for LBC cases like (51). Assuming Chomsky's (1981) proposal that a theta role can only be assigned to a chain which is either Case-marked or headed by PRO, t_i in (51) cannot receive a theta role. (51) is thus ruled out by Thematic Theory. In order for this account to go through, genitive Case assignment cannot be as in (27iv), but the genitive Case assigner must be *'s*, as suggested here. Huang's account, however, does not extend to LBC cases involving the extraction of a QP, as in (i),

(i)   *How many$_i$ did you read [t_i books]?

since the trace of the QP *how many* need not be assigned a theta role.

14. NP$_i$ is also ungoverned, but its trace is K-governed by INFL, which assigns Nominative Case to it. This Case is inherited by NP$_i$ in the manner normally assumed (Chomsky 1981) for movement to A-bar positions.

15. It is not crucial for the argument whether *cuándo* 'when' is adjoined to V' or to VP in D-structure.

16. See Contreras (1982) for arguments that [+wh]-movement in Spanish is adjunction to S. See Baltin (1982) for related discussion. The argument here goes through, however, whether we take this view of [+wh]-movement or the more widely accepted one that it is movement/adjunction to COMP.

17. The grammaticality of (i) below suggests that perception verbs either do not take small clauses or are also subcategorized for the frame [___ NP PP].

(i)   Vi café en la cocina
       'I saw coffee in the kitchen'

For discussion of perception verbs, see Akmajian (1977), Gee (1977), Suñer (1982b), and Zagona (1982).

18. M. Suñer points out that (i) is also ungrammatical.

(i)   *Ahora consideraremos [$_{NP}$ *e* café]
       'Now we will consider coffee'

This indicates that *considerar* 'consider', like *terminar* 'finish' (see (13) and (14) above), is incompatible with a nonuniversally quantified object. This, however, is unrelated to the ungrammaticality of (71), since in this case, *considerar* subcategorizes for an AP, and has no access to the subject of that NP as far as K-government is concerned.

19. As stated above, I am following Chomsky 1982 and Hurtado 1983 in assuming that topics are coindexed with variables at LF'. This implies that condition (78) can only apply al LF', and it would seem to follow from this that the ECP must be allowed to apply at LF'. This would conflict with the position I have defended elsewhere (Contreras 1983) that the ECP is an S-structure principle. In fact, the latter position can be maintained without contradiction. If (78) is interpreted as a filter, the variable in (79) will have a complex internal structure throughout the derivation. If that is the case, (77b) is ruled out at S-structure exactly the same way as *Es caro [e café] 'Coffee is expensive' is. We are of course free to choose a variable without internal structure for (77b), in which case there is no ECP violation at S-structure. But then condition (78) is violated at LF'.

20. The NP *e café* is also ungoverned, but it inherits Case from its trace.

21. Independent arguments for ergativity in Spanish have been presented by Bordelois (1983).

Predication and passive*

Violeta Demonte, *Universidad Autónoma de Madrid*

0. INTRODUCTION

In classical analyses of clausal structures lacking inflection and the copula it has been assumed, either implicitly or explicitly, that these structures fall into two well-distinguished sets: subcategorized or argument small clauses and non-subcategorized (sometimes called adjunct) small clauses. (1) illustrates the former set, (2) shows non-subcategorized structures:

(1)   The news made [Mary happy]

(2)   a. He left the room [tired]
         b. She eats the meat [raw]

To a certain extent, subcategorized structures are the core cases for the "small clause" analysis of this type of construction (Stowell 1981, 1983, Chomsky 1981, and Contreras 1982 for Spanish) while non-subcategorized are the nucleus of the "predication" analysis (Williams 1980, 1983, Rothstein 1983).

In this paper we will try to explain some properties of the second type of structures (those illustrated in (2)) and we will refer to them indiscriminately as predicates and/or small clauses. In particular, the way adjectival predication is licensed in passive sentences will be the focus of our study.

1. SOME FORMAL PROPERTIES OF SUBJECT-ORIENTED AND OBJECT-ORIENTED PREDICATES

There are two subclasses of non-subcategorized small clauses which are well distinguished in the literature: object-oriented and subject-oriented predicates. Examples of them are shown, respectively, in (3) and (4):

* This paper was written during the author's stay as Visiting Scholar in the Department of Linguistics at MIT, and was partially supported by a grant from the Comité Conjunto Hispano-norteamericano para la Cooperación cultural y educativa. I would like to thank M. Baker, A. Belletti, N. Chomsky, H. Contreras, K. Johnson, E. Torrego, A. Varela, and K. Zagona for helpful suggestions. Errors are all my own.

(3)   a. Comió la carne cruda
        'He ate the meat raw'
        b. Goya pintó a la maja desnuda[1]
        'Goya painted the woman naked'
        c. Encontré las sardinas secas
        'I found the sardines dry'
        d. Juan pintó la casa roja
        'Juan painted the house red'
        e. Cortó la hierba corta
        'He mowed the grass short'

(4)   a. Pedro lloraba desconsolado
        'Pedro cried disconsolate'
        b. La soprano cantó el lied adormilada
        'The soprano sang the lied sleepy'
        c. María confesó ingenua que su hija la engañaba
        'Maria confessed naively that her daughter lied to her'
        d. El bote se hundió lento
        'The boat sank slowly'
        e. María volvió contenta
        'Maria returned happy'

What the category label of the non-subcategorized adjectival predicates is and where they are attached, are two aspects of the analysis of these structures which are controversial. (See Chomsky 1981 and Stowell 1983 for arguments related to the former topic, and Williams 1981 and 1983 with regard to the latter.) However, we will not enter into this controversy in any detailed fashion in this paper. Now, to set a point of departure for our analysis we will maintain, for the time being, the following three assumptions first established in Williams' (1980) analysis of predication:

(i)   Subject-oriented predicates are daughters of INFL" (= S) and they are grammatically governed.
(ii)   Object-oriented predicates are in the VP and they are thematically governed.
(iii)   The NP subject of the predication must c-command the adjective predicate.

Assumption (iii) can be easily justified by mentioning the fact that there are no small clauses or predicates of indirect objects, as (5) shows:

(5)   *Juan le regaló el libro [pp a su hermano] [contento]
        'Juan gave the book to his brother happy'

Indirect objects being PP's–as is usually assumed for English and Spanish (see Jaeggli 1982)–there is no possible c-command relation between the NP in the indirect object–the subject–and its predicate. (More evidence for this structural requirement will be provided when we consider predication in passives.)

Assumptions (i) and (ii) now follow from (iii) and thus the facts of (3) and (4) are accounted for. To avoid circularity, though, they can be independently motivated, albeit sketchily.

In brief, productivity and contiguity are two aspects of the formal structures of sentences under which both types of predicate seem to diverge.

1.1. Regarding the productivity of the two types of structures, it should be noted that the adjectival predications of (3) appear only with a restricted set of transitive verbs-approximately those listed in (3) and a few others lexically connected to them: *devorar* 'to devour', *beber* 'to drink', *vender* 'to sell', *fotografiar* 'to photograph'. These adjectival predicates, on the other hand, always refer to a state which is a phase in a process and which can be seen either as temporary or final. Predicates like those in (3a)-(3c) have been named "depictives", while the ones in (3d) and (3e) are considered "resultatives" (see Simpson 1983 and Rothstein 1983).

The contrast with subject-oriented predicates is clear in this regard. They constitute a very productive class. Almost all verbs which assign a thematic role to their subjects license an adjectival predication: (4a) is an intransitive non-ergative verb; in (4b) and (4c) there are transitive verbs taking, respectively, an NP and a sentential object; (4d) is an inchoative or anticausative construction; and (4e) is a lexically ergative verb.[2]

The descriptive generalization which seems to underlie this difference is that object-oriented predicates are in some sense selected by the main verb while subject-oriented predicates are unselected. The former are similar, in this regard, to subcategorized small clauses, as the comparison between (6) and (7) suggests. ((6) is a causative sentence whose main verb presumably s-selects a small clause; (7) is our previous (3d).)

(6)   a.   Tu sugerencia hizo [viable la solución]
            'Your suggestion made the solution viable'
       b. *Tu sugerencia hizo [elaborada la solución] (*cf.* una solución elaborada)
           'Your suggestion made the solution elaborated'

(7)   a.   Pintó la casa roja
            'She painted the house red'
       b. *Pintó la casa enorme (*cf.* una casa enorme)
           'He painted the house enormous'

1.2. A second shallow property which seems to establish a sharp distinction between the two types of predicates is what we have called "contiguity". It is illustrated by the contrasts in (8):

(8)   a.   Juan le devolvió [el perro] [muerto] a Enrique
             'Juan returned the dog dead to Enrique'
       b.   Juan le devolvió a Enrique [el perro] [muerto] y a Luis se lo
             devolvió vivo
             'Juan returned Enrique the dog dead, but he returned it to Luis
             alive'
       c.   *Juan le devolvió [el perro] a Enrique [muerto]

Actually, (8c) shows that a thematically oriented predicate appearing in an active sentence must be adjacent to its subject for the predication relation to be correctly licensed, as it is in (8a) and (8b). This contiguity requirement, however, does not need to be met when the predicate is subject oriented, as all the examples in (4) illustrate.

A principled explanation for this difference would take us too far afield of the goal of this paper, so we will put this question aside (see Demonte 1985). But the existence of the distinction is enough, for the time being, to justify the claim that subject-oriented and objected-oriented predicates attach to different nodes.

2. AGENT ORIENTED PREDICATES IN PASSIVES

2.1. The standard analysis of passive constructions in the present theory of formal syntax establishes that one of the defining properties of passive morphology is its capacity to absorb the θ-role which the verb generally assigns to its external argument. When this θ-role is also present in the *by* phrase optionally subcategorized by the passive morphology, it is assumed that a strategy of transmission of the θ-role from the verb through the preposition is at work.

This general conception has been instantiated in different ways. In recent work, Jaeggli (1984) interprets the notion of "absorption" of the θ-role in the sense that the passive suffix is in fact assigned this θ-role. Actually, as Chomsky (1984, Fall lectures) has pointed out, there appears to be interesting evidence for the claim that there are no passives with implicit or understood agents (or whatever other role the transitive verb assigns to its external argument), and that in a sentence like:

(9)   Los culpables fueron castiga*dos*
       '(The) guilty ones were punished'

The passive morpheme has to be taken as an overt argument which bears the θ-role assigned by *castigar* 'to punish' to its external argument, namely, θ-role of agent.

More explicitly, it has been shown (Jaeggli 1984, Baker and Johnson 1985) that agent-oriented adverbs, (10a), control effects, (10b), and binding configuration, (10c), can appear in certain passives licensed presumably by the agent passive morpheme:

(10) a. Los culpables fueron castigados deliberadamente
        'The guilty ones were punished deliberately'
      b. Los culpables fueron castigados para mostrar el poder de la policía
        'The guilty ones were punished to show the power of the police'
      c. No es sano ser castigado por el placer de uno mismo
        'It is not wise to be punished for one's own pleasure'

One crucial idea of Baker and Johnson's analysis is that the passive morpheme *-en* is generated under INFL, separate from the main verb, and that there it receives the θ-role of agent which the verb generally assigns outside the VP. The verb then moves up, attaches to the suffix, and assigns case to the passive morpheme. A second important point of this hypothesis is that *-en* can either be an argument or not, its argumental nature being derived from other independently motivated principles.

With this general framework in mind, let us now study how adjectival predication is realized in passive sentences.

2.2. Consider, to begin with, the following agent-oriented predicates appearing in passives in which the *by* phrase is absent and with which some arbitrary agent interpretation can be associated:

(11) a. El aria del acto III de Turandot debe ser cantada emocionado
        'The aria of act III of Turandot should be sung with emotion'
      b. Una regañina no puede ser oída contento
        'A scolding cannot be listened to happy'
      c. El Papa puede ordenar que la misa sea dicha dormido
        'The Pope could order that mass be said sleepy'

These sentences appear to contrast with similar ones in which a *by* phrase appears. As a matter of fact, what the (i) examples in (12) indicate is that predication is not possible in passives with a *by* phrase, although a predicative-like constituent formed by an adjective preceded by a modifier, the (ii) examples, in (12), is licit in this configuration:

(12)   a.   La carrera   { fue ganada / puede ser ganada }   por el corredor belga   (i) #agotado
(ii) extemadamente ago-
tado

'The race   { was / could be } won   by the Belgian racer   (extremely) exhausted'

(12)   b.   La canción   { fue cantada / debe ser cantada }   por la soprano   (i) #borracha
(ii) completamente borracha

'The song   { was / should be } sung   by the soprano   (completely) drunk'

(12)   c.   Juan no   { fue despertado / debe ser despertado }   por María   (i) *angustiada
(ii) angustiada por la noti-
cia

'Juan   { was not / should not be } awakened   by María   excited (by the news)'

(The # in the preceding examples indicates that the predication interpretation is not available although other readings are possible.)

Examples (13), parallel to those in (12), reveal that the order relation between
the NP in the *by* phrase and its hypothetical adjectival predicate differ from
the pattern of order which some adjectival predicates exhibit in Spanish. In fact,
in many cases these predicates can precede their subjects; consider, for
instance, *Juan toma caliente el café* or *Econtró completamente rota la vajilla.*

(13)   a.   La carrera fue ganada (*agotado) por el corredor belga
       b.   La canción fue cantada (*borracha) por la soprano
       c.   Juan fue despertado (*excitada) por María

The explanation for the facts in (11) follows straightforwardly if our assumption (i) is taken together with the hypothesis that the passive morpheme is an
explicit external argument bearing the θ-role of agent. (14), which carries a
slight modification of our assumption (i), is the underlying structure of
sentence (11a):

(14) $[_{INFL''} [_{NP}$ El aria...$_i] [_{INFL'} [_{INFL}$ modal -en$_j] [_{VP}$ ser cantada e$_i]$
$[_{Pred}$emocionadao$]]]$

Note, incidentally, that in (14) we generate the predicate under INFL'. This
representation (together with the assumption that the internal branching of
the INFL head does not count for the effects of c-command) seems to be
necessary if we want to use a strict definition of c-command, i.e., c-command
up to the first branching node, to characterize the relation subject-adjectival
predicate. However, up to this point there does not seem to be a principled

way of choosing between the above-mentioned possibility and that of using Aoun and Sportiche's (1983) extended definition of c-command, that allows c-command up through the maximal projection. If this second alternative is taken, our initial assumption (i) can be maintained without modification and the predicate in (14) could be generated as a daughter of INFL".

Coming back now to the core of our discussion, the same set of assumptions that explains (11) could account for the lack of predication in the (i) sentences of (12) if some qualification is made with regard to the hypothesis that -*en* can be plus or minus argumental. Suppose that -*en*, being a clitic-like element, forms a chain with another NP similarly to regular clitics which enter into doubling configurations in Spanish. If the second member of the chain is lexical, a preposition will have to be inserted for the NP to receive case in an appropriate way (Kayne's generalization; see Jaeggli 1982), similarly, again, to what happens in configurations of clitic doubling. Furthermore, if the *by* phrase is present, the clitic will transfer to it its argumental properties through the transmission of the θ-role of agent which the clitic would otherwise bear. This transmission is necessary in order to avoid a violation of the Theta Criterion. If this is the situation, what will qualify now as the subject of the predicate is the NP in the prepositional phrase and not the passive morphology. But this NP will not be able to be coindexed with the adjectival predicate, thus licensing the predication relation, for given that it is within a PP it will not c-command its potential predicate. This is the reason why the (i) sentences of (12) are ruled out.

This analysis, then, automatically classifies the heavy final constituents of the (ii) sentences of (12) as non-predication. This result, I believe, is not implausible.

Although there were no clear ways of distinguishing between predications and normal adverbials, there are some reasons in this case to think that this adjective-plus-modifier sequence could be an adverbial. Note, first, that this will be the only case, among the many contexts in which predication occurs, in which a predicate will *have to* be modified in order to be licensed. Of course predicates *may* be modified, as sentence (15), a variant of (11a), shows:

(15)   El aria del acto III de Turandot debe ser cantada muy emocionado
        'The aria of act III of Turandot should be sung with a lot of emotion'

Secondly, there appears to be a clear contrast between sentences like those in (11) and the (ii) sentences in (12) with regard to intonational breaks. Those sentences which are characterized by our analysis as instances of predication do not accept any comma break between the predication and the preceding constituent, as is usual in this type of structure:

(16)   ??El aria del acto III de Turandot debe ser cantada, emocionado

The comma intonation is not only possible but preferred in the (ii) sentences in (12).

2.3. As the alert reader will have noticed, we have built our argument for the analysis of agent oriented-predicates in passives taking into consideration only passive sentences inserted under a modal verb. (Observe the data in (11).) As a matter of fact, predication does not seem to be possible in bare passives, as the corresponding sentences of (11) appearing in (17) suggest:

(17)   a. ?El aria del acto III de Turandot fue cantada emocionado
       b. *La regañina fue oída contento
       c. *La misa fue dicha dormido

The same contrast, incidentally, is found in English, where, for instance, binding effects do not occur in bare passives with "implicit arguments" but do not appear in passives within a modal:

(18)   a. *The boat was sunk for oneself
       b. The boat shouldn't be sunk for oneself

These facts, nevertheless, should not be a problem for our analysis if we think that in certain sentences with passive morphology the speaker is computing a chain formed by a clitic and an NP position. In fact, in recent developments of generative syntax (Rizzi 1984, Fall lectures), it has been argued that *pro* with arbitrary interpretation can be licensed in non-subject contexts if it is supposed that licensing and interpretation of *pro* are independent conditions.

We could assume, then, that in the cases in (11) there is a *pro* inside the VP to which a generic (rather than simply arbitrary) interpretation is associated.[3] In other words, this *pro* will be licensed by the verb and will be identified by the passive morpheme (and presumably by other features appearing in INFL). In non-modal sentences like (17) the presence of this generic *pro* is not very plausible, because the elements in INFL do not have the required features to identify this *pro*.

Our underlying structure (14) could then be modified as in (19), where we assume that the *pro* doubled by the clitic occurs in the same position in which the *by* phrase would appear, i.e. at some level inside VP:

(19) $[_{INFL''} [_{NP}$ El aria...$_i] [_{INFL'} [_{INFL}$ modal -$en_j] [_{VP}$ ser cantada e_i $pro_j]$
       $[_{Pred}$ emocionado]]]

This formalization implies that when the passive clitic is linked to a *pro* it retains its argumental properties, thus acting as subject of the adjectival predicate, and that it only transmits or loses its capacity to act as an argument when it is linked to an element in a *by* phrase. The deep reason for this strategy is not clear to us at this moment; but observe that the same contrast seems to be found in sentences with clitic doubling where adjectival predication can be found only when the clitics are in a chain with an empty position ((20a) and (21a)), but not when they appear in a true clitic doubling configuration ((20b) and (21b)):

(20) a. La$_i$ encontré e$_i$ cansada
    'I found her tired'
  b. ??La$_i$ encontré a la mujer$_i$ cansada
    'I found the woman tired'

(21) a. Pedro la$_i$ come e$_i$ hervida
    'Pedro eats it (fem.) boiled'
  b. ??Pedro la$_i$ come a la gallina$_i$ hervida
    'Pedro eats the chicken boiled'

In summary, what we have tried to say is that in some cases (for instance, in generic type sentences) *-en* should be coindexed with some element to get its right interpretation. In sentences with indefinite reading like *Fue vendida la casa* 'The house was sold', this would not be necessary. It is precisely in the former type of sentences where predication is possible. It appears then, intuitively speaking, that adjectival predicates need a subject strong enough from a semantic point of view–much stronger, actually, than the implicit agent required by controlled PRO and agent-oriented adverbs, which sound perfectly natural in modal and non-modal contexts.

2.4. Note, finally, that contrasts like those we have observed in sentences with passive morphology do not seem to be so neat in *se*-passive or *se*-middle sentences:

(22) a. Estas canciones $\left\{ \begin{array}{l} \text{se cantan} \\ \text{pueden cantarse} \end{array} \right\}$ emocionado (en las fiestas de año nuevo)

  'These songs $\left\{ \begin{array}{l} \text{are sung} \\ \text{may be sung} \end{array} \right\}$ with emotion (at New Year's parties)'

  b. Las informaciones $\left\{ \begin{array}{l} \text{se presentan} \\ \text{deben presentarse} \end{array} \right\}$ documentado (en un lugar como éste)

  'The information $\left\{ \begin{array}{l} \text{is presented} \\ \text{should be presented} \end{array} \right\}$ with documentation (in a place like this)'

  c. En esta casa, los invitados $\left\{ \begin{array}{l} \text{se reciben} \\ \text{deben recibirse} \end{array} \right\}$ contento

  'In this house, guests $\left\{ \begin{array}{l} \text{are received} \\ \text{should be received} \end{array} \right\}$ happy'

As a matter of fact, but with some lexical idiosyncrasies which need to be explored, adjectival predicates sound quite natural in bare *se*-middle sentences and are perfect when the *se*-middle construction is under a modal verb. This difference could be related to the fact that the *se* is always argumental, for it is a true pronominal.

3. THEME-ORIENTED PREDICATES

3.1. To complete our study of predication in passives, we want to consider now how the predication relation is set when the adjectival predicate is connected to the theme argument of the passive verb, i.e. when the predicate is thematically governed.

Consider, to start with, the following minimal pair of passive sentences:

(23)   a.   Las frutas fueron comidas maduras
              'The fruits were eaten ripe'
        b. #Fueron comidas las frutas maduras
              'The raw fruits were eaten'

(The # in (23b) indicates, again, that *maduras* is not a predicate of *las frutas*, though the modifier reading is of course available.)

The question which immediately arises looking at these data is why we cannot construe a thematically oriented predicate when the subject is "inverted". And the answer to this question is not obvious, given that we find thematically oriented predicates in active sentences of similar configurations (recall sentences (3) above) and that other types of predicates are available in sentences with inverted subjects such as in *Telefoneó mi amiga angustiada* 'My friend phoned distressed'.

Two lines of explanation could be given to explain the contrast in (23). Intuitively speaking, we might think that these facts derive from some generalization related to the syntactic properties of the subject of the predication, or we can suppose that it is the predicate itself which cannot act as such in (23b). We will explore both possibilities in this section, but before entering into the lines of argumentation we want to add other data to the minimal pair in (23).

Relevant evidence which could be taken into consideration comes from other sentences with inverted subjects in which blocking of the predication relation also holds. Consider the following structures. (24) is a *se*-middle construction, (25) is a *se*-inchoative structure:

(24) a. Los coches se vendieron nuevos
           'The cars were sold new'
      b. #Se vendieron los coches nuevos[4]
           'The new cars were sold'

(25) a. El bote se balancea tranquilo
           'The boat swings quiet'
      b. #Se balancea el bote tranquilo
           'The quiet boat swings'

3.2. Let us consider now the possibility that for some reason the potential subject of the predication is not visible at the appropriate level so that the predication relation cannot be correctly established.

A property shared by sentences (23)-(25) is that in all of them the grammatical manifestation of the agent external argument is in some sense blocked. More precisely, the role of the external argument is, let us say, reconverted through two different mechanisms: "absorption" by some element of the morphology of the sentence (a concept which we have examined in the preceding section) and "deletion" (probably in the lexicon, see Zubizarreta 1983) in (25). As a consequence of such absorption or deletion, the canonical position of the external argument–the position of the grammatical subject–becomes dethematized and is left available for movement. As discovered by Burzio (1981), assignment of thematic role to the subject and assignment of case to the object are mechanisms which interact in a principled way. Actually, what happens in sentences like (23)-(25) is that objective case is not assigned to the theme argument of the main verb. Now how does the theme NP get case, if it is not through the verb which governs it? We can assume that in pro-drop languages, where by parametric option the position of the external argument can be occupied by an empty pronominal, case assignment to the theme NP can proceed in either of the following two ways: either the theme is moved to receive case in preverbal position (the canonical position of the external argument) or it remains in situ and an expletive *pro* is inserted in D-structure forming an expletive-argument chain where the first member has case and the second receives a theta-role, and where case is presumably "transferred" from the head to the terminal position of the chain to void a Case filter violation.

Suppose now, following Chomsky (forthcoming), that these expletive-argument chains–which actually involve a coindexing distinct from that involved in the Binding Theory, i.e. superscripting–have to share the properties of true chain links, and suppose also that this requirement follows from the Binding Theory, which is assumed now to be restricted (at least some part of it) to LF. This requirement, together with a principle of Full Interpretation that stipulates that every element of LF and PF must receive an appropriate interpretation, compels us to assume that the expletives should be, so to say, eliminated at LF. More explicitly, it could be said that in structures like the ones we are considering, the movement which did not take place in the syntax takes place at LF, where the argumental NP substitutes for the expletive, thus forming a true A-chain (with an argument as a head) which satisfies Principle A of the Binding Theory.

Applying this analysis to (23)-(25) we can say that the relevant difference between (a) and (b) of each pair is that in the (a) cases the NP with the theta role of the [NP, VP] is moved to the canonical position of the grammatical subject (the grammatical external argument), while in the (b) cases such movement does not take place in the syntax. A central assumption of all analyses of predication structures is that coindexing is not possible in the (b) sentences of (23)-(25) because, since the expletive-A chain has not yet been rebuilt, the potential subjects are still not visible at this level of the analysis.

Now, the first thing to say with regard to this hypothesis is that it is extremely strong and that it carries undesirable consequences for the notion of visibility: actually it implies that visibility is checked at different levels for different types of syntactic relations. It seems hardly plausible, for instance, that a constituent which is visible for control effects could not be active in the same way for predication, and control is possible in passives with inverted subjects:

(26)   Fue invitada María a [PRO dar una conferencia] y Pedro a [PRO organizar la exposición]
'Maria was invited to give a lecture and Pedro to organize the exhibition'

I do not see any independently motivated argument which could support such a claim.

On the other hand, any solution which attributes the contrasts in (23)-(25) to the interaction between case and theta assignment will need to explain why such a contrast does not appear in ergative sentences. Actually, as (27) shows, ergative constructions in Spanish do not pattern like passive, middle, and inchoative sentences; i.e. predication is possible when the subject appears inverted:

(27)   a. Volvió María cansada
'Maria returned tired'
b. Llegaron los hombres derrotados
'The men arrived defeated'

3.3. We can begin the second line of explanation suggested above by asking what the descriptive generalization is which captures the difference between ergatives, on the one hand, and passive, middle, and inchoative constructions, on the other.

If the analysis that we have proposed in the preceding section is correct, we can say that in the second type of construction (inchoative, passive, and middle sentences) there are two positions available for the attachment of the external argument, following from the lexical properties of transitive verbs tied to the properties of passive, middle, and inchoative morphology: the dethematized canonical positions of the grammatical subject, and the one under INFL in which lexical external arguments (*se* and *-en*, for instance) could appear. This situation does not hold with ergative verbs that assign just one θ-role–the θ-role of the internal argument–and that have only one position for the externalization of the internal argument–the dethematized position of the grammatical subject.

Recalling that there are only two types of adjectival predicates which can occur in the sentences of the language, i.e. grammatically oriented and thematically oriented predicates, we could assume that the following stipulation holds in the grammar of predication:

(28)   Attach predicates to external arguments if they are available

where stipulation (28) could be paraphrased by the statement that predicates tend to be subject oriented (i.e. grammatically governed) in the unmarked case.

Suppose now that the level of attachment of adjectival predicates does not follow only from the requirement of c-command between the subject and the predicate, but rather that such a requirement is a consequence of our quasi-principle (28). The last two statements taken together imply that in those structures in which a theme can appear as external argument, its predicate will probaby not be in the VP, but in a position in which it could be c-commanded without ambiguity by an external argument, i.e. outside the VP and outside INFL', which is the domain of the other external argument. If this is the situation, then the lack of predication in (23b)-(25b) follows from the fact that a potential lexical subject will not be in a position from which it could c-command the predicate, and the other available external arguments will not be able to play the role of subject of the predicate: the element under INFL' because it cannot be coindexed with the predicate, and the expletive *pro* because it is not argumental and as such cannot act as subject of a predicate.

From this stipulation it follows also that the regular level of attachment of adjectival predicates in active sentences (our assumptions (i) and (ii) in section 1) is in some sense inverted in passive sentences, a consequence which, anyhow, can be derived also from the properties of passive morphology. If the Theme can move (and in some languages *must* move) to the position of the external argument, it is expected that the predicates of the Theme in passive and similar structures could be grammatically governed.

Independent evidence that the thematically oriented predicates in passive sentences attach to the level of the grammatically external argument and are not inside the VP comes from the contrast which arises between active and passive sentences with regard to the occurrence of the two types of adjectival predicates. Observe the following pair of sentences:

(29)   a.   Juan toma el café caliente relajado
             'Juan drinks the coffee hot relaxed'
        b.   *El café debe ser tomado caliente relajado
             'Coffee must be drunk hot relaxed'
             (cf.El café debe ser tomado caliente
             El café debe ser tomado relajado)

(29a) suggests that there exists a still poorly understood principle of the grammar of predication that precludes the simultaneous occurrence of two predicates associated to external argument positions of a single verb, although they appear alternatively in independent sentences. It does not happen in (29a), where the predicates are coindexed to subjects which bear a different argumental relation to the main verb: one is an internal argument (although it behaves as external with regard to the adjectival predicate; see Williams 1983), the other is external both with regard to the main verb and with regard to the predicate.

In the case of the ergative sentences, now, we want to say that the c-command relation holds when the ergative subject appears after the verb, and there seem to be two ways to obtain this result. One way is to assume that in ergative sentences, due to lexical properties of verbs of this type, the position after the verb *is* the position of the external argument, given that subjects normally appear inverted in ergative sentences. This assumption, however, would predict significant differences between ergative and non-ergative verbs with regard to those principles of the grammar in which the notion of lexical government is relevant, but these implications are still unexplored for Spanish. It seems more natural to assume, then, that ergatives behave like all the verbs of the language which carry one and only one slot for the external argument, i.e. if the predicate is thematically governed it appears in the VP. If the predicate is in the VP, now it will be predicated of the Theme of an ergative structure both when it remains internal to the VP and when it moves to the grammatical position of the external argument, because in both cases it will be c-commanded by a coindexed subject and there will be no other intermediate external argument which could force the option to become grammatically governed.

The solution that we propose, then, seems to account for the data of

(23)-(25) and (27) without recourse to ad hoc reformulations of basic principles of the theory. The problem with it, however, is that it remains in part at a stipulative level and that the interesting step of relating it to other principles of the grammar is still to be taken.

3.4. Let us consider, finally, certain sentences which appear to be counter-examples to the generalization that we have just proposed. In fact, there are passives in Spanish in which the subject appears after the verb and where the predication interpretation nevertheless obtains. Do they contradict our claims?

There are two possible configurations which could be brought up in this regard:

(30)   a. Me dijo que fueron devueltos destrozados todos los coches
           me (he) said that were returned smashed all the cars
           'He said to me that all the cars were returned smashed'
        b. En esta fiesta disparatada, fue servida la sopa fría, la carne quema-
           da y la fruta pasada
           in this crazy party, was served the soup cold, the meat burned and
           the fruit rotten
           'In this crazy party, the soup was served cold, the meat burned and
           the fruit rotten'

A reasonable hypothesis is that (30a) is a case of subject inversion, a rule of Spanish grammar which applies with many verbs of the language. This configuration presumably interacts with the rule or process which locates the adjectival predicate immediately after the verb. Some contrastive interpretation is usually added to this configuration. Example (30b), on the other hand, shows a characteristic pattern of subject-verb inversion triggered by the presence of an adverbial constituent sentence initially (see Piera 1982). In both cases, then, it could be assumed that the postposed subject has been landed previously in the position of the grammatical subject, thus licensing the predication relation and satisfying our stipulation (28).

4. SUMMARY

In the first section of this paper we reviewed certain descriptive properties of subject-oriented and object-oriented predicates in active sentences which motivate the assumption that the two types of predicates have different levels of attachment. In the second and third sections we studied the licensing of both types of predicates in passive structures. Two empirical and analytical contributions arise from this study. First, if it is assumed that the external agent argument is overtly expressed in passive morphology, there is an explanation for why predicates of implicit agents are construed in passive sentences while predicates of the Theme NP in situ are not. Second, the study of predication in passives indicates that the attachment of predicates to grammatical external arguments is the core case in the grammar of predicates, while attachment to internal arguments seems to be more restricted. The descriptive properties pointed out in the first section follow from this analysis.

NOTES

1. This *a* should not be confused with the identical preposition appearing in indirect objects. This *a*, named "*a* personal" by traditional grammarians, is obligatory in front of animate direct objects. Following the standard line of analysis among generative grammarians, we will assume that the (possible) insertion of this *a* does not change the categorial nature of the direct object; i.e. this is an NP.
2. The initial "almost" is not accidental. Some verbs of psychological state which select a Theme subject do not seem to allow this type of small clause. Observe: *??Le temo al terremoto despierto* 'I fear the earthquake awake' or *??Me gusta la música cansado* 'I like music tired'. (I owe this observation to L. Rizzi.) Actually, there seems to be in Spanish a complementary distribution between subject- and object-oriented predicates with regard to the semantic nature of their subjects: object-oriented predicates have subjects which are always theme, while subject-oriented predicates admit all kinds of semantic subjects except Themes. Recall the preceding examples and observe the following ones:

(i)   **Este libro* pertenece a Pedro *roto* (subject theme)

(ii)   *Pedro* recibió el premio *feliz* (subject goal)

(iii)   *Pedro* canta *contento* (subject agent)

(iv)   *Despojaron *al libro limpio* de su cubierta (object source)

3. This idea was suggested to me by M. Baker and K. Johnson.
4. These examples should be distinguished from those in which strong comma intonation precedes the adjectival predicate. In these cases the predication reading is always available. We assume, as usual, that these sentences have a different analysis.

The structure of the sentence in Spanish

Anneke Groos and Reineke Bok-Bennema, *Tilburg University*

The structure of the Spanish sentence is generally assumed to be like the English one, i.e. consisting of a subject NP, followed by INFL and the VP. Despite this general assumption, there are several proposals which claim that the verb is initial in Spanish, for instance Bordelois (1974) and Contreras (1982), who argues that the Spanish S should be treated as a small clause with an initial (verbal) head.

In the following we will present a systematic analysis of Spanish word order; in particular, we will explore more in detail Contreras's proposal and try to find arguments for it.

In order to illustrate word order, Gili y Gaya, in his Spanish grammar (1973), gives the following sentence, together with all the possible and impossible permutations of its constituents:

(1)   El criado trajo una carta para mí
        'The servant brought a letter for me'

In the grammatical sentences the verb is either in first or in second position. In the ungrammatical ones the verb is in some other position. Therefore, the following are ungrammatical:

(2)   a. *El criado una carta para mí trajo
        b. *El criado una carta trajo para mí

Besides this restriction on the position of the verb, Gili y Gaya's examples also show that the arguments of (1) can take any position in the sentence. In (3) there are some examples that illustrate this:[1]

(3)   a. Trajo para mí una carta el criado
        b. Trajo el criado una carta para mí
        c. Trajo una carta para mí el criado
        d. Para mí trajo el criado una carta

As a first approximation to Spanish word order, one might argue on the basis of these facts that in Spanish there is an optional first position that can be filled by any argument. This position is followed by the verb; the verb is followed by a series of constituents that may appear in any order. (4) characterizes these facts:[2]

(4)   (XP) V XP*

Spanish, seen in this way, looks very much like Hungarian and other so-called "topic languages" that have one or two pre-sentential positions which are characterized as "topic" or "focus", and a fixed position for the verb. As in Spanish, the order of the other constituents in Hungarian is also free. This freedom of word order in Hungarian has led to the claim that Hungarian is a non-configurational language, a language that lacks fixed argument positions or hierarchical structure within S (see for instance, É. Kiss 1981).

In the first part of this article we shall discuss the status of the optional XP in (4). The second part will be dedicated to the postverbal part of the sentence.

1. THE PREVERBAL POSITION
*1.1.*The assumption that in Spanish all arguments–including the subject–are generated postverbally and that, when an argument occurs preverbally, this is the result of movement to a base-generated empty position (XP of (4)), has certain advantages over the traditional view that the Spanish preverbal position is the base position for subjects.

We claim that the preverbal XP position is optional; this means that in sentences like (3a,b,c) it is simply absent. Furthermore, the idea that the first position is the target of movement predicts correctly that Spanish does not allow two constituents–e.g. a subject and a preposed *wh*-constituent–to occur before the verb, as in the following ungrammatical sentences:

(5)   a. *¿A quién Juana dio el libro?
           'To whom Juana gave the book?'
       b. *¿Con quién Paco vendrá hoy?
           'With whom Paco will come today?'

Within the traditional SVO view on Spanish, one has to assume that Spanish either has a rightward movement rule for subjects and/or a leftward movement rule for verbs, in order to account for the fact that only one preverbal constituent is allowed. In an interesting article on *wh*-movement in Spanish, Torrego (1984) does both: she claims that Spanish has a rule of "free subject inversion", which is identical to the rule proposed for Italian by Rizzi (1980), as well as a verb-preposing rule. The latter is triggered by a preposed *wh*-constituent and accounts for the correct order in *wh*-questions, whereas the former is responsible for sentences like (3a,b,c). Though our analysis is radically different from Torrego's, her data are extremely relevant for the present article and we will make frequent use of them below.

Notice that our view on the ungrammaticality of (5a,b) implies that the preverbal XP position can be occupied either by a *wh*-phrase or by a (non-*wh*) subject NP. Other (non-*wh*) major constituents can appear in it as well, but when this happens there is a requirement that the constituent under consideration bear focal stress, as in (6).[3]

(6)   a. Un viaje a las CaNArias hizo Antonio este verano (Torrego 24)
         'A trip to the Canary Islands made Antonio last summer'
    b. Para MI trajo el criado una carta   (= 3d)
         'For me brought the servant a letter'

We propose that the preverbal position, like the topic and focus position in Hungarian, is base-generated to the left of S. An alternative would be that this position is created by means of an adjunction rule that adjoins the relevant constituent to S. However, this alternative, which is chosen by Contreras (1982), requires some special restriction on multiple adjunction in order to exclude sentences with more than one preverbal constituent, such as (5a,b).[4]

1.2. There is one type of *wh*-phrase that can precede a preverbal subject in Spanish. We refer to *wh*-adjuncts like *por qué* 'why', *cuándo* 'when', and *cómo* 'how'. Some relevant examples are in (7):

(7)   a. ¿Por qué Juana se fue a las Canarias?
         'Why did Juana go to the Canary Islands?'
    b. ¿Cuándo Juana se fue a las Canarias?
         'When...'
    c. ¿Cómo Juana se fue a las Canarias?
         'How...'

In Torrego's analysis these *wh*-phrases do not trigger the rule of verb preposing. If we assume in our analysis that the subject occupies the XP position, it is clear that the *wh*-phrases cannot occupy this position as well. We propose therefore that they are in an adjoined position. Note that their non-*wh*-counterparts show exactly the same possibility of preceding subjects:

(8)   a. Por esta razón Juana se fue a las Canarias
         'For this reason Juana went to the Canary Islands'
    b. Ayer Juana se fue a las Canarias
         'Yesterday...'
    c. Así Juana se fue a las Canarias
         'This way...'

It is quite plausible that adjunction is involved in the cases in (8), and that adjuncts of the same type bearing the feature +*wh* undergo the same adjunction process.

1.3. The cases we have been examining so far have all been root sentences. We want to claim, however, that the preverbal XP position we are discussing can also be present in embedded sentences. In this respect, Spanish is similar to Hungarian, whereas it differs from, say, Dutch and German. Hungarian (see É. Kiss 1981) has a "focus position", with characteristics very similar to the Spanish one, that occurs both in root and in embedded (tensed) sentences. Dutch and German also have such a position, but only in root sentences.

Whereas subjects occur preverbally quite freely in finite embedded sentences (9a), +*wh* constituents do so only if the sentence is an indirect question. Furthermore, non-root sentences never contain a preverbal focused constituent. These facts are illustrated in (9).

(9) a. Sé que Juana se fue a las Canarias
        'I know that Juana went to the Canary Islands'
     b. No sé qué viaje ha hecho Juana   (indirect question)
        'I don't know what trip Juana has made'
     c. Ha dicho qué viaje ha hecho Juana
        'He has said what trip Juana has made'
     d. Ha dicho que un viaje a las Canarias ha hecho Juana
        'He said that a trip to the Canary Islands Juana has made'

The restricition on *wh* and focused constituents exemplified in (9c) and (9d), however, is a restriction on *lexical* constituents. Data from Torrego show quite clearly that for the *trace* of such constituents this restriction does not exist. Consider in this respect the following sentences:

(10) a. ¿*Qué* pensaba Juan que Pedro le había dicho que *la revista* había
         publicado?   (Torrego 19c)
         'What did John think that Peter had told him that the journal had
         published?'
      b. ¿*Qué* pensaba Juan que le había dicho Pedro que había publicado
         la revista?   (Torrego 19b)
         (gloss same as 10a)

In (10a) the subject of the S' that contains the trace of *qué* precedes the verb, which means, in our analysis, that it occupies the XP position of this S'. Extraction of *qué* through this position is therefore excluded. Torrego shows that in Spanish, successive cyclic *wh*-movement can skip one S' cycle, i.e. that in Spanish–as in Italian, see Rizzi (1978)–S is not a bounding node for subjacency. In (10a) the subject *Pedro* of the S' that immediately dominates the lowest S' again precedes the verb, i.e. occupies the XP position in this S', so that the XP position in this S' is also inaccessible to the *wh*-phrase. Direct extraction of *qué* to its surface position is excluded by subjacency.

In (10b) *la revista* follows the verb, which implies that the XP position of the lowest S' is free to serve as an "escape hatch" for the extraction of *qué*. *Qué* can subsequently move to the XP position of the next S'–which is also free, because *Pedro* does not precede the verb–and from there to its surface position.

Notice that Torrego's claim about S' not being a bounding node for subjacency in Spanish predicts the following variant of (10a)/(11a), to be correct. In this variant, the XP position of the second S' cycle is free, so that the derivation can proceed as indicated in (11b).

(11) a. ¿Qué pensaba Juan que había dicho Pedro que la revista había publicado?

  b. qué$_i$ pensaba Juan [$_S$, que e_i había dicho Pedro [$_S$, que la revista había publicado e_i]]

The examples in (12) illustrate that extraction of a focus constituent is also excluded when there is no XP position at the relevant distance, whereas it is permitted when such a position is available.

(12) a. Un viaje a las Canarias dice Juan que la gente quería que Antonia hiciera este verano   (Torrego 26b)
    'A trip to the Canary Island John says that people wanted that Antonia make this summer'

  a.'.un viaje a las Canarias$_1$ dice J. [$_S$ que *la gente* quería [$_S$, que *Antonia* hiciera e_1 este verano]]

  b. Un viaje a las Canarias dice Juan que quería la gente que hiciera Antonia este verano   (Torrego 26a)

  b'. un viaje a las Canarias dice Juan [$_S$ que e_1 quería la gente [$_S$ que e_1 hiciera e_1 Antonio este verano]]

Our assumption that embedded finite sentences have the same XP position as root sentences correctly predicts the extraction facts exemplified above. It also predicts that when a subject precedes the verb in such sentences, there cannot be a fronted *wh*-phrase as well, unless, of course, this *wh*-phrase is of the adjunct type. This prediction is correct, as shown in (13).

(13) a. *No sabía qué esos dos querian   (Torrego 8b)
    'I didn't know what those two wanted'

  b. No sabía qué querian esos dos   (Torrego 8a)

    c. *Es impredecible con quién Juan vendrá hoy   (Torrego 9b)
    d.   Es impredecible con quién vendrá Juan hoy   (Torrego 9a)
    e.   No sé cuándo Juan llegará
       'I don't know when John will arrive'

To finish this section we want to return briefly to the ungrammaticality of (9c) and (9d). The ungrammaticality of (9c) shows that Spanish does not allow lexical +*wh*-phrases to appear in the XP position of non-*wh* Ss. Lasnik and Saito (1984) propose the following, probably universal, filter to exclude fronted +*wh* constituents in other than +*wh* Ss:

$$* \begin{bmatrix} \text{COMP} \\ \text{-WH} \end{bmatrix}, \text{ if it contains a } +wh \text{ element } (+\text{wh lexical})$$

This filter has to be slightly adapted, if we want it to hold for Spanish S-structure, where *wh*-phrases are not in COMP but in the XP position (whether they move to COMP in LF, or are interpreted in the XP position itself is a question we leave open here). We propose that the following holds in Spanish:

$$* \begin{bmatrix} \text{COMP} \\ \text{-WH} \end{bmatrix}, \text{ if it has a } +wh \text{ element in its local domain}^5$$

The restriction on lexical focused constituents is even stricter: they only appear in root sentences. Pending further study on the rule of focusing and of focus stress assignment, we leave open the exact formulation of this restriction.

1.4. Spanish non-finite verbs usually occur in initial position. This can be illustrated quite clearly by means of the absolute construction, which contains a lexical subject that can never precede the verb, cf. (14):

(14)   a.   Por decir estas cosas mi abuela...
           'Because of my grandmother saying these things'
      b. *Por mi abuela decir estas cosas
      c.   Estando Juan en casa, ...
           'John being at home'
      d. *Juan estando en casa, ...

Another fact that illustrates the initial position of the verb in tenseless sentences is that the clitic node, which in finite sentences must precede the verb, follows it in these sentences, cf. (15):

(15)   a.   Te lo doy
               'I give it to you'
        b.   *Dóytelo
        c.   Para dártelo
               'In order to give it to you'
        d.   *Para te lo dar
        e.   Diciéndomelo tú
               'You saying it to me'
        f.   *Mc lo diciendo tú

A possible hypothesis for non-finite sentences is that the verb in these sentences is obligatorily preposed to the XP position. This hypothesis, however, is immediately falsified by the existence of infinitival indirect questions such as those in (16):

(16)   a. No sé a quién darlo
            'I don't know to whom to give it'
        b. No sabía qué hacer
            'I didn't know what to do'

In (16), the XP position is occupied by *a quién* and *qué*, respectively.

An alternative hypothesis is that the verb is fronted to a position between the clitic node, which in this view has a fixed position, and the XP position. Let us suppose that INFL in Spanish is the head of S', and that it governs S to its right, INFL and S being adjacent. Let us assume, furthermore, that INFL in Spanish has to be lexically filled. In finite sentences it is filled by the agreement and other verbal features that in surface structure appear as an affix on the verb. In non-finite sentences there are no such features. In order to satisfy the requirement of lexical material in INFL, the verb of non-finite sentences has to move to the INFL node.[6]

If INFL is the head of S' in Spanish, S is inflectionless. This means that S is typically a small clause. We thus agree with Contreras on the status of Spanish S as V^{max}. Just like other clauses, S is transparent for government of the subject from outside. In the case of a finite sentence, the relevant governor is INFL[+tense]; in the case of non-finite sentences, INFL, which is [−tense], cannot act as a governor. It follows that in non-finite sentences there is no governor at all and that the subject is PRO, just as in the case of other ungoverned small clauses (e.g. *John entered the room PRO nude*); an exception on this point is the absolute construction (see below).

(17) graphically represents verb fronting in non-finite sentences.

(17)

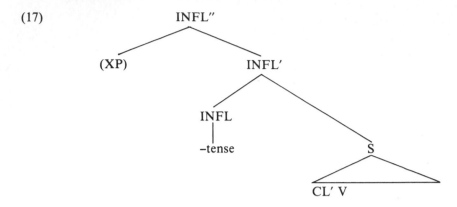

The optional XP node in (17) has the status of a specifier of INFL, the head of S'. The only case in which a lexical phrase can appear in the XP of infinitivals is that of infinitival indirect questions. In these constructions the phrase in XP has to be +*wh*, as required by their COMP. Lexical focused phrases in infinitivals are excluded by the condition that phrases of this kind can only appear in root sentences. PRO subjects, of course, never appear as lexical NPs. Absolute constructions with lexical subjects seem to be degenerate in that they never have an XP position. The non-selection of the XP in this case can be made dependent on the presence of the lexical subject if one assumes that the inflectional head of such absolutives has a special feature [+nom]. This feature would make it possible for INFL to act as a Case-assigner for the subject and would at the same time be responsible for the non-selection of XP.

2. THE STRUCTURE OF S

2.1. In this section we will discuss the structure of S (= V^{max}). In the beginning of this article we claimed that word order is free, and some examples to illustrate this fact were given in (3). Some more examples follow in (18):

(18)   a.   Queremos regalar un libro a Juan
        b.   Queremos regalar a Juan un libro
            'We want to give John a book'
        c.   Considero inteligente a Juan
        d.   Considero a Juan inteligente
            'I consider John intelligent'
        e.   Hacemos traer otro plato al camarero
        f.   Hacemos traer al camarero otro plato
            'We have the waiter bring another plate'
        g. *Hacemos al camarero traer otro plato

The sentences in (18c-g) containing small clause complements are included to show that they do not behave differently from S. We'll return to these examples below. Examples like those in (18) raise the question of how this free word order in Spanish must be accounted for.

Basically, there are two hypotheses available. We represent them in (19).

(19) a. V^{max} → V XP*
      b.

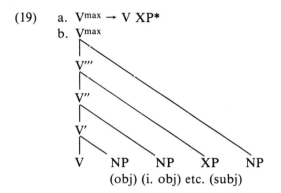

The fact that the constituents that follow V can appear in any arbitrary order can be taken to indicate that the structure of S, and mutatis mutandis that of (other) small clauses, is in fact flat. S can then be characterized as in (19a). Such a structure is assumed, for instance, for Hungarian, cf. É. Kiss (1981).

Alternatively, one may take the view that S is configurational, and that its configurational character reflects the thematic structure of the verb. The structure in (19b) expresses this idea. It represents a right-branching tree, and the basic word order is VOS, as in Contreras (1982). In what follows we will argue for (19b).

Taking (19b) as basic, we assume that the different surface orders are derived by the rule Move-alpha, in the spirit of a proposal by Saito and Hoji (1983) for Japanese. Japanese is another apparently non-configurational language with one fixed position, namely the position of the verb. The verb in Japanese is final in S, and Move-alpha in Japanese has the character of a leftward adjunction rule. In Spanish, however, the structure of S is exactly the reverse from Japanese: the verb is initial in S, and the rule that accounts for the different surface orderings is a rule that adjoins to the right. We will assume that this type of adjunction is completely free–specifically, that phrases may adjoin to any higher level of the governing projection. In (20) we illustrate this adjunction process:

(20)   a. V^{max}

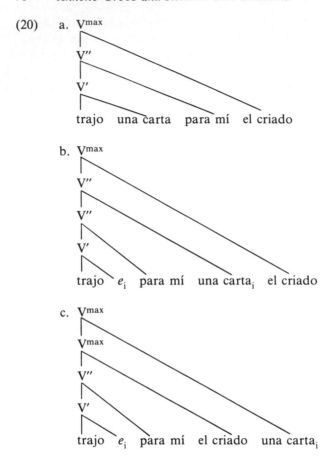

b. V^{max}

c. V^{max}

From the basic structure in (20a) we derive both (20b) and (20c); in (20b) the object is adjoined to V"; in (20c) the direct object is adjoined to V^{max}. The other possible surface orders we will not illustrate here.

The ordering differences shown in (18) can be derived in a similar way: (18a) is the base order; (18b) is derived from (18a) by adjoining the direct object to V". (18d) is derived from (18c), the basic order, by adjoining the head of the small clause *inteligente* to either V" or V^{max}, depending on the position of the *pro* subject. (18e) is again a base structure; in (18f) the direct object of the small clause is adjoined to the small clause itself. (18g), however, is not a possible sentence. Its derivation would involve the adjunction of the head of the small clause *traer* to some projection of the matrix verb *hacer*. This sentence can be excluded if we assume that verbs are the only category that is never subject to this type of adjunction process.

2.2. The question that we wish to establish in this section is the correct characterization of S in Spanish. Is there any evidence that (19b) is superior to (19a)?

One piece of evidence that (19a) cannot be correct comes from the contrast shown by the (a) sentences and (b) sentences in (21) and (22). These sentences, from Torrego (1984), are examples of extractions out of *wh*-islands:

(21)   a. ¿Quién no sabes cuánto pesa?   (Torrego 40)
           'Who don't you know how much weighs?'
       b. *¿Cuánto no sabes quién pesa?   (Torrego 43)
           'How much don't you know who weighs?'

(22)   a. ¿A quién no sabes qué diccionario ha devuelto Celia?
           'To whom don't you know what dictionary Celia has returned?'
       b. *¿Qué diccionario no sabes a quién ha devuelto Celia?
           'What dictionary don't you know to whom Celia has returned?'

The grammaticality of (21a) and (22a) indicates that it is possible to *wh*-move out of a *wh*-island. In (21a) it is the subject that undergoes long extraction; in (22a) it is the indirect object that is extracted out of the *wh*-island. The direct object in both cases is subject to short extraction. (21b) and (22b) show that in these sentences the direct object cannot undergo long extraction. What needs to be explained is why this should be the case. Note that it is only in sentences of the type illustrated in (21) and (22) that the direct object cannot be subject to long extraction, since the sentences in (23) are perfectly grammatical:

(23)   a. ¿Cuánto crees que pesa Juan?
           'How much do you think that John weighs?'
       b. ¿Qué diccionario piensas que ha devuelto Celia?
           'What dictionary do you think that Celia has returned?'

The ungrammaticality of (21b) and (22b) can be accounted for if we assume that their structure is as in (24a) and (24b), respectively:

(24)   a. cuánto$_i$ no sabes quién$_j$ pesa e_i e_j
       b. qué diccionario$_i$ no sabes a quién$_j$ ha devuelto e_i e_j Celia

Their ungrammaticality can be attributed to the fact that the configurations in (24) violate the crossing constraint of Bordelois (1974). But then it follows that we must reject (19a) as the characterization of S in Spanish, since (19a) claims that there is no relevant ordering of arguments in S in Spanish. On the other hand, the crossing constraint can be formulated on the base structure of (19b), given, of course, the natural assumption that *wh*-movement takes place out of base positions only, not from adjoined positions. Notice that the crossing constraint holds only in a linear way, not structurally;[7] it is therefore an argument against (19a), not an argument in favor of (19b).

A positive argument in favor of the structure that we propose in (19b), together with adjunction, involves a certain type of parasitic gap, illustrated by the examples in (25)-(27):

(25)   a. *Ayer compré dos trajes sin probarme e
           'Yesterday I bought two suits without trying on'
    b. Ayer compré e_i sin probarme e_i dos trajes$_i$

(26)   a. *Vamos a fregar estos platos tan sucios antes de poner e en la mesa
           'We are going to wash these very dirty dishes before putting on the table'
    b. Vamos a fregar e_i antes de poner e_i en la mesa estos platos tan sucios$_i$

(27)   a. *Devolví las novelas que me habían prestado sin haber leído e
    b. Devolví e_i sin haber leído e_i las novelas que me habían prestado$_i$

The contrast between the (a) examples and the (b) examples follows directly if we assume the base structure in (19b). The (a) examples are ungrammatical since the object gap in the infinitival adjunct receives no interpretation: it violates the Theta Criterion. The direct object in the matrix sentence cannot bind this gap. In the grammatical (b) examples, on the other hand, the parasitic gap is licensed by the variable in object position. In the (b) cases the object has undergone Move-alpha, and is adjoined to V^{max} where it functions as an A'-binder with respect to the trace it has left behind in its original position. Notice that the situation sketched here is the same as in English, where parasitic gaps are licensed by the trace of constituents that have undergone Heavy NP Shift (Engdahl 1983), cf. (28):

(28)   John offended e_i by not recognizing e_i immediately his favorite uncle from Cleveland$_i$

We take these facts as strong evidence for the configurational structure proposed in (19b).

NOTES

1. We will assume these permutations of arguments to be completely free from the point of view of syntax. The choice of a particular order is partly determined by pragmatic considerations like

choice of focus and heaviness of constituents. Apart from the fact that we will remark on the focused status of some preverbal constituents, we will not be concerned with pragmatic factors in the present article. We refer the interested reader to the works of Contreras (1976) and Suñer (1982a) and references therein.

2. It should be noted that (4) simplifies the state of affairs somewhat. The preverbal position is actually not the absolute initial position of Spanish sentences. Elements occurring to the left of the preverbal position are:

a. topicalized phrases, e.g. *La carta* Juana la ha recibido hoy 'The letter Juana has received it today'

b. complementizers, e.g. Dijo *que* Juana vendría 'He said that Juana would come'

c. adjuncts of the type *por esta razón* 'for this reason'; these adjuncts will be treated below in the text

d. relative pronouns, e.g. El hombre *a quien* Juana ha visto 'The man whom Juana has seen'; we assume, following Contreras (1982), that relative pronouns adjoin to S'.

3. Torrego shows that exclamatives, comparatives, and the Spanish equivalent of *Bad though the road may be, I'm still going to New York* have exactly the same characteristics as sentences with *wh*- or focus-fronting. In our terms they all involve movement of the relevant element to the preverbal XP-position.

4. Whereas focus and *wh*-constituents (as well as the constituents involved in the constructions mentioned in note 3) form a natural class in many languages (see e.g. É. Kiss 1981 for Hungarian), it may seem strange that non-focused, non-*wh* subject NPs pattern in the same way in the configuration we are considering here. It is possible that we are in fact overgeneralizing and that these subjects in preverbal position do not occupy the XP position, but rather the topic position, which occurs at the extreme left of S'. The grammaticality of sentences like (i) and (ii):

(i)   ¿Juana a quién ha dado el libro?
        'Juana to whom did (she) give the book'

(ii)   ¿Juan con quién vendrá hoy?
        'Juan with whom will (he) be coming today'

shows that Spanish subjects can occur in topic position. A case like:

(iii)   Juan vendrá hoy

does not (obligatorily) show the typical comma-intonation of topic constructions, however. The question of the status of the XP position clearly requires more research.

5. We define "local domain" as follows:

x is in the local domain of y, iff

(a) y c-commands x.

(b) there is no major category boundary between y and x.

In section 1.4 we will argue that S in Spanish is the maximal projection of V, i.e. that S constitutes a major category boundary. *Wh*-phrases in situ thus will never be in the local domain of a COMP.

6. Fronting of the verb in Spanish non-finite sentences is also proposed in Schroten (1978).

7. As pointed out in the text, the argument based on crossing shows that the order of complements is relevant, but it only shows the necessity of linear order; it has nothing to say about hierarchical structure. Pesetsky has proposed a more elaborated version of the crossing constraint for a whole range of constructions: The Path Containment Condition (Pesetsky 1982). This condition requires that wherever we find overlapping paths–where a path is seen as a line formed by the nodes connecting the A'-binder and the variable–between two A'-binders and two gaps bound by them, it must be the case that one path contains the other. The Path Containment

Condition, however, makes the wrong predictions for the sentences in (21) and (22). It predicts that the direct object should undergo long extraction, since it is more deeply embedded than either the subject or the indirect object (given the structure proposed in (19b)). In other words, Path Containment predicts that Spanish should behave like English, where direct objects can (marginally) be extracted out of *wh*-islands, but not subjects. Pesetsky's elaboration of the crossing constraint is based on languages with initial subjects. It may well be the case that it needs a re-elaboration for languages with final subjects. Further research is clearly needed on this point. It also appears that the crossing facts of (21) and (22) do not hold in other similar cases, as Torrego points out; cf. the following examples:

(i)   ¿Qué$_i$ no sabes a quién$_j$ querían sus amigos regalarle e_i e_j?   (Torrego 58)
       'What don't you know to whom his friends wanted to give?'

(ii)   ¿Qué preso dices que no sabes por qué otro iban a canjear?   (Torrego 59)
       'What prisoner do you say that you don't know for what other they were going to exchange?'

In the sentences above, the *wh*-island is an infinitival clause. This question also needs further research.

Arbitrary subjects in finite clauses*

Carlos P. Otero, *U.C.L.A.*

0. INTRODUCTION

GB theory is widely recognized as a major breakthrough in the study of language, something that can be better appreciated in its historical perspective.[1] It is true that the Pisa theory "develops directly and without a radical break from earlier work in transformational generative grammar, in particular work that falls within the framework of the Extended Standard Theory (EST)". But it is no less true that "earlier transformational grammar was in part on the wrong track in attributing [the full complexity of natural language] to the variety of phrase structure rules and transformations". With the advent of GB theory "the phrase structure rules can be largely and perhaps completely eliminated ..., and the components of transformations in the sense of earlier work are virtually abandoned; they did not have the independent significance that should be manifested in the right choice of basic abstract features, as Heny (1981) observes" (Chomsky 1982,3,89; cf. Stowell 1981).

Today we may be a good bit closer to identifying these fundamental elements, so it seems fair to say, as Chomsky does in his *Lectures on Government and Binding* (henceforth, LGB), that "for the first time in the long and rich history of the study of language, we are now in a position to put forth theories that have some of the right properties, and that have significant explanatory power over a considerable range, as well as at least the beginnings of a deductive structure" (p.344).

From the present perspective, the question of the nature of "empty categories" (ECs) is a particularly interesting one for a number of reasons. "In the first place, the study of such elements, along with the related investigation of anaphors and pronouns, has proven to be an excellent probe for determining properties of syntactic and semantic representation and the rules that form them. But apart from this, there is an intrinsic fascination in the study of properties of empty elements. These properties can hardly be determined inductively from observed overt phenomena, and therefore presumably reflect inner resources of the mind. If our goal is to discover the nature of the human language faculty, abstracting away from the effects of experience, then these elements offer particularly valuable insights" (LGB, 55; from now on, a page number not otherwise identified refers to LGB). This is one of the reasons why some of the questions examined below now attract generally far more interest among generative grammarians than they did in 1965 or even in 1976. And, more importantly, they are less elusive.

A particularly interesting type of EC is the one associated with the parameter Luigi Rizzi refers to as the "Null Subject parameter". The main purpose of this paper (which is part of a larger effort) is to study some aspects of a class of EC subjects characteristic of Spanish and other Romance languages that appears to have considerable theoretical interest. This class may be exemplified with a paradigm such as (1). Abstracting away from the effects of the presence/absence of "tense" (see note 41), in each example the subject is interpreted as the PRO subject with arbitrary variable-like interpretation of, e.g. *it is possible PRO to be a victim of circumstances*, which is why I gloss it as ARB:[2]

(1)   (i)   *Copulative*
              a. Se es víctima de las circunstancias
                 'ARB is a victim of circumstances'
              b. O se es/está alta o no
                 'Either ARB is tall (for her age) or not'
       (ii)   *Intransitive*
              c. Se trató de muchos temas
                 'ARB dealt with many topics'
       (iii) *Transitive*
              d. Se trató muchos temas
                 'ARB discussed many topics'
              e. Se explota a los indefensos
                 'ARB exploits the defenseless'
       (iv)   *Passive*
              f. Se es explotado (por los poderosos)
                 'ARB is exploited (by the powerful)'

This paper provides evidence that in the class of constructions exemplified in (1) the subject is interpreted as an "arbitrary PRO" (= ARB), and proposes an analysis of pronominals that derives these effects. As a point of departure I will take Belletti 1980, a very insightful contribution to a full understanding of the problems involved, and Chomsky's more widely known and more readily accessible analysis of the constructions at issue (which draws on Belletti's), together with the revised version of Belletti's paper (published in 1982), Burzio 1981, Zubizarreta 1982, and Manzini 1983b. I will avoid complexities when at all possible, keeping to simple properties of these constructions that are relevant to the point under discussion. Given the space limitations, it will not be possible here to go beyond a few initial remarks.

The exposition is organized as follows: I begin (section 1) with some general remarks about the theoretical framework and the comparative approach that it makes possible. I next present (section 2) the essentials of the Belletti/Chomsky analysis. Section 3 outlines a new approach to the functional role of the clitic in (1). Section 4 deals with the question of government and related issues, and section 5 examines a presumably universal aspect of the logical form of the structures of this class. The results are briefly summarized in the final section.

1. A COMPARATIVE APPROACH TO ROMANCE SYNTAX

I will adopt and presuppose the essentials of the framework presented in LGB, as modified in Chomsky 1982, with some minimal changes that at the very least make explicit some crucial assumptions that often prove misleading when they are tacitly assumed. I will depart, however, from both works in particulars that do not appear to be compatible with the results of the investigation partially reported in this paper.

In LGB lexical substitution is assumed to be at the base level, "largely as a matter of execution" (p.93). Here, however, it will be assumed that "only abstract features are generated in the base (which is now limited to the categorial component) in positions to be filled by lexical items" (Chomsky and Lasnik 1977, note 18), and that no new features can be added in the course of the derivation (cf. Borer 1984, 2.4). What may and must be added are some value specifications, e.g. for structural Case (cf. Freidin 1985, ch.5). As is well known, phonological matrices play no role in either "syntactic structures" in the narrow sense or in purely grammatical LF structures, both of which appear to require nonphonological feature specifications.[3] Under the assumption adopted here, every "pronoun" (in the traditional sense) is an "empty category" before insertion of the phonological matrices, but only some pronouns will always lack a surface phonetic realization.[4] In this paper, then, the term EC is to be understood as an empty pronoun that is not associated with a phonological matrix at any point in the derivation. A pronoun has some property or properties that distinguish it from a "full" NP (an NP that is not a pronoun).[5] I will tentatively identify these properties with a feature specification matrix defined by a feature complex including [αI, βII], where α, β range over $\{+, -\}$ and I, II stand for first and second "grammatical person", respectively;[6] however, for ease of exposition I will resort to the descriptive feature specification [+Pronoun]. A null position (i.e. an empty node) is a position without specific grammatical feature specifications. In the spirit of Emonds 1970, 1976, movement is permitted only to a null position–never to a position that is "filled", i.e. a position occupied by a specific abstract feature matrix; in the same spirit, only an NP (hence no clitic) can occupy an argument position, the class of NPs (both pronominal and nonpronominal) being disjoint with the class of clitics at all grammatical levels.

In the first quarter century of generative grammar (see Newmeyer 1980), it became fairly clear that "a great deal can be learned about UG from the study of a single language, if such study achieves sufficient depth to put forth rules of principles that have explanatory force but are underdetermined by evidence available to the language learner" (p.7); this is in sharp contrast with studies based on a sampling of several languages.[7] Naturally enough, it is possible to learn even more from the study in depth of more than one language. A particularly good research strategy is "to consider languages that differ in some cluster of properties but have developed separately for a relatively short time, so that it is reasonable to suppose that a difference in the values of only a few parameters accounts for the apparent typological difference" (Chomsky 1982, note 7). Study of closely related languages in this way "is particularly valuable for the opportunities it affords to identify and clarify parameters of UG that permit a range of variation in the proposed principles" (p.7).

Recent work on the syntax of the Romance languages has exploited these possibilities quite effectively. Careful formal analyses of various syntactic domains of several languages, in particular Romance languages,

> "have provided new types of empirical evidence for testing the general theoretical framework and have suggested significant refinements of the theory and sometimes also radical modifications of specific hypotheses ... Descriptive problems traditionally belonging to the domain of comparative syntax and linguistic typology have been revisited from a sophisticated theoretical perspective, which has permitted important progress ..." (Rizzi 1982, viii)

This is particularly true of the investigation of the NS parameter.[8]

2. A NOVEL ANALYSIS OF TWO ROMANCE CONSTRUCTIONS

As a result of the developments of the last few years, the kinds of claims the theory can make about what is significant within a language and across languages differ fundamentally from the kinds of claims that could be made in the earlier theories (Heny 1981, 4ff). The new analysis of some complex data has obvious advantages, crosslinguistically, over the earlier ones.[9] Of particular interest for us is the fact that the passive rule defined by the earliest generative theory was not very illuminating in the case of the "passivizing clitic" (*si, se*) constructions in Romance (which we will examine directly), while the range of options is now quite different. In GB theory, what is usually called "passive" has these two basic properties:

(2)   (I) [NP, S] does not receive a θ-role
        (II) [NP, VP] does not receive Case within VP, for some choice of NP
        in VP

Moreover, it can be argued that these two properties can be reduced to one, so
that "the unique property of the passive morphology is that it in effect
'absorbs' Case (p.124). More precisely, Chomsky argues that (I) can be
derived from (II) if we assume the "uniformity principle" (3), so we have the
general conclusion (4):

(3)   Each morphological process either
        (i) transmits θ-role uniformly, or
        (ii) blocks θ-role uniformly, or
        (iii) assigns a new θ-role uniformly
(4)   If some NP governed by V is assigned no Case, then the VP of which V
        is the head assigns no θ-role

2.1. The passive construction

Given (2)-(4), (5) can be seen as a passive sense construction without canonical passive morphology:[10]

(5)   le mele si mangiano
        'the apples PASS(IVE) eat'   (similar in sense to 'the apples are
        eaten')

The derivation (5) that Chomsky sketches leaves no doubt as to its "passive"
character. As a base form, he gives the following:

(6)   [$_{NP}$ *e*] si mangia [$_{NP}$ le mele]

In his view, "*si*, like passive morphology, can 'absorb' the objective Case-
marking of a transitive verb. ... If this happens, then NP-movement from
object position is obligatory by virtue of the Case Filter, converting (6) to (5),
which is interpreted as an impersonal passive. The impersonal passives have
the two basic properties of passive discussed in 2.7 [= (2)]: Case is absorbed
by some element other than the object, and the subject position [NP, S] lacks
a θ-role, though *si* retains the θ-role of subject, thus, incidentally, excluding
agent phrases in these constructions" (p.271, with the numbering adjusted to
the numbering in this paper, something I will do from now on).[11]
    The S-structure he gives for (5) is (7):

(7)   le mele [$_{INFL}$ Tense, AGR, si] [$_{VP}$ mangi- t]

In other words, in the "passivizing clitic" construction, like in any other passive, the verb fails to assign Case to its object, and, consequently, the subject is not θ-marked. Only the application of Move α can save the construction.[12]

2.2. *The active construction*

What about the active sentence (8ii), which I pair below with the two forms, "noninverted" (a) and "inverted" (b), of the "passivizing clitic" construction?[13]

(8) (i) a. le mele si mangiano   SG = singular
          b. si mangiano (NON-SG) le mele (NON-SG)
              'the apples PASS eat'
     (ii)   si mangia (SG) le mele (NON-SG)
              'ARB eats the apples'

As Chomsky writes, "in each case, *le mele* is understood as the direct object of *mangiare* at LF; ... by the projection principle and the assumption that the lexicon is maximally simple, we conclude that there is a common base form, namely (6), underlying all the examples of (8)".

For Chomsky, case (8ib) is not problematic, since it can be reduced to case (8ia), that is, it derives from (8ia) by the inversion process that he takes to be characteristic of NS languages. Turning to (8ii), Chomsky assumes, following Rizzi, that *si* is a clitic related to the subject; furthermore, that it is in INFL in D-structure. If his rule R (which is reminiscent of Affix-Hopping) applies in the syntax, *si* along with AGR will be in VP at S-structure and LF. The S-structure he postulates for (ii) is (9), where PRO is coindexed with *si* and ungoverned, as required:

(9)   PRO [$_{VP}$ si-mangia le mele]

Assuming the analysis in (9), how are Case and θ-role assigned? In (9), the object *le mele* receives objective Case in the normal way. It is then natural to assume, Chomsky continues, that, in contrast with the "passivizing *si*", which "absorbs objective Case, triggering NP-movement and yielding the impersonal passive (8ia), which may then be converted to (8ib) by the normal inversion process", "in the D-structure (6), *si* may be assigned nominative Case, yielding the active sentence (8ii)". In the latter case, "the θ-roles of object and subject are assigned to *le mele* and *si* respectively" (p.270-1).

3. THE FUNCTIONAL ROLE OF SE

As we have seen, the underlying structure of the SE construction is essentially (6), irrelevant details omitted, provided the subject NP is an argument position with a thematic role (hence is not an empty node). This is in keeping with the LGB analysis of languages like Spanish as having obligatory underlying subjects (pp.28,327), an analysis which appears to be well established. Since, as we will see, there are reasons to reject the assumption that the clitic itself is the subject, the fact that sentences lacking a surface argument subject actually do have EC subjects at D-structure forces us to assume that there is an EC subject in (8ii), as posited in (9).

(6) cannot be the underlying structure of *se*-passive, however, if the subject position is not empty (i.e. is not an empty node). Under the assumptions we have adopted, if the subject position is already occupied by an abstract feature matrix, the direct object does not have a position to move to (see section 4.2).[14] On the other hand, if there is no feature matrix in subject position in the D-structure, there is no way of inserting one in the course of the derivation.[15] We have therefore the following contrast:

(10)   (i)   [EC se comió las manzanas]   (SE-active)
          (ii)   [Δ se come las manzanas]   (*se*-passive)

Now we may ask whether the morpheme *se* is an instantiation of the same abstract element in both (10i) and (10ii). Note that under the analysis of section 2 the verb assigns objective Case in (10i) (cf. (8ii)), but does not assign Case in (10ii) (cf. (8ia)). Therefore, either the two instances of *se* are underlyingly different, or other properties of (10ii), in particular Δ, conspire with *se* to bring about the movement of the object NP.[16]

What is the nature of the EC in (10i)? A structure essentially identical to (10i) was proposed in Strozer 1976.[17] It might be helpful to reconstruct and slightly develop here the reasoning that led to that proposal. Consider the following structures:

(11)   a.   Ana (se) fue a la sierra
             'Ana went (away) to the sierra'
      b.   Ana (se) comió las manzanas
             'Ana ate (up) the apples'

As the parentheses indicate, *se* is syntactically optional (i.e. its presence or absence does not change the basic nature of the structure, nor does it affect grammaticality) in both (11a) and (11b); when present, it introduces an additional aspectual specification (as the English particle in the gloss suggests): Inchoativeness (initialness) in the intransitive construction (11a),

terminativeness (completeness) in the transitive one (11b). Since tense-aspect is part of INFL, in (11) *se* alters the content of INFL.[18]
    Consider now the NS counterpart to (11):

(12)   a.   EC (se) fue a la sierra
        b.   EC (se) comió las manzanas

If *se* is left out, the understood subject can only be 'he/she' and the meaning of each sentence is as in (11) minus *Ana* and the parenthesized particle in the English gloss. If, on the other hand, *se* is part of the string, both examples are ambiguous in a parallel way: On one reading, they mean the same as before (in particular, the subject can only be understood as 'he/she') except that the particle has to be included in the English gloss ('he/she went away ...'; 'he/she ate up ...'); on the other reading, the meaning of the predicate is exactly the same as when *se* is left out, and the subject is understood, not as 'he/she', but as 'ARB', as in (13), where the notation EC* stands for an EC with an arbitrary variable-like interpretation:

(13)   a.   EC* se fue a la sierra
              'ARB went to the sierra'
        b.   EC* se comió las manzanas
              'ARB ate the apples'

Note that *se* is no longer syntactically optional; if it is not present, the subject is not open to an arbitrary variable-like interpretation. Note also that a lexical subject is excluded: If it is right to posit an EC* in (13a,b), such an EC is not only phonetically unrealized, but unrealizable. It is also clear that the functional role of the obligatory *se* of the SE construction is not the same as that of the syntactically optional *se* of (11). It is less clear whether they have something non-trivial in common, in addition to being an instance in each case of the least specified clitic in the language, as (14) makes explicit:

(14)   *se* is a non-nominative, non-I/II person (and the only MORPHOLO-
        GICALLY "reflexive", hence nonreferring) Spanish clitic, which is
        not specified for definite/indefinite, for masculine/feminine or for
        singular/nonsingular (see tables in Strozer 1976, 103,119; also, (23)
        below).

One possibility is that, in the SE construction also, *se* alters the content of INFL, that is, it is a surface manifestation of part of the content of INFL.[19] This is what I will try to show directly.
    Consider the following contrast:

(15) a. A juzgar por sus actos, EC se sobornan fácilmente
   b. A juzgar por sus actos, ellos se sobornan fácilmente
    'To judge from their acts, they bribe easily'

Example (15a) is open to a generic interpretation, whereas (15b), with the pronoun *ellos* in place of the EC, is not. An overt pronoun cannot replace the EC in this case. The opposite is also true, as (16) shows:

(16) Ana ama a sus hijos$_i$, y *(ellos$_i$) lo saben
   'Ana loves her children, and they know it'

There is a crucial difference, then, between a phonologically specified (definite) pronoun and a definite EC. Perhaps a necessary step towards the characterization of this difference is to assume that in Spanish, and perhaps in the (Romance) NS languages in general, an overt pronoun is always a "personal pronoun" in the sense that "I" (= the speaker) and "you" (= one of the addressees) are "personal pronouns".[20] More precisely, it appears that in Spanish an overt pronoun is always an "indexical", i.e. a word whose referent is dependent on the context of use.[21] This is of course not true of non-overt pronouns.

 There is also an important difference, as we have seen, between an ordinary pro and a finite clause EC* subject. Recall that the two partial structures that can be assigned to each of the examples in (12) when *se* is part of the string differ in two ways, and that one of the ways has to do with the interpretation of the EC, which in one case is understood as 'he/she' and in the other as 'ARB' (see (13)).

 How is this difference to be represented? Since there is no question that *he/she* are [+Definite] (cf. Hawkins 1978, Holmback 1982, Heim 1982), as a first approximation we might say that, in contrast, an EC* is [−Def]. It is easy to see that in the case of ordinary pro the [+Def] interpretation can only be due to the content of a finite INFL (cf. Rizzi 1982,IV, (43ii)). Compare (a) and (b) in (17):

(17) a. Es posible EC INFL comer todos los días
    'It is possible ARB to eat every day'
   b. Posiblemente, EC INFL come todos los días
    'Possibly, he/she eats every day'

It is therefore reasonable to assume that in (17b) INFL includes [+Def], whereas in (17a) it does not. Compare now (18a) and (18b), where again EC* stands for an EC with arbitrary variable-like interpretation:

(18)   a. Es posible EC*   INFL   comer todos los días
                            [–Def]
        b. Posiblemente, EC*   INFL   come todos los días
                            [...se...]

(18) suggests that a necessary functional role of *se* in (18b) is to make the indefinite interpretation possible in a finite clause; perhaps equivalently, the functional role of *se* in (18b) is to "absorb" the definiteness of a finite INFL.

Some of the advantages of this proposal seem clear. To begin with, it allows us to take the morpheme *se* (see (14)) for what it is (the null hypothesis): It is a clitic, not an NP;[22] paradigmatically (morphologically), it is a non-nominative clitic (just as *le(s)*, *la(s)* are non-nominative clitics in the clitic paradigm), not a bearer of nominative case;[23] it is generated essentially in place, not moved by transformation ("just like other NPs", Burzio (1.3.1) writes). Under our analysis, there is no need to assume (in fact, it is impossible not to disallow) the movement of SE in the Raising structures exemplified in (19b) and the Copular and Passive ones exemplified in (1a,b,f), repeated below:[24]

(19)   a. Parece EC (ser) consciente
           'He/she seems EC (to be) conscious'
        b. SE parece EC (*ser) consciente
           'ARB seems EC (to be) conscious'

(1)   a. SE es víctima de las circunstancias
        b. O SE es/está alta o no
        f. SE es explotado por los poderosos

Furthermore, our theory of clitics does not limit their functional role to that of identifiers of empty categories. It is plain that not every clitic is an identifier or "licenser" of an associated empty category. We have already seen three functional roles of *se*, namely, those exemplified in (11), (13) and (15), in which the clitic is not an NP identifier. A fourth one is no less plain. Thus Burzio, among others, assumes that both "inherent" and "ergative" *se* (*si* in Italian)–as in *Ana se desmayó* 'Ana fainted' and *el buque se movió* 'the ship moved', respectively–may be taken to be "the morphological reflex of the 'loss' of subject-thematic role", that is to say, "a marker indicating that the subject position has no thematic role" (1981, 1.4.3;1.8).

By assuming that SE is simply a marker of INFL, we automatically account not only for the fact that the NP associated with SE "can be a derived subject" (which makes any transformational movement of SE unnecessary) but also for the fact that SE "is a clitic that can be related to subject positions only" (read: to finite INFL only), and therefore there is no need to "regard this as a peculiarity of the syntax of SI" or SE, as Burzio (1.3.1) does.[25]

Another important fact that is accounted for by the hypothesis that the functional role of SE is to "absorb" the plus value of [+Def] in a finite INFL is illustrated by contrasting pairs such as those in (20):[26]

(20) (i) a. Es posible EC* comer (*se) todos los días (= (18))
　　　　 b. Posiblemente, EC* *(se) come todos los días
　　　　　　 'Possibly, ARB eats every day'
　　 (ii) a. Impidieron EC* comer (*se) todos los días
　　　　　　 'They impeded EC* to eat every day'
　　　　 b. Impidieron que EC* *(se) coma todos los días
　　　　　　 'They impeded that EC* eat every day'

Since the class of EC* infinitival constructions exemplified in (a) and the class of (EC*) SE constructions exemplified in (b) are in complementary distribution, we can explain this complementarity if we assume that the content of EC* is the same in both classes of sentences (nonfinite and finite), and that SE simply makes an EC* possible as subject in a finite clause.[27] We also have an explanation for the fact that EC* is interpreted the same way (i.e., as "arbitrary human") in both finite and nonfinite clauses, and for the related fact that predicational agreement is also the same in both cases (singular in Spanish, nonsingular in Italian; see note 35). Furthermore, EC* is always a free pronominal in finite clauses, since it always receives an arbitrary variable-like interpretation in the constructions exemplified in (20b). It does not have one property of PRO, however, since the EC* in a finite clause is not open to control, as the contrast between (i) and (ii) in (21) shows:[28]

(21) (i) a. EC* se llegó a saber PRO estudiar (*se) todos los días
　　　　　　 'ARB came to know how to study every day'
　　　　 b. EC* se llegó a saber PRO estudiando (*se) todos los días
　　　　　　 'ARB came to know studying every day'
　　 (ii) a. EC* se insistió en que EC* se estudia todos los días
　　　　　　 'ARB insisted that ARB studies (IND) every day'
　　　　 b. EC* se insistió en que EC* se estudie todos los días
　　　　　　 'ARB insisted that ARB study (SUBJ) every day'

PRO is controlled by the EC* to its left in the infinitival embedded in (21i), but the EC* immediately after the complementizer *que* 'that' in (21ii) is not (and cannot be) controlled by the EC* to its left, the "mood" (IND/SUBJ) of the embedded clause making no difference, as the examples show. This fact is predicted by the "opacity condition" (Chomsky 1978, LGB: cf. George and Kornfilt 1981). We therefore conclude that the subject in SE clauses is a free pronominal that can be a controller but is not open to control (therefore, not PRO), which, however, cannot be identical to ordinary pro.

If this is essentially correct, the basic contrast between a finite structure such as (17b) and a finite structure such as (18b) is between an ordinary ([+Def]) pro subject and a type of pro subject that differs from ordinary pro in that it is [−Def], respectively (henceforth, I will tentatively use pro* to refer to this empty indefinite pronominal). This difference can now be stated in a precise way: It is the difference between a definite pro-NP, i.e. [−V, +N, +Pronoun, +Def, . . .]″ and an indefinite pro-NP, i.e. [−V, +N, +Pronoun, −Def, . . .]″, where [Pronoun], a content feature complex (cf. Rizzi 1982,IV,(75)), should not be confused with the descriptive feature [pronominal] of Chomsky 1982. Note that this distinction is not available under any recent analysis of the clitic structures, in particular under the ones given in Jaeggli 1982 or in LGB, which characterize every EC subject as PRO.[29]

Further evidence in support of our hypothesis comes from contrasts such as the one exemplified in (22):

(22)   a. (Ana) se admira a sí misma
           'Ana admires herself'
        b. pro* SE admira a *sí/?una misma
           'ARB admires oneself'

The main reason why there is no fully successful "clitic doubling" structure in (22b) is that Spanish lacks a non-definite objective pronoun corresponding to pro*. In other words, Spanish does not have a pronoun that would correspond exactly to English *oneself* in (22b), that is, the pronoun that *una* (which, unlike English *one* in the gloss, is an indexical) is sort of filling in for in (22b). This is shown in (23):

(23)   a. Ana cree que [PRO alimentarse a sí misma) será difícil
           'Ana thinks that PRO to feed herself will be difficult'
        b. Ana cree que [PRO alimentarse] será difícil
           'Ana thinks that PRO to feed oneself/herself will be difficult'

(23b) is ambiguous, as the gloss indicates (evidence that *se* is not [+Def]–cf. (14)–whereas *sí* is), and there is no way of disambiguating it in favor of the non-definite meaning in Spanish. Another relevant contrast is the following (cf. Parisi 1976):

(24)   a. Ana es muy conocida en su casa
           'Ana is very well-known in her home'
        b. pro* SE es muy conocida en [*su casa]/[?en casa de una]
           'ARB is very well-known in one's house'

The first alternative in example (24b) is bad because Spanish lacks a possessive corresponding to pro*; the second, again, is not quite right, but there is no better option.

This contrasts sharply with what we find in French, as shown in the following examples, due to Ruwet (1972,114):

(25)   a. En periode troublée on/chacun ne pense qu'a soi
           'In a troubled period one/each one thinks of oneself/himself'
       b. Quand on parle très souvent de soi(-même), on risque de faire fuir ses amis
           'When one speaks about oneself too often, one risks to make one's friends flee'

For Ruwet, who acknowledges Kristian Sandfeld and Richard Kayne, *soi* is no longer the stressed form corresponding to *se*, but rather an indefinite object pronoun.[30]

We therefore have the following conclusion (cf. p. 258):[31]

(26)   The non-overt subject of a clause is [+Pronoun, –Def]
         iff INFL does not contain [+Def]

If (26) is on the right track, it is possible that there is no distinction in internal constitution between free (arbitrary) PRO and pro* but simply functional differences.[32]

Thus we have a unified account of infinitival (more generally, non-finite- see (21ib)–with the necessary qualifications, but this is beyond the scope of this paper) and finite constructions with a pro* subject, and an explanation for the exclusion of SE from non-finite constructions (a non-finite INFL is not [+Def], so it does not have to be de-definitized).[33] We also have the beginning of an explanation for the fact that pro* is invariably interpreted as 'indefinite human' in both finite and non-finite constructions, a question to which I return in Section 5.

4. GOVERNMENT, CASE, AND THETA-ROLE

It is widely assumed that the subject of a finite clause is governed by INFL and that the governing element in INFL is AGR.[34] Nothing said so far leads us to expect that pro* is not governed by INFL, in particular if we assume that a SE sentence, being finite, contains AGR, just like any other finite structure (the null hypothesis). It is reasonable to further hypothesize that AGR is some instantiation of the feature complex including [αI, βII, γDef, δSg], superficially realized as a "person-number" suffix on the verb in Spanish (in contrast with, e.g., Breton, where it can be realized on both [–N] categories). We therefore conclude that pro* (an NP that includes an instantiation of the aforementioned feature complex) is governed and that its governor is AGR, which locally determines the content of pro and pro*.[35] There is nothing unusual about this (p.162; cf. p.140 n.24). Under this analysis, it is still the case that PRO may be arbitrary in reference only "in a position that is assigned neither agreement with AGR nor Case", namely, "only in the position of subject of an infinitive or gerund" (LGB, 262; Chomsky 1982, 18). However, we now have an EC that is cosuperscripted with AGR, hence not subject to control, which nevertheless is arbitrary in reference, a possibility not contemplated in LGB.[36] On the other hand, we have no reason to believe that PRO can be coindexed with (a definite) AGR (cf. p.262).[37]

More generally, we can say that, aside from the difference in specification with respect to the feature [Def], pro* in (13) has exactly the same properties that pro has in (12). These include the possibility of agreeing with a [+Feminine] predicate, as in (27) and (28b):[38]

(27)   pro/pro* se fue a la sierra descalza
        'He/she went away to the sierra barefooted'
        'ARB went to the sierra barefooted'
(28)   a. O pro está embarazada o pro no lo está
           'Either she is pregnant or she is not'
        b. O pro* se está (*n) embarazada (*s) o pro* no se está(*n) embarazada (*s)
           'Either ARB is pregnant or ARB is not pregnant'

(On number agreement, see note 35.)

4.1. Case. The only Case that can be assigned in the domain of a finite INFL is nominative Case. The following has been proposed as a rule of universal grammar (cf. LGB, 266; Borer 1984a):

(29)   At S-structure, assign nominative Case to NP co-superscripted and governed by AGR.

We know that the obligatoriness of PRO in certain positions such as a subject of an infinitive or a subject of NP follows from Case Theory (71). Neither is the case in SE structures. Therefore, nominative Case assignment should be exactly the same in either of the two structures that it is possible to assign to (12). There is no reason to suppose that nominative Case is assigned to SE, as there is no reason to suppose that it is assigned to *se* in, e.g. *pro se fue a la sierra*, a variant of *pro fue a la sierra*, where evidently nominative Case is not assigned to the clitic.[39] In fact, as pointed out before, the *se* in *pro se fue a la sierra* is syntactically optional (i.e., its presence does not affect grammaticality and it alters the meaning only slightly and in a systematic way, as we have seen). It seems reasonable to conclude that in this respect the parallel structures that can be assigned to (12) do not differ essentially in structure. If so, SE is not assigned Case either.

4.2. Theta-role. As has often been emphasized, Case Theory and Theta Theory are closely related. In LGB, θ-role is assigned to a chain that "has Case or is headed by PRO" (p.334), since PRO is not an instance of the NP[e] but an element base-generated in place bearing a grammatical function that contains features, being therefore "visible" (pp. 251,176). Since in our analysis, PRO is simply a pro* that is not in the domain of a finite INFL, the simplest and most natural assumption is that pro* is treated in a unified fashion by θ-theory everywhere. We therefore assume the homogeneity of θ-role assignment to pro*, evidently the null hypothesis pro* must, then, assume an (independent) θ-role in any syntactic context, finite or non-finite. There seems to be no reason not to assume that in (12) pro* is an argument, whereas pro is an argument.[40]

In a word, there are reasons to conclude that SE is assigned neither nominative Case nor the θ-role of subject, contrary to what has been repeatedly assumed.

5. LOGICAL FORM

Twenty years ago, in the earliest non-pregenerative study of the SE construction (Strozer, 569-71), it was concluded that in this class of structures the subject is necessarily understood as "human" and that, consequently, only if a verb admits a human subject can it give rise to a SE construction. Thus, the examples in (30) are not grammatical (except that the first one can be understood metaphorically):

(30)   a. SE rebuznó
          'ARB brayed'
    b. SE transcurrió
          'ARB elapsed'
    c. SE llovió mucho en 1789
          'ARB rained a lot in 1789'

Similarly, we cannot have

(31)   Es posible rebuznar/transcurrir/llover
        'It is possible to bray/elapse/rain'

nor can we have in (32a) the systematic ambiguity we find in (32b), where the EC subject may be understood as human or nonhuman:

(32)   a. Es posible EC rodar montaña abajo
            'It is possible ARB to roll down the hill'
        b. Posiblemente, EC rodó montaña abajo
            'Possibly, he/she/it rolled down the hill'

This brings to mind an analysis of the English equivalent to (32a) which takes the subject of the infinitive to be 'a variable bound by some operator'', the domain of this variable being restricted, since the sentence "may be taken as referring to people rolling down the hill, but hardly to rocks, though the properties of 'roll down the hill' permit either subject and there is no general restriction of PRO to humans in D", i.e. in a domain of individuals associated with arguments at LF as values of variables, denotata of names, etc. (p.324-5). To this we can now add that it can be further restricted to female humans (cf. (27)-(28)). It should also be added that the nature of the operator binding pro* in the domain of a finite INFL seems to be akin to the existential quantifier.[41] In contrast, a definite subject of a *se*-passive construction under generic interpretation is akin to a universally quantified expression, and the definite subject of a *se*-passive interpreted non-generically is essentially a universally quantified expression.[42]

The two observations about the indefinite human subject are brought together in (33), where, as before, pro* = empty indefinite pronoun:

(33)   In some languages pro* in the domain of INFL is necessarily inter-
        preted as [+Human]

An important question, however, is whether (33) might not be derivable from some general principle of (universal) grammar. Is there a plausible candidate among the principles already known?

Consider a language L with structures equivalent to the following, where the words in capitals stand for actual words in L:

(34)   a. STICK-c1 MAN-c2 HIDES
            'Man hides stick'
        b. MAN-c1 [e] HIDES-se

The morphological element *se* stands for the L-equivalent to Spanish *se*, and c1 and c2 stand for Case markers. How is the EC interpreted in (34b) in such a language? Suppose that there are two possibilities, the most obvious one being 'himself' (the whole sentence meaning 'Man hides himself'). What could the other one be? A priori at least there is a possibility that it is understood as 'indefinite inanimate', i.e. as (roughly) 'someTHING' ('Man hides something'). Compare the Spanish counterparts to (34):

(35)   a. El hombre esconde el palo
          'The man hides the stick'
    b. EC SE esconde el palo
          'ARB (i.e. roughly, someONE) hides the stick'

As a matter of fact there is at least one actual language that is essentially like L in the respects under consideration, if my understanding of the facts is not too far off. Such a language is Dyirbal, a true ergative language in terms of Marantz's definition of the Ergative parameter (1984, ch.6). Could this parameter be the principle we are looking for? If so, given the contrast between (34) and (35), the Ergative parameter would predict that in control structures in ergative languages, free "PRO" is interpreted as 'indefinite inanimate', i.e. as (roughly) 'someTHING', in contrast with the (roughly) 'someONE' interpretation we find in Spanish, Italian, and other non-ergative languages. This prediction, however, is still to be put to the test, since apparently no clear cases of control structures in ergative languages are yet known.[43] This lack of clear cases of control structures might very well be a promising sign, given the limited attention the Ergative parameter has received so far (in contrast with the NS parameter, for example). The reason is that the typical main verbs of control structures (e.g. *persuade, promise, appeal, plead, ask, tell,* and so on) take only human subjects. The test would have to come exclusively from something like (32a) or like *it is unclear* [*how pro* to roll down the hill*].

Marantz's formulation of the Ergative parameter may be slightly simplified as follows:[44]

(36)   (i) A subject is assigned [α Theme] by the predicate (alternatively, is
           indirectly θ-marked as [α Theme] by the verb)
    (ii) [α theme] → [−α Animate]

"True ergative" languages are those, such as Dyirbal, that take the value [+Theme], non-ergative languages are those, such as Spanish, that take the value [−Theme]. Can this be the principle we are looking for? It is not immediately obvious, since a SE construction may have a Theme subject, provided that it is human, or at least this is what examples such as (1a,f) and (37 suggest:

(37)   O SE está de pie o SE está sentado
    'Either ARB is standing up or ARB is sitting'

If this principle is not the right one, is there another formulation of the parameter that might be? Suppose we have something like the following:

(38)   (i) A pro* in the domain of INFL is assigned [α Animate] by the predicate
       (ii) [α Animate] iff [−α Ergative]

The additional auxiliary assumption that is needed is that animate subjects are paradigmatically [+Human], which is quite natural. If correct, (38) offers a clear advantage over Marantz's formulation, since it defines an absolute principle, not just a preference.

   To appreciate the significance of this question, it should be kept in mind that, as David Pesetsky has emphasized (1982, 16, 203), primitive categories that meet the criterion of epistemological priority are the key to all the subsystems of universal grammar. There is little reason to doubt that the child has to begin by learning some of the most elementary properties of specific lexical items that are central in the system. To be able to do so, the child must make some connection with the world around him. In the case of the SE structures, this connection can be kept to a bare minimum, given an innate system of concepts which includes the feature [Animate] and the relation [+Animate] → [+/−Human]. It therefore comes as no surprise to find that tokens of strings that are superficially identical to tokens of the SE structure type are used by children "long" before they are three years old, whereas they apparently do not produce *se*-passives until they are almost three.[45] In other words, puzzling as they are for some adults (in particular linguists), strings superficially identical to SE structures (which represent a radical innovation in the history of the language) are among the earliest used by children.[46] This is compatible with the idea that [−ergative] is the unmarked value of the parameter (38) and that the child tentatively sets up this value before he/she encounters any positive evidence for the other value, much as the value [+null subject] is set up as a point of departure, if Hyams's view of the matter is essentially on the right track.[47]

6. CONCLUSIONS

The preceding remarks are meant as a contribution to a better understanding of Spanish (and, more generally, Romance) constructions with *se*, particularly those I refer to as SE constructions as part of a study of the nature of syntactic representations. I hope that the outlines of the approach to the problem are tolerably clear from this brief sketch.

   It is generally assumed, more or less explicitly, that a finite INFL includes the feature specification [+Def], thereby identifying the EC subject as definite. I believe that it is also reasonable to assume that an infinitival INFL is unspecified for definiteness (an obvious exception being the Galegan/Portuguese "inflected infinitive"), thus providing the proper environment for arbitrary PRO, an indefinite empty category.

If the preceding discussion is on the right track, at least two classes of clitic structures must be recognized:[48] Structures with what we might call an "Identifier(Id) clitic" such as *Ana la vio EC* 'Ana saw her' or *Ana se mató EC* 'Ana killed herself' (to illustrate with object clitics, the only Id clitics found in Spanish) and structures with what we might call an "Absorber clitic", e.g. *Ana se comió las manzanas* 'Ana ate up the apples' (= 17b), the absorber always being a "reflexive" (i.c. nonreferring) clitic, and in some structures (in particular, those of section 2) always the minimally specified clitic *se* (see (14)). In other cases, such as the one illustrated in (11) or in the constructions with "anti-causative" clitics, e.g. *el buque se movió, tú te moviste(s)* 'the ship/you moved' ("ergative" or "unaccusative") or *Ana se desmayó, tú te desmayaste(s)* 'Ana/you fainted' ("inherent"), the absorber is not always *se*. An interesting question is what the theoretical status of the EC associated with the Id clitic is. The view implicit in this paper is that the EC identified by an NP clitic is pro, that is, a non-overt pronoun.[49]

The distinction between "ids" and "absorbers", which cannot be elaborated here, plays a crucial role in this paper, which presupposes that it is necessary to begin by determining whether SE structures belong to one or to the other class.

There is little doubt that the Spanish morpheme *se* (*si* in Italian) has multiple functional roles (Burzio, 1.4.3; Zubizarreta 1982, III.2.2; cf. Williams 1981, 107). The analysis of the functional role of SE (again, the minimally specified clitic) outlined in section 3 takes SE to be an "Absorber clitic". If this analysis is essentially correct, the functional role of SE in the construction under study is not what I refer to as an "Id clitic", associated with an empty NP (as, essentially, its identifier), but what I refer to as an "Absorber clitic"; in particular, SE "absorbs" the definiteness of a finite INFL, of which it is a part, thus partially assimilating it to an infinitival INFL—partially, because an indefinite finite INFL is still an INFL including Tense and AGR, if the assumptions of this study are correct.

This implies that SE is not directly associated with the empty NP subject and that it does not bear Case or Theta-role, as assumed in earlier studies. In SE structures there is no relation of identification between the clitic and the subject pro* simply because *se* is an object clitic that can only identify an object NP. Therefore, in SE structures the subject pro* is simply cosuperscripted with the verbal inflection (and indirectly with the clitic). Put another way, the pro* subject of a SE construction is not cosubscripted with any empty category; it is related only to INFL (including SE), the relation being one of agreement (in the precise sense of cosuperscripting). This relation is therefore structurally similar to the relation between the (non)overt subject and INFL (including *se*) in (17)-(18). It is true that in (17)-(18) *se* may be replaced by *me/te/nos (Yo (me) fui a la sierra, tú (te) fuiste* . . ., and so on), whereas a characteristic property of SE is that it is irreplaceable, but this is a consequence of an independent fact, namely, that there are no I or II person indefinite pronouns, overt or non-overt.[50] Needless to say, from this perspective the question of whether SE is Case-marked or Theta-marked does not arise: SE is not associated with the subject NP as an Id clitic. More generally, *se* can never be the identifier of a subject NP in a Spanish structure (cf. (14)).

As pointed out in section 3, a significant advantage of this proposal is that it allows us to take the morpheme *se* for what it is: It is a clitic, not an NP; paradigmatically (morphologically), it is a non-nominative clitic, not a bearer of nominative case; it is generated essentially in place, not moved by transformation.

If it is true that SE structures belong to the Absorber clitic class (not to the Id class, as generally assumed, often implicitly, since the question, to my knowledge, has never been explicitly raised), some non-trivial consequences follow, and a number of features of some of the analyses so far proposed in the literature immediately come into question. One of those consequences is a new view of the non-overt subject NP involved, which appears to be a close kin of PRO. This view, in turn, might shed some light on the theory of non-overt NPs and, indirectly, on the theory of binding.

NOTES

*I am grateful to the participants in the First Workshop on Spanish Syntax (Simon Fraser University, 1982) for their interest in my sketchy presentation and for their comments, in particular to Alfredo Hurtado, who showed unusual understanding not only during the workshop but also afterwards. I am also grateful to Luigi Burzio for the many hours he gave to sharing with me his vast knowledge of the matters dealt with here at the very time he was busy completing his monumental doctoral dissertation. It was at that time that I discovered that Tom Roeper and Jay Keyser were zeroing in, from a different angle, on some of the questions I was concerned with, and I also profited from discussions with them. Numerous discussions with Judith Strozer have contributed considerably to my present understanding of some of the topics explored here. I am also indebted to John A. Hawkins, Heather Holmback, Susan Plann, and to the editors of this volume, in particular to Karen Zagona, who provided me with a detailed and extremely thoughtful list of suggestions that greatly facilitated the preparation of this (hopefully improved) shortened version of the paper.

1. For an attempt in this direction see Otero 1984, in particular the introductory chapter.
2. This practice is also adopted in Zubizarreta 1982.
3. Cf., e.g., LGB, 115f, 176f, 181-2, 257f, passim; Rizzi 1982, 46; Pesetsky 1982, 460, 475; Giorgi 1984; Picallo 1985, 2.2.
4. Cf. Jaeggli (1982, 181) and Aoun (1981, 159)–see Chomsky 1982, 86–who take pronominals to always be generated as a set of non-phonological features in D-structure, the set of features being phonetically realized in the PF component and "pronounced" only when the Avoid Pronoun principle introduced in LGB is not applicable.

5. As pointed out in Postal 1966, a so-called pronoun is actually a pro-NP; more precisely, pronominal NP (e.g. *she*) appears to be the only kind of underlyingly determinerless NP there is. See Sloat 1969, Burge 1973 (cf. Bar-Hillel 1970, 81).

6. On the significance of the notion "grammatical person" in Spanish, see Strozer 1976 (III, 1.1); see also the references given there, and Enç 1983. Complexities arising with respect to the specification of non-singular forms will be ignored in this paper. Cf. Ingram 1978.

7. Cf., e.g., Huang's (1982a) dissertation with the study he mentions on page 116, based on a sampling of fourteen languages.

8. See Borer 1984, Chomsky 1981, Rizzi 1982, Jaeggli 1982, Zubizarreta 1982, Zagona 1982, Safir 1982, Bouchard 1984, 1985, Manzini 1983b, Montalbetti 1984, among other recent studies.

9. Cf., e.g., Stump 1984 and the studies on Celtic it builds on.

10. In LGB (p.122), (i) is given instead of (5) as one of two exemplications of "passive sense with neither passive morphology nor movement":

(i)   si mangia (SG) le mele (NON-SG)

This appears to be an oversight (see, however, Chomsky 1982, 80). It is true that the generation of (i) involves no movement, but this is because sentences such as (i) "are not passive sentences", as is repeatedly emphasized in Belletti 1980. Chomsky himself refers to (i) as an "active sentence" later in his book (p.271). On the other hand, on the same page and in other places, he refers to (5) as an "impersonal passive". Notice also that the translation he gives for (i) on page 122 is adequate only for (5)–in fact, it seems a more correct translation (cf. LGB, p.121) than the one he gives for the inverted version of (5). Another approximate translation would be "apples are eatable/to be eaten" (cf. the generic interpretation of *la mela si mangia* 'the apple is eatable/to be eaten'–see (8i)). (With a possibility modal the equivalence is near perfect. For instance, in Spanish *estas bellotas pueden comerse* 'these acorns can be eaten' in one of its senses means exactly *estas bellotas son com(est)ibles* 'these acorns are eatable'.) Observe that example (5a) is parallel to (ii) in both structure and general sense:

(ii)   La gente mangia le mele
         'People eat the apples'

11. I will just note in passing that the identical remark does not appear to be empirically correct, at least for Spanish. Thus, we have structures with by-phrases such as the following:

(i)   a. Los indios se tienen por los españoles por esclavos
            'The Indians PASS consider by the Spaniards (to be) slaves'
(ii)   b. Las normas se dictarán por el gobierno
            'The regulations PASS will dictate by the government'
         c. Los tipos de cotización se fijarán por el gobierno
            'The types of dues PASS will establish by the government'
         d. Las posibles discrepancias se resolverán por la autoridad laboral
            'The possible discrepancies PASS will resolve by the labor board'
         e. Se podrán presentar candidatos por los sindicatos de trabajadores
            'Candidates PASS may present by the workers' unions'

To avoid questions about the status of this class of examples, I give only attested ones. Example (a) appears in a XIVth century text (Biblioteca de Autores Españoles 65, 200); the other are only a sample of the instances found in some recent Spanish labor legislation, namely, the Estatuto de los Trabajadores (14 March 1982), 33.6, 69.2, 81, DF.4. There are much older examples. I will give only two medieval ones as illustration:

(iii)   An se a vencer los buenos por los malos
         'The good ones PASS are to conquer by the bad ones'
(iv)   El sacrificio ... se faze sobre altar por preste que es derechamientre ordenado
         'The sacrifice ... PASS makes on the altar by a priest that is properly ordained'

(iii) is from the *Crónica General* (Nueva Biblioteca de Autores Españoles 5.397); (iv) is from the *Fuero Real* (II.7).

12. A more refined derivation is given in the last chapter of LGB (p.341).

13. I prefer the term "non-singular" to "plural" here because, strictly speaking, there is no first person "plural" (there is only one "I").

14. This assumption seems implicit in Ruwet 1972, III, in contrast with Kayne 1975, 5.9.

15. This brings to mind "the ... 'irreflexivity' principle that prevents formation of *John killed t* from *PRO kill John* by an NP-movement rule" (Chomsky 1978).

16. Comparative evidence that SE and passive *se* are functionally distinct is provided by languages like Trentino (cf. Brandi and Cordin 1983) "in which one but not the other exists", as pointed out in Zubizarreta 1982, III, 2.2.3, where the facts are reviewed.

17. See, in particular, p.266. This is in contrast with other studies, e.g. Bustos 1960, Rizzi 1976, or Burzio 1981. Rizzi assumes that the clitic *si* is under the NP subject node at the level of D-structure. Burzio (1.3.1) argues that this analysis is necessary to account for movement. It seems that one of the virtues of GB theory is that it makes it possible to avoid treating the clitic as an ordinary NP, a treatment which does not seem natural. This observation applies also to Schroten 1981, where *se* is placed in the subject position in the course of the derivation. See below.

18. The question whether *se* is generated under INFL in the constructions exemplified in (11) is not addressed in this paper (cf. Zagona 1982, 5.1.1). Another question not addressed here is the precise delimitation of the class of verbs that properly includes *ir, comer*; for a basic condition the NP in (11b) must meet, see Strozer, IV, n.4, p.564.

19. Perhaps it should be added that this characterization does not entail a structural identity between the constructions exemplified in (11a/b) and (13a/b), respectively.

20. This includes, but is not limited to, the property responsible for the star in (i):

(i)   Pedimos los libros$_i$, y (*ellos$_i$) llegaron enseguida
       'We ordered the books, and they arrived right away'

21. See Kaplan 1977 and Bar-Hillel 1954 (in particular III); cf. Montalbetti 1984.

22. Contra Burzio 1981, Manzini 1983b.

23. Contra Oca 1914, Belletti 1980, 1982, Chomsky 1981, Burzio 1981, Manzini 1983b.

24. The questions raised by the star in (19b), which, to my knowledge, is still to be explained, would take us too far afield.

25. Burzio in fact argues that when *si* moves from the subject position to the clitic postion, it leaves a trace, which is then filled by Object Preposing, and he assumes that "in derived structure SI properly "binds" the subject position, in spite of the fact that the latter is not c-commanded by SI" (1.3.1). If SI (which only by fiat can be made a subject NP) left behind a trace, we would have two overlapping chains, a problem that would require a revision of the theta-criterion, as Chomsky had pointed out (1984, III, 5.2.4).

26. It might be thought that the necessity/impossibility of *se* in (20) simply correlates with, respectively, the presence (FINITE) / absence (NON-FINITE) of AGR in a narrow sense (i.e., in the sense of [αI, βII]). Observe, however, that the latter difference obtains in (i) also, but no special device is needed:

(i)   Puede comer todos los dias
       'He/she can eat every day'

27. It is also necessary to assume something like a "principle of non-redundancy" such as that proposed in Zubizarreta 1985, which she states as (i):

(i)   Attachment of redundant morphology is prohibited.

28. Compare (21i) to (i), suggested by an example that was brought to my attention by Osvaldo Jaeggli:

(i)   Es necesario [PRO estudiar todos los días] para [PRO llegar a saber]
        'It is necessary PRO to study every day in order PRO to come to know'

The lower PRO is controlled by EC* in (21i) and by the higher PRO in (i) as excepted. On the other hand, in (21ii) the EC* in the embedded clause, being in the domain of a finite INFL (indicative or subjunctive), cannot be controlled, and as an indefinite non-overt NP is not open to a "proximate" interpretation (coreference).
29. It is made, however, in Strozer 1976 (within a pre-GB theory framework), where the content of the EC in (17b) is essentially that of what is called pro in Chomsky 1982, 79–and the content of what we are referring to as EC* includes the feature specification [–Def].
30. Incidentally, one might be tempted to think that the construction in (25) is independent of the NS parameter contrary to what has sometimes been assumed, since it is found in Catalan (together with the construction with the rough equivalent of English *one* as subject, we might add), and it was also found in Old Spanish, both NS languages, side by side with the construction under study. It should be kept in mind that in Spanish it disappeared half a millenium ago (cf. Brown 1931), and in Catalan it is no longer natural, as stressed in Badia Margarit, I, sect. 132. (I am indebted to Maria Soledat Jacas-Santoll for having reminded me of this reference.) cf. n.32 below.
31. Here again the present proposal represents the null hypothesis, which is to relate the "indefiniteness effect" to the content of the EC in the environment of the (de-definitized) INFL, not to simply assume that "the particle *si* [or *se*] has approximately the indefinite meaning of 'one/you/people'" (Burzio, 1.3.1), particularly because *si/se* does not have such a meaning in any other construction type.
32. In Strozer 1976, 264 the feature specification [–Specific], at one time taken to be a partial characterization of the informal notion 'indeterminate" (cf. Chomsky 1977, 200), is also included; in Zagona 1982, 5.1.1 it is the basic property of this type of NP. Since it is not clear that [Specificity] is a feature in the grammar (in a class of cases it is a direct consequence of scope relations), [–Def] seems preferable as a first approximation. Correspondingly, it seems reasonable to assume that the contrast illustrated in (22)-(23), which is of a grammatical nature, in independent of the (un)availability of a specific interpretation.
   It might be helpful to emphasize here that there is a fundamental difference between an overt indefinite NP (which is open to a specific interpretation) and a non-overt indefinite (cf. (15)). (On the difference between the construction with *uno* 'one' as the subject and the construction under study, see Perlmutter 1971, 2.3.2 and the references given there.)
33. The non-occurrence of SE in nonfinite constructions has been repeatedly pointed out, e.g., in Otero 1974 and in Strozer 1976, 266-7 for Spanish and in Burzio 1981 for Italian. Thus SE/SI is possible (and necessary) only in a class of finite construction, namely, the one under study. (I am idealizing slightly the data and ignoring some occasional apparent counterexamples, and a class of constructions that superficially might look like counterexamples, e.g., *puede comerse las manzanas* 'ARB can eat the apples'). The single Spanish example given by Belletti (1982, n.35), *estas ideas son difíciles de defenderse en estas circunstancias* 'these ideas are difficult of ARB defend in these circumstances', is clearly not a grammatical SE construction for the speakers I worked with (see, in particular, her 4.1.2.2, where, referring to the Italian equivalents of her

Spanish example, she remarks that they "should not be derivable"–cf. Zubizarreta 1982, 1985); in fact, closely related examples don't seem to be interpretable as SE constructions at all when no other interpretation is available, as in the alternatives with *SE* in (i):

(i)　　a.　Es difícil comer(*SE) todos los días (cf. (19b))
　　　　　　'It is difficult ARB to eat every day'
　　　　b.　Es difícil vivir(*SE) momentos felices
　　　　　　'It is difficult ARB to live happy moments'
　　　　　　(Cf. SE vive momentos felices)

Also clearly not grammatical are the Spanish cases of the analogue to the configuration that "never yields perfect results" in Italian (Burzio, ch.1, (19)):

(ii)　　a.　Parecía comer(*SE) todos los días
　　　　　　'It seemed ARB to eat every day'
　　　　b.　Resulta vivir(*SE) momentos felices
　　　　　　'It turns out ARB to live happy moments'

Needless to say, all other classes of examples of SE cooccurring with an infinitive, in particular those in (iii), are not grammatical for anyone:

(iii)　　a.　SE ordena comer(*SE) todos los días
　　　　　　'ARB orders ARB to eat every day'
　　　　b.　SE prefiere vivir(*SE) momentos felices
　　　　　　'ARB prefers ARB to live happy moments'

34. LGB, 52, 164; cf. George and Kornfilt 1981.
35. This means that we lose one of the explanations suggested for the "sort of paradox" exemplified in (i):

(i)　　(a)　(In questo paese) pro* si vive (SG) sempre nervosi (NON-SG)
　　　　　　'In this country ARB always lives nervous'
　　　　(b)　Non è chiaro come pro* essere allegri (NON-SG)
　　　　　　'It is unclear how ARB to be happy'

As Belletti points out, at the observational level there is no surface agreement between *nervosi* (like *allegri* a non-singular adjective form) and the finite verb form (*vive*) in (ia). In view of this, she proposes that in Italian *SI* "is not only in INFL, but is in fact the realization of AGR in these cases", so that *vive*, è in (i) "are unmarked stems" (271). Such a proposal is not beyond question. For one thing, *mangio/mangiera/mangierebbe* are not identical to *mangia-* (the unmarked stem), in (ii):

　　　　　　Si mangiò/mangiera/mangierebbe le mele
　　　　　　'ARB ate/will eat/would eat the apples'

and the spelling out procedure will not be able to operate adequately in (ii) if the verb feature specification matrix does not contain "AGR". More importantly, an alternative that appears to be preferable in any case is to exploit the necessary (and crucial) distinction between the cosuperscripting of the subject with AGR (presumably part of core grammar) and the (free) association between the subject and the predicate, which plausibly involves no indexing (see Higginbotham 1984). A feature complex with unmarked values such as pro* can easily be open to either singular or non-singular interpretation under predication (a binary relation). From this perspective, it is not surprising to find examples not unlike the Italian ones in Spanish, e.g.:

(iii) a. Con libertad pro* se ha de andar en este camino, puestos (NON-SG) de la mano de Dios
'With freedom ARB is to walk in this path, placed (NON-SG) in the hand of God'
b. Así pro* se debía estar en el cielo, aunque un proco más anchos (NON-SG) y sudando menos
'Thus ARB should be in heaven, although a little more spacious (NON-SG) and sweating less'

(The first one is found in a XVI century literary work (Teresa, *Vida*) and the second is taken from a modern author. Both are documented in Kärde 1943.) Consider also the following:

(iv) a. Es posible pro* ser arrestados juntos
'It is possible ARB to be arrested (NON-SG) together'
b. pro* SE puede ser arrestado(s) juntos (en grupos de diez)
'ARB may be arrested (NON-SG) together in (in groups of ten)'

Conversely, a sentence such as (v) used in a preface by a single author referring to his/her book (a not uncommon practice) might make an adjective in the singular form desirable even in Italian:

(v) SE es consciente de los escasos méritos de esta obra
'ARB is conscious of the limited merits of this work'

In any case, not all [+V] categories are pluralized in SI constructions in Italian, and the predication approach might account for this contrast.
36. It is generally assumed that PRO with arbitrary variable-like interpretation, as in (17a), appears "only in the positions that are 'transparent' in the sense of the binding theory, that is, the positions in which overt anaphors need not be bound by an antecedent within the same major category (clause or NP)" (Chomsky 1982, 18, 27; 1984, 3.3.4.2, 3.5.5). This is not true of pro*. The following pairs contrast in that (iib) is grammatical:

(i) a. They want each other to be happy
b. *Each other want to be happy
(ii) a. (Ellos) quieren PRO ser felices
b. pro* se quiere PRO ser feliz

On the other hand, in (iia) PRO is controlled by the higher subject (see also (21)), but in (iii) it cannot be:

(iii) (Ellos) quieren que pro* se sea feliz
'they want that ARB be happy'

Observe that if it is true that SE constructions are structures "deprived" of definiteness, it can still be the case that AGR is the crucial element determining opacity in these structures (cf. p.210).
37. Suñer (1982a, 1983) has defended a different view. She claims that ECα in (i) is interpreted as ARB:

(i)   ECα llaman a la puerta
           'they are knocking at the door'

Limitations of space do not allow me to argue here against this claim. Suffice it to say that a use that permits leaving a referent at the outer limits of definiteness (i.e. sufficiently vague that the referent can be taken to be a person or persons not clearly definite), which might be particularly appropriate when "it is immaterial for what is being stated to identify the referents", is not necessarily "a formal way to indicate arbitrariness of reference in contemporary Spanish" (Suñer 1983, 189)–see note 41). The claim just quoted is difficult to reconcile with the widely accepted fundamental leading idea that a finite INFL (without SE) invariably determines a non-overt subject as [+def]. Notice also that (i) differs from its English analogue only in that the remote obviative interpretation is not possible with a pronoun with a phonetic matrix in place of an EC, a direct consequence, it would appear, of the NS parameter (see above, in particular (15)). Cf. p.289.

38. It has sometimes been assumed that feminine predicates are not possible in SE structures. For a reference for the following attested example, see Kärde 1943:

(i)   Cuando se nace honrada, no es tan fácil dejar de serlo
           'When ARB is born honest (Fem), it is not easy ARB to stop being it'.

Cf. Manzini 1983b.

39. Since we have a very natural account of the fact that SE never appears in non-finite constructions, there is no need to appeal to Case Theory to exclude it form the subject position of non-finite constructions as Burzio does (cf. Oca 1914).

40. The expletive analysis of what I am referring to as pro* (in a finite clause) is argued for in Hyams 1983. It is to be observed that, contrary to what has been claimed, it makes no difference whether the predicate is or is not an idiom. Thus, in

(i)   Cuando menos pro* se espera, pro* se ve las estrellas
           'When ARB least expects it, ARB sees the stars'

ve las estrellas can be understood in its literal sense ('sees the stars') or in its idiomatic sense (roughly, 'feels sharp pain').

41. For some discussion and initial qualifications, see Lo Cascio 1974, 182-5. There is no question that a statement such as *SE es mortal* 'ARB is mortal' may be understood as a universally quantified expression, but this is not generally the case, and in particular it is not the case in *SE dice que va a nevar* 'ARB says that it is going to snow', contrary to what is suggested in Epstein 1984, 503. In terms of quantification, EC* and PRO are quite different, the main reason being that as a rule EC* is part of an "indexical expression" (see the references in note 21), whereas arbitrary PRO is not, as hinted just immediately before (1).

42. See Chomsky 1977, 29ff; cf. Evans 1982, 59-60. From this perspective the use of some tokens of the SE construction type is intriguing. Here is an example that has recently come to my attention (*Cambio 16*, March 11, 1985, p. 66a):

(i)   Alli se cambia, se compra, se buscan [N.B.-CO] componentes de conjunto o, simple-
           mente, se está
           'There ARB exchanges, ARB buys, ARB look [NON-SG] for set components or,
           simply, ARB is there'

Presumably it was examples similar to *se buscan componentes* in (i) that led Burzio (1981, 1.3.2) to write that "in some ... dialects [object preposing, i.e. NP-movement] is near-obligatory". This is no way out of the problem, however. Under the analysis presented above, NP-movement cannot be obligatory in a SE structure, since it is not possible (cf. (10)), and it is clear from the linguistic context that each of the clauses in (i) is a SE construction (not a *se*-passive). Even in isolation, the string *se buscan [NON-SG] componentes* with the intended meaning of *se busca componentes* would not be unremarkable (cf. Cinque 1976a). More significantly, not even the passive derivation made available by GB theory makes it possible to account for the use of, e.g. (iia), instead of the imperative sentence in (iib), even out of context, since passives are not used as imperatives:

(ii)   a. Ejecútense [NON-SG] las órdenes dadas
       b. Ejecútese (SG) las órdenes dadas
          'Execute (you ARB) the orders given'

Several facts to keep in mind when considering *se buscan (NON-SG) componentes, ejecútense (NON-SG) las órdenes,* and similar data, when intended to be understood (and generally understood as) *se busca componentes, ejecútese las órdenes,* etc., are the following: (1) No speaker has the slightest difficulty with structures of the form (iii)

(iii)   SE V(SG)NP(NON-SG)

which are generally understood as SE constructions and easily pass unnoticed to anyone in spontaneous conversation, a fact usually neglected by students of these constructions in Spanish, though not by students of Italian. (2). Many speakers that use structures of the form (iii) in spontaneous conversation consciously substitute a non-singular verb form on occasion, particularly in writing or in public speaking. (3) Although they obviously are peculiarly Romance innovations, with no remote parallel in Latin, structures of the form (iii) have been around for centuries. In fact, the earliest example of the SE construction attested, which goes back to the second half of the XIII century, happens to be of the form (iii):

(iv)   Si se cree los mágicos, ...
        'If ARB believes the magicians, ...'

(cf. Martín Zorraquino, 151-2). It should be added that structures of the form (iii) are used earlier than *si*-passives by Italian children. See note 45.

The questions that arise in relation with these data are, however, beyond the scope of this paper. For dated but still relevant discussion, see the latest version of Otero 1974 and the references cited there (cf. Westphal 1980, perhaps the most recent monograph on the topic); for a very informative general survey, see the 1979 book by María Antonia Martín Zorraquino I have just referred to.

43. "Unfortunately", writes Marantz (1984, 199-200), "the good candidates for ergative languages for which I have data do not exhibit clear cases of control constructions in which this prediction might be tested".

44. Here is Marantz's characterization:

(i)   (1) a. Agent roles are assigned by predicates
             b. Theme and patient roles are assigned by verbs
       (2) a. Agent roles are assigned by verbs
             b. Theme and patient roles are assigned by predicates

"True ergative" languages choose (i2), whereas non-ergative ones choose (i1). (i) brings to mind Jackendoff's (1972, 2.5) "thematic hierarchy", repeated below as (ii), except that in (i) no reference is made to his second option:

(ii)   (1) Agent
        (2) Location, source, goal
        (3) Theme

We might ask whether Jackendoff's second option could fall together with either the first or the third at a deeper level of generalization. Marantz's work suggests that goal falls together with the first, whereas source and location (which is sometimes placed at the bottom of the "subject hierarchy" for non-ergative languages) fall with the third. The basic contrast, then seems to be between themes and non-themes.

The following are examples of SE structures with non-theme subjects:

(iii)   a. pro* SE cruzó las dos plazas   'ARB crossed the two squares'
         b. pro* SE recibió las cartas   'ARB received the letters'
         c. pro* SE vio las estrellas   'ARB saw the stars'

In (a), the subject is assigned the θ-role agent, even though the predicate also assigns theme (as in *el patín cruzó las dos plazas* 'the roller skate crossed the two squares'); in (b), the subject is assigned the θ-role goal or recipient; in (c), that of experiencer. Now consider

(iv)   d. pro* SE toca el piano cada vez que pro* SE pasa junto a él
            'ARB plays/touches the piano every time ARB passes by it'

If *tocar* is interpreted as 'play', the subject can only be agent; if it is interpreted as 'touch', the agent interpretation is at the very least overwhelmingly the preferred one. (It is observed in Strozer, 571 that although *Este guía me costó muy caro* 'This guide (person) cost me a lot', with a human subject, is possible, *SE me costó muy caro* 'ARB cost me a lot'–cf. *SE me dijo muy poco* 'ARB told me very little'–is questionable). If the theme interpretation is possible, (i) could still hold if for θ-theory each sense is an independent θ-role assigner, since in its nonagentive sense *tocar* 'touch' would assign only theme. Something of the sort might be necessary to maintain the θ-criterion unmodified (cf. 139). See Pesetsky (1982, 57-8) for what I take to be supporting evidence from Russian. Significantly, (36i) subsumes both his Agent rule and his Theme rule.
45. See Hyams 1983, IV.3.1, and the reference she gives, for Italian. In Randeri 1980, the earliest case of a string of this type given for Spanish-speaking children of the Los Angeles area is recorded as uttered at 5.3, but this seems to be an artifact of the sample, which is almost exclusively from children between the ages of five and nine.
46. On the other hand, it is well known that, at least in English and some other languages, the ordinary passive construction is acquired quite late. Cf. Valesio 1976, n.1.
47. If the results reported in Marantz 1982 are essentially correct, the value of the ergative parameter need not be known before age five.
48. This is not an exhaustive classification. See Strozer, III.
49. This is the view presented in Strozer 1976, within what from the present perspective is a rudimentary empty category approach to clitic constructions (cf. Bok-Bennema 1981) in which the clitics are, consequently, base-generated. (Strangely enough, this approach, the real motivation in the earliest proposal of this kind, is not taken over in subsequent analyses that adopt the base-generation idea, an important difference from Strozer's analysis that has generally passed unnoticed). The EC is also taken to be an empty pronoun, within the LGB framework, In Zubizarreta 1982, II.4. For an updated, lucid, and carefully argued presentation of the empty pronoun view, within a modified version of the GB framework, see Sportiche 1983, III (cf. Goodall 1984, perhaps the latest sustained study of Spanish clitics, sect. 3.5). I assume that Sportiche's theory of clitics, which is close to my own view, particularly in his analysis of non-reflexive clitics, is independent of some of his more general conclusions.

50. This is the reason why SE was dubbed "non-paradigmatic *se*" twenty years ago, a label later (1973) used as part of the title of a doctoral dissertation on the topic (see Suñer 1982a: 369). For a similar view about Italian *si*, see Napoli 1976, Burzio 1981, 5.7.5 (cf. Cinque 1976b, Manzini 1983b).

A note on the visibility condition*

M. Carme Picallo, *Columbia University, New York*

1. This note is concerned with the status of the principles of Case in the theory of grammar. I would like to support a hypothesis proposed by Aoun (1981) and Chomsky (1981, forthcoming), suggesting that the function of Case is that of making arguments of predication "visible" for theta-role interpretation–i.e. the visibility condition. The empirical evidence for this claim will be provided by data drawn mainly from Spanish.

The visibility hypothesis entails that all governed categories which have the status of arguments in a thematic relation must bear Case features or be in a Case-marked chain. This has been partially argued against in Safir (1982), who suggests that sentential arguments cannot appear in Case-marked chains. Thus, according to this view, the Case filter cannot be subsumed under the Theta Criterion,[1] the filter being an independent condition applicable to a subset of the argument structure that the projection principle would require for a given predicate, namely, to governed NPs exclusively.[2]

In this note I would like to argue that features for Case appear to be realized in the nominal and sentential arguments of all major categories characterized by the features [+/–N, +/–V].

2. I will first suggest that the Case filter can be reformulated as in (1), and that Case is realized under the conditions specified in (2):

(1)   *[α] when α is governed and/or lexically specified and α is not in a
        Case-marked chain.[3]

(2)   (i)   α is nominative if governed by [+AGR][4]
        (ii)   α is accusative if governed by V
        (iii)   α is genitive if governed by N or A
        (iv)   α is oblique if governed by P

The formulation of the Case filter as given in (1) excludes from the require-

* This article is a revised version of a part of Chapter III of my doctoral dissertation *Opaque Domains*, C.U.N.Y. 1985.

ment of Case marking argument chains which contain the null element PRO as their only member as well as those representing the derivational history of PRO, while including all the rest.

The visibility hypothesis is an attempt to eliminate the stipulatory character of Case requirements by deriving them from the θ-Criterion: every governed category which receives a θ-role must be Case marked for its proper interpretation at logical structure. Thus, Theta Theory and the Projection Principle become a central notion of the theory of Case under this view. The visibility condition is stated as follows:

(3)   If a position P is marked with the θ-role R and $C = (\alpha_1, \ldots, \alpha_n)$ is a chain, then C is assigned R by P if and only if for some i, α_i is in position P and C has Case or is headed by argument PRO.

(Chomsky 1981, 334)

Condition (3) predicts the ungrammaticality of infinitive sentential structures exhibiting a subject argument other than the pronominal anaphor PRO.[5]

(4)   a. *Era necesario [[la recuperación]$_i$ ser controlada [e]$_i$ cuidadosamente]
       'It was necessary [[the recovery]$_i$ to be monitored [e]$_i$ carefully]'
       b. *Ignorábamos por qué [[PRO cantar]$_i$ parecer [[e]$_i$ estar prohibido]]
       'We ignored why [[PRO to sing]$_i$ to seem [[e]$_i$ to be prohibited]]'

In (4a) the lexically specified NP argument of a passive predicate does not receive Case; it is not possible either to assign structural Case to the derived clausal subject in (4b). If the NP or the clause are governed by [+AGR], the sentences are grammatical:

(5)   a. Era necesario que [[la recuperación]$_i$ [+AGR] fuera controlada [e]$_i$ cuidadosamente]
       'It was necessary that [[the recovery]$_i$ was monitored [e]$_i$ carefully]'
       b. Ignorábamos por qué [[PRO cantar]$_i$ [+AGR] parecía [[e]$_i$ estar prohibido]]
       'We ignored why [[PRO to sing]$_i$ seemed [[e]$_i$ to be prohibited]]'

It may be assumed that the absence of structural Case marking to the surface subject is what rules out examples (4a,b). No principles of grammar such as the Empty Category Principle (ECP) or the (Extended) Projection Principle (see Chomsky 1981) appear to be violated, and the c-command and local binding requirements between the argument antecedent and the trace are fulfilled. However, the absence of Case marking to the head of the argument chain violates the visibility condition.

As is known, elements with the grammatical function of subject may appear postverbally in null-subject languages, such as Catalan, Italian, or Spanish. Chomsky (1981) and Rizzi (1982) have suggested that nominative arguments in postverbal position, whether base generated in [NP,VP] (see Burzio 1981) or adjoined to VP via Move α (see Rizzi 1982), are linked by chain formation to an expletive pronominal-like element in the [NP,S] position.[6] In these cases the expletive pronominal[7] heading the argument chain is governed and Case marked by [+AGR]. The chain is assigned nominative through the governed expletive in its head. Chain composition is represented by co-superscripting (irrelevant details omitted):

(6)   a. [pro^i cantaba [yo]^i]
          '[(It)^i was singing [I]^i]'
    b. [pro^i nos divertía [PRO bailar]^i]
          '[(It)^i amused us [PRO to dance]^i]'
    c. [pro^i era obvio [que Isabel estaba contenta]^i]
          '[(It)^i was obvious [that Elizabeth was happy]^i]'

It is generally assumed that expletive elements must be linked by chain formation to an argument they c-command.[8] Expletives may be viewed as having a double function in the sentence: on the one hand, they may occupy a syntactic position for the purposes of formally licensing a predicate (cf. note 6); on the other hand, they may act as Case holders for the chain they head, transmitting these features to the argument they are co-superscripted with. This prevents some structures which would otherwise be permitted (or required) by θ-theory and the Projection Principle from being barred by the visibility condition through the Case filter.

Safir (1982) has noticed that expletive PRO appears to be excluded from the set of empty categories. The fact that the grammar seems to prohibit expletive ungoverned elements may be accounted for by Aoun's (1981) and Chomsky's (1981) hypothesis that argumenthood needs to be marked by the realization of Case features in order to be properly interpreted at some level of representation.

Suppose that the sentences exemplified in (6a-c) above with a postponed subject were in the infinitive. The absence of [Tense/AGR] features would leave the element in [NP,S] position ungoverned and unable to be assigned structural Case. PRO is the only element which may appear in the subject position of infinitive clauses. In the cases under consideration, the empty ungoverned category could only be expletive PRO, otherwise the presence of an argument pronominal anaphor would rule out the structure as ungrammatical because the chain would then contain two arguments: argument PRO and the postposed subject.

The visibility condition, through the Case filter, would exclude structures such as those exemplified in (7) showing an ungoverned (and non-Case-marked) expletive in [NP,S] position in the head of an argument chain which may not receive Case otherwise:[9]

(7)   a. *Era necesario [PRO$^i_{(ex)}$ [-AGR] cantar [yo]^i]
          'It was necessary [PRO$^i_{(ex)}$ to sing [I]^i]'
       b. *No sabíamos por qué [PRO$^i_{(ex)}$ [-AGR] divertirnos [PRO bailar]^i]
          'We didn't know why [PRO$^i_{(ex)}$ to amuse us [PRO to dance]^i]'
       c. *Le molestaba [PRO$^i_{(ex)}$ [-AGR] ser obvio [que Isabel estaba contenta]^i]
          'It bothered him/her [PRO$^i_{(ex)}$ to be obvious [that Elizabeth was happy]^i]'

These structures might be assumed to be ruled out by a condition such as visibility, contingent on Case marking, and not by syntactic requirements of well-formedness such as the predication rule. Given that the ungrammaticality of (4a) and (7a) appears to be in all respects parallel to (4b) and (7b,c), respectively, it may be claimed that clauses as well as NPs must be in a chain where Case is realized when having the function of arguments of predication.

3. Earlier versions of Case theory, such as Rouveret and Vergnaud's (1980), assumed that nominal categories such as Adjectives and Nouns were not Case assigners. This was based on the fact that their complements must always appear preceded by a preposition in order to preserve grammaticality:

(8)   a. *Estábamos orgullosos Juan
          'We were proud John'
       b. Estábamos orgullosos *de* Juan
          'We were proud *of* John'

(9)   a. *Un buen ambiente de trabajo era imprescindible Pilar
          'A good working environment was essential Pilar'
       b. Un buen ambiente de trabajo era imprescindible *para* Pilar
          'A good working environment was essential *for* Pilar'

(10)   a. *Observábamos el aterrizaje los aviones
          'We were observing the landing the planes'
       b. Observábamos el aterrizaje *de* los aviones
          'We were observing the landing *of* the planes'

The unacceptability of (8a), (9a), (10a) led to the assumption that only [-N] categories such as verbs and prepositions, as well as the [Tense/AGR] marker in the head of INFL, were able to assign Case.

Van Riemsdijk (1980) argued, however, that German adjectives must be considered Case assigners. Morphological marks for Case (genitive or dative, according to the lexical idiosyncrasies of the adjective) appear overtly in the NP complement of an adjective without a mediating preposition:

(11)　a. Das Franzoesische ist *ihm* ungelaeufig
　　　　'French is *to him* not fluent'
　　　b. Dieser Mann muss *des Franzoesischen* maechtig sein
　　　　'This man must *of French* in command of be'

(van Riemsdijk 1980)

He questions an initial hypothesis that Case could have been assigned to the NP by the verb *to be* through previous reanalysis with the adjective. He points out that such an assumption leads to the problem of properly accounting for the fact that the complex predicate, obtained under the hypothetical reanalysis operation, conforms to the idiosyncrasies of the adjective with respect to Case selection, not to the properties of the copula. Moreover, nominal complements of prenominal predicative adjectives in German also appear inflected for genitive or dative. In those cases there is no verbal element with which the adjective could be reanalyzed in order to assign Case to its object:

(12)　a. Ein [*ihm* ungelaeufiges] Wort
　　　　'A [*to him* unfamiliar] work'
　　　b. Der [*seiner Freundin* ueberdruessige] Student
　　　　'The [*of his girlfriend* weary] student'

(van Riemsdijk 1980)

Overt Case features may also appear in the nominal complements of some adjective predicates in Spanish, such as the one exemplified in (9) above. If the NP is pronominalized, as in the corresponding sentence (13), a clitic marked for dative heads a chain interpreted as the benefactive argument of the adjective:[10]

(13)　Un buen ambiente de trabajo *le*[i] era imprescindible [*e*][i]
　　　'A good working environment *for him/her*[i] was essential [*e*][i]'

In Romance languages with a more extensive clitic system than Spanish, such as Catalan or Italian, the arguments of adjective predicates which undergo cliticization show morphological Case as well; either dative, in constructions similar to the Spanish example above, or genitive. Consider the following examples in Catalan:

(14)   a. Estaba orgullós del [seu èxit]
            '(He) was proud of [his/her success]'
         b. Estava content de [PRO haver-te vist]
            '(He) was happy of [PRO to have seen you]'
         c. Estava segura [que vindries]
            '(She) was sure [that you would come]'

The genitive clitic *en/ne* stands for the clausal or nominal arguments of the adjective if those undergo cliticization:

(15)   a. N^{i}' estava orgullós $[e]^{i}$
            'He *of* NP^{i} was proud $[e]^{i}$'
         b. N^{i}' estava content $[e]^{i}$
            'He *of* S^{i} was happy $[e]^{i}$'
         c. N^{i}' estava segura $[e]^{i}$
            'She *of* S^{i} was sure $[e]^{i}$'

Arguments of nouns may also undergo genitive cliticization in Italian (see Cinque 1980) or in Catalan (see Argente 1976):

(16)   a. Observàvem l'aterratge de [l'avió]
            'We were observing the landing of [the plane]'
         b. Teníem la sospita [que s'havia equivocat]
            'We had the suspicion [that he/she erred]'

(17)   a. N^{i}' observàvem l'atterratge $[e]^{i}$
            'We *of* NP^{i} were observing the landing $[e]^{i}$'
         b. En^{i} teniem la sospita $[e]^{i}$
            'We *of* S^{i} had the suspicion $[e]^{i}$'

The transitive verb may not have assigned Case to the argument internal to the NP it subcategorizes for. The complex NP is marked for accusative by this predicate:

(18)   a. l^{i}' observàvem $[e]^{i}$ (cf. (16a))
            'We it^{i} observed $[e]^{i}$'
         b. La^{i} teníem $[e]^{i}$ (cf. (16b))
            'We it^{i} had $[e]^{i}$'

In Manzini (1983b) the property of being a Case assigner is extended to Nouns. She suggests that the preposition *of* or its correlate in other languages (*de* in Spanish or Catalan) has no semantic content in those cases but serves the purposes of morphological inflection. The preposition may be considered, in some notional sense, an "expletive" element inserted to preserve grammaticality. The idea behind Manzini's proposal would be that languages, when losing Case inflection, may substitute the function of the desinence of Case by prepositions such as *of*, or other syntactic elements like the *'s* marker in English, allowing the argument to be properly interpreted with respect to the θ-role it bears.

Chomsky (forthcoming) suggests that the θ-role assigned by [+N] categories, which are not structural Case assigners (such as [+AGR], V, or prepositions with semantic import),[11] has to be morphologically expressed in their arguments. Under the assumption that the base component is category neutral (see Stowell 1981) the Projection Principle predicts that major categories semantically related such as Verbs and deverbal Nouns have the same complement system. However, structures containing predicative Nouns and Adjectives would be ruled out for lack of Case realization in their arguments. In these cases, the grammar resorts to other mechanisms such as preposition insertion in order to meet the Case filter.

Arguments of Nouns and Adjectives in Spanish, whether clausal (tensed or untensed) or Nominal, require preposition insertion:

(19) a. Teresa estaba convencida *de* [que ya lo dijo]
          'Therese was convinced *of* [that (he/she) said it already]'
      b. Juan estaba orgulloso *de* [PRO haber ganado]
          'John was proud *of* [PRO to have won]'
      c. Estábamos avergonzados *de* [la actitud de su amigo]
          'We were embarrassed *of* [the attitude of his/her friend]'

(20) a. El temor *de* [que contara aquella historia]
          'The fear *of* [that he/she) told that story]'
      b. El deseo *de* [PRO bailar]
          'The desire *of* [PRO to dance]'
      c. La sospecha *de* [su traición]
          'The suspicion *of* [his/her treachery]'

It must be noticed that *of* insertion or its equivalent does not apply in English, Catalan, or Italian if the complements of [+N] categories are [+AGR] clausal arguments:

(21) a. She was happy [that we called]
      b. Estava contenta [que *pro* telefonéssim]   (cf. (19a))

In English *of* is not inserted, either, if the complements of Adjectives and Nouns are infinitive clauses:

(22)   Your attempt [PRO to finish early]

Stowell (1981) has suggested that the particle *to* found in English infinitive structures might have the function of preposition insertion for the purposes of fulfilling the visibility condition.[12]

As discussed above, clitic pronouns manifest morphological Case in Romance, unlike NPs. Then, similarly to what occurs in the instances of NP complements of Adjectives in German, the licensing properties of [+N] categories as θ-role assigners are already morphologically realized in their arguments if cliticization applies, that is, the argument chains are visible. Following Stowell's suggestion it might be claimed that *of* insertion may not necessarily apply if the head INFL of the clausal argument already has a "Case" feature. In the cases of [+AGR] clausal complements this would be a Case-assigning feature which is morphologically realized. I would like to suggest that it is this morphological marker which makes the clausal argument already visible at the relevant level.[13]

NOTES

1. The θ-criterion dictates that each expression requiring a θ-role be assigned one, and that each θ-role determined by the lexical properties of a predicate be uniquely assigned to an argument:

(i) θ-*Criterion*: given the structure S, there is a set K of chains K $= C_i$, where $C_i = (\alpha_1^i, \ldots, \alpha_n^i)$, such that:
(a) if α is an argument of S, then there is a $C_i \epsilon K$ such that $\alpha = \alpha_j^i$ and a θ-role is assigned to C_i by exactly one position P.
(b) if P is a position of S marked with the θ-role R, then there is a $C_i \epsilon K$ to which P assigns and exactly one α_j^i in C_i is an argument.

(Chomsky 1981, 335)

2. I am referring to *governed* NPs and not only to *lexical* NPs, as originally stated in the Case filter proposed in Rouveret and Vergnaud (1980), Chomsky (1980), in order to include *pro*, a non-anaphoric pronominal without phonetic features (c*f*. Chomsky 1982), into the elements subject to the filter.
3. The Case filter was originally formulated as follows:

(i)   *NP to VP   (Chomsky and Lasnik 1977)

This represents the English instantiation of a condition expressing that no lexical element can appear in the [NP,S] position of an infinitive sentence.
4. I am assuming the following definitions of Government and c-command:

(i)   Given $[_\beta \ldots \gamma \ldots \alpha \ldots \gamma \ldots]$, where
(a) $\alpha = X^0$.

(b) where φ is a maximal projection, if φ dominates γ then φ dominates α.

c. α c-command γ, α governs γ.

(Chomsky 1981, 165)

(ii) α c-commands β iff

(a) α does not contain β.

(b) Suppose that $\gamma_1, \ldots, \gamma_n$ is the maximal sequence such that

(i) $\gamma_n = \alpha$

(ii) $\gamma_i = \alpha^j$

(iii) γ_i immediately dominates γ_{i+1}

Then if δ dominates α, then either (I) δ dominates β,

or (II) $\delta - \gamma_i$, and γ_1 dominates β.

(Chomsky 1981, 166)

5. N. Chomsky (p.c.) has suggested that argument PRO may have inherent features which make this element intrinsically visible. These features are [+animate] and [±plural].

6. The presence of a syntactic subject (argumental or pleonastic) is required, at least at S-Structure, in order to satisfy well-formedness conditions such as the Predicate Linking Rule (see Rothstein 1983, 27). This condition establishes that all syntactic functions must be saturated. See Zagona (1982) and Rothstein (1983) for discussion on this issue.

7. Expletive elements have no phonological matrix in the null subject languages (cf. *pro*). Hyams (1983) attributes this characteristic of Romance expletives, as well as the possibility of having phonologically unrealized subjects, to the intrinsic characterization of the AGR marker in the head of INFL.

8. See however Safir (1982), who argues against this proposal.

9. The ungrammaticality of expletive PRO as a consequence of the visibility hypothesis was first pointed out, I believe, by L. Burzio.

10. I am assuming that a clitic can head an argument chain despite being in an A' position (see Chomsky 1982, Kayne 1983).

11. These would be prepositions other than *de* 'of' and *a/para* 'to/for'. Kayne (1975, 145ff) points out that two types of preposition *à* appear to exist in French. He refers to it as the "Double-A Hypothesis": one type of [à-NP] complements allows dative cliticization, the other type of [à-NP] constructions does not allow it. This may suggest that in the first instance *à* is a morpheme with the function of making visible the θ-role of the external argument of the verb, in a fashion similar to *of* discussed above; whereas in the second case *à* is a structural Case assigner, the NP being the object of this preposition.

12. Reuland (1981) has indicated as well that the particle *to* could be considered a "dummy" Case marker in some sense.

13. Specification for a structural Case assigner such as [+AGR]/Tense (and perhaps "dummy" *to* - see note 12) in the head of clausal arguments appears to trigger obligatory movement of sentential arguments to a peripheral position. Stowell (1981) has argued that categories exhibiting a Case-assigning feature in their head may not receive *structural* Case directly, although if they receive a θ-role they must be in a Case-marked chain in order to fulfill the visibility condition. Stowell's suggestion tries to explain, in terms of a subprinciple of Case theory (cf. the Case Resistance Principle), the observation of some authors such as Rosenbaum (1967), Kuno (1973), Emonds (1976), and Koster (1978), among others, that sentences may not appear in argument positions where Case is structurally assigned, that is [NP,S] and [NP,VP]. See Stowell (1981) for extensive discussion on this issue, and Picallo (1985), who supports Stowell's basic hypothesis with data from null-subject languages.

Substantive: A neutralized syntactic category in Spanish*

Susan Plann, *U.C.L.A.*

The purpose of this study is to determine the syntactic category of elements such as *encima, debajo, cerca, lejos.*[1] Such elements have been classified in various ways by traditional grammarians of Spanish. For example, according to some grammarians these words are adverbs, while according to others they are prepositions.[2] In what follows I present a different analysis, arguing that these words, which share certain properties with both nouns and adjectives, belong to a neutralized syntactic category, referred to here as "substantive" (S).

I shall assume here the analysis of Chomsky (1974), according to which verbs have the syntactic features [−N +V], nouns are [+N −V], adjectives are [+N +V], and prepositions are [−N −V]. This analysis is crucial for Case Theory,[3] according to which the [−N] categories, that is, verbs and prepositions, assign Case, while the [+N] categories, nouns and adjectives, receive Case. The Case Filter specifies that lexical noun phrases must bear Case.

This analysis provides us with an explanation for the use of *de* in examples like the following:

(1) a. $[_{VP} [_V$ desear] (*de) $[_{NP}$ la paz]]
        to-desire of the peace
     b. nuestros deseos $[_{PP} [_P$ para] (*de) $[_{NP}$ la paz]]
        our desires for of the peace
     c. $[_{NP}$ el $[_N$ deseo] *(de) $[_{NP}$ la paz]]
        the desire of the peace
     d. $[_{AP} [_A$ deseoso] *(de) $[_{NP}$ la paz]]
        desirous of the peace

The verb in (1a) and the preposition in (1b) can assign Case directly to the noun phrase complement, *la paz.* But in (1c), (1d), neither the noun nor the adjective can assign Case, and consequently *de* must be inserted in order to assign Case to the noun phrase, and thus avoid violation of the Case Filter.

Turning now to the question of the syntactic category to which words such

*Thanks are due to Carlos Otero, whose comments on an earlier version of this work led to significant improvements in the analysis.

as *encima*, *debajo* (our "substantives") should be assigned, I have already observed that many traditional grammars classify them as adverbs, a category which has traditionally been the catch-all for many elements with diverse syntactic properties.[4] I shall not explicitly address this traditional analysis here. Nevertheless, the evidence presented in this study, which demonstrates that substantives represent a neutralized syntactic category that resembles both the noun and the adjective, automatically refutes the hypothesis that these words are adverbs.

I have also noted that some grammarians consider these words to be prepositions. Although I shall ultimately reject this analysis, let us first briefly review some possible arguments in its favor. Semantically, some substantives have very near prepositional equivalents, for instance, $[_P$ *bajo*$]$ *la mesa*/$[_S$ *debajo*$]$ *de la mesa* 'under the table'. Furthermore, substantive phrases (SP) may occur in positions that require prepositional phrases, for example, as the complement of verbs like *estar* 'to be', *poner* 'to put', and *dejar* 'to leave':

(2)　　a.　El libro estaba $[_{PP}$ en la mesa$]$/$[_{SP}$ encima de la mesa$]$ the book was on the table/on-top of the table

　　　　b.　Pon/Deja esos papeles $[_{PP}$ en el sobre$]$ $[_{SP}$ dentro del sobre$]$ put/leave those papers in the envelope/inside of-the envelope

Moreover, it is clear that historically some substantives were once prepositional phrases. For example, *encima* 'on top' and *enfrente* 'in front' once had the respective structures of (3a), (3b):[5]

(3)　　a.　$[_{PP}$ $[_P$ en$]$ $[_{NP}$ cima$]]$
　　　　b.　$[_{PP}$ $[_P$ en$]$ $[_{NP}$ frente$]]$

That is, such phrases had the same syntactic structure as prepositional phrases like *en contra* 'against', *en medio* 'in (the) middle', *a la ribera* 'on the shore':[6]

(4)　　a.　$[_{PP}$ $[_P$ en$]$ $[_{NP}$ contra$]]$
　　　　b.　$[_{PP}$ $[_P$ en$]$ $[_{NP}$ medio$]]$
　　　　c.　$[_{PP}$ $[_P$ a$]$ $[_{NP}$ la ribera$]]$

But such arguments are far from compelling. A grammar in which the syntactic component is autonomous will have little use for semantically based arguments. As for the distributional arguments, while substantives can occur in positions that subcategorize a PP, these same positions also subcategorize AP, as will be discussed below. And finally, as for the historical arguments, while some substantives were at one time prepositional phrases, others, *lejos*, for instance, may once have been adjectives.[7]

The arguments in favor of classifying substantives as prepositional phrases, then, are by no means conclusive. But the evidence against so classifying them is, to my mind, overwhelming. Let us now turn to that evidence.

In what follows, we shall see that substantives share certain properties with both nouns and adjectives, and these same properties distinguish all three categories–substantives, nouns, and adjectives–from prepositions. Note first that substantives, like the [+N] categories (noun and adjective) but unlike the [–N] catgories (one of which is the preposition), do not assign Case. To avoid violation of the Case Filter, substantives, nouns, and adjectives require the insertion of *de* before an NP complement (5)-(7), while prepositions disallow it (8):

(5)   a. la [$_N$ defensa] *(de) [$_{NP}$ la ciudad]
         the defense of the city
      b. el [$_N$ orgullo] *(de) [$_{NP}$ los profesores]
         the pride of the professors

(6)   a. [$_A$ contento] *(de) [$_{NP}$ sus notas]
         content of his grades
      b. [$_A$ orgulloso] *(de) [$_{NP}$ su hija]
         proud of his daughter

(7)   a. [$_S$ lejos] *(de) [$_{NP}$ su hogar]
         far from his home
      b. [$_S$ alrededor] *(de) [$_{NP}$ la casa]
         around of the house

(8)   a. muchos saludos [$_P$ para] (*de) [$_{NP}$ toda la familia)
         many greetings for of all the family
      b. su interés [$_P$ en] (*de) [$_{NP}$ la física]
         his interest in of the physics

Moreover, substantives can receive Case. In this respect as well, they resemble the [+N] categories, that is, nouns, which according to the Case Filter *must* receive Case, and adjectives, which *may* receive Case,[8] and they differ from prepositions, [–N], which cannot receive Case. Thus, *de* is obligatory in (9) and (10) but inadmissible in (11):

(9)   a. los argumentos *(de) [$_{NP}$ los anarquistas]
         the arguments of the anarchists
      b. los miembros *(de) [$_{NP}$ ese comité]
         the members of that committee

(10)   a. las casas *(de) [_SP_ alrededor]
        the houses of around
    b. el vecino *(de) [_SP_ enfrente]
        the neighbor of in-front

(11)   a. tu preocupación (*de) [_PP_ por el dinero]
        your preoccupation of for the money
    b. los regalos (*de) [_PP_ para los niños]
        the gifts of for the children

Another argument in favor of the claim that substantives, like nouns and adjectives but unlike prepositions, can receive Case has to do with the syntactic distribution of a construction I shall refer to as the "quantified clause". Examples of quantified clauses containing substantive phrases appear in (12):[9]

(12)   a. *Lo lejos que vive Tomás* impide que llegue a tiempo
        the far that lives Tomás impedes that arrive-III-sg on time
        'How far away Tomás lives impedes his arriving on time'
    b. Juan duerme mal, debido a *lo cerca que está su casa de la carretera*
        Juan sleeps badly, due to the close that is his house to the highway
        'Juan sleeps badly, because his house is so close to the highway'

In Plann (1984b) I argue that these constructions should be analyzed as clauses. If this analysis is correct, the S-structure of the quantified clause in (12a) is (13):[10]

(13)   [_S_ [_COMP_ [_SPi_ lo [_Q_ *e*] [_S_ lejos] [_-QU_ que]]
    [_S_ [_Vj_ vive] Tomás *e_j* *e_i*]]

In my analysis, these constructions are clauses in which a *wh* phrase has been fronted to COMP. The *wh* phrase can be, in addition to a substantive phrase, a noun phrase (14a), an adjective phrase (14b), or a prepositional phrase (14c):

(14)   a. Nadie sabe [_NP_ los novios] que ha tenido Luisa
        No one knows the boyfriends that has had Luisa
        'No one knows how many boyfriends Luisa has had'
    b. Nadie sabe [_AP_ lo terriblemente inteligente] que es esa mujer
        No one knows the terribly intelligent that is that woman
        'No one knows how terribly intelligent that woman is'
    c. Nadie sabe [_PP_ con las mujeres] que ha salido Guillermo
        No one knows with the women that has gone-out Guillermo
        'No one knows how many women Guillermo has gone out with'

The respective partial surface structures are (15a,b,c):

(15) a. [$_S$, [$_{COMP}$ [$_{NP_i}$ los [$_Q$ e] novios] [$_{-QU}$ que]] [$_S$ [$_{V_j}$ ha tenido] Luisa $e_j e_i$]]
  b. [$_S$, [$_{COMP}$ [$_{AP}$ lo [$_Q$ e] terriblemente inteligente] [$_{-QU}$ que]] [$_S$ [$_{V_j}$ es] esa mujer $e_j e_i$]]
  c. [$_S$, [$_{COMP}$ [$_{PP_i}$ con las [$_Q$ e] mujeres] [$_{-QU}$ que]] [$_S$ [$_{V_j}$ ha salido] Jorge $e_j e_i$]]

For the purposes of this study, it is important to note that constructions in which a substantive phrase is moved to COMP have the same syntactic distribution as those in which a noun phrase or an adjective phrase is moved to COMP, and that this syntactic distribution differs from that of constructions in which a prepositional phrase is moved to COMP. More specifically, when SP, NP, or AP is in COMP, the quantified clause can occur in positions to which Case is assigned, but the same is not true when PP is in COMP. For example, when SP is in COMP, the quantified clause may occur as object of passive *por* (16a), as object of prepositions like *sobre* 'about' and *contra* 'against' (16b), in conjunction with a noun phrase (16c), between the verb and its complements (16d), and as subject of a small clause (16e):[11],[12]

(16) a. El comité fue impresionado por [$_{SP}$ lo [$_Q$e] lejos] que estaba Juan de comprender la teoría
    the committee was impressed by the far that was Juan of to-comprehend the theory
    'The committee was impressed by how far Juan was from comprehending the theory'
  b. Gustavo sólo hablaba sobre [$_{SP}$ lo[$_Q$ e] lejos] que quedaba el hotel de la estación
    Gustavo only talked about the far that remained the hotel of the station
    'Gustavo spoke only about how far the hotel was from the station'
  c. [$_{SP}$ lo [$_Q$ e] lejos] que está mi casa de la universidad y el hecho de que camino muy lentamente me hacen llegar tarde
    the far that is my house of the university and the fact of that walk-I-sg very slowly me make arrive late
    'How far my house is from the university and the fact that I walk very slowly make me arrive late'
  d. De ser [$_{SP}$ lo [$_Q$ e] cerca] que vives un factor importante, ya te habrían dado el puesto
    of to-be the near that live-II-sg a factor important, already you would-have-III-pl given the position
    'If how close you live were an important factor, they would have already given you the job'

e. El jefe considera [$_{SP}$ lo [$_Q$ e] lejos] que estás de terminar el proyecto
prueba de que no has trabajado mucho
the boss considers the far that are-II-sg of to-finish the project
proof of that NEG have-II-sg worked much
'The boss considers how far you are from finishing the project
proof that you have not worked very much'

The respective examples of (17) and (18) reveal that quantified clauses in
which NP or AP is in COMP have the same syntactic distribution:

(17)   a. El comité fue impresionado por [$_{NP}$ los [$_Q$ e] artículos] que había
publicado Raquel
'The committee was impressed by how many articles Raquel had
published'

        b. Gustavo sólo hablaba sobre [$_{NP}$ los [$_Q$ e] problemas] que pudieran
tener sus hijos, sin pensar en cuántos tenían los demás
'Gustavo spoke only of how many problems his children might
have, without thinking about how many the others had'

        c. [$_{NP}$ las [$_Q$ e] amantes] que ha tenido Juan y la cantidad de alcohol
que consume han sido las causas principales de su divorcio
'The many lovers that Juan has had and the quantity of alcohol
that he consumes have been the main causes of his divorce'

        d. De ser [$_{NP}$ el [$_Q$ e] dinero] que pueda tener en el banco lo único que
te gusta de Juan, no debes casarte con él
'If how much money he may have in the bank is the only thing that
you like about Juan, you should not marry him'

        e. Luisa considera [$_{NP}$ los [$_Q$ e] millones] que pueda tener Juan en el
banco los más atractivo de él
'Luisa considers the many millions that Juan may have in the bank
the most attractive thing about him'

(18)   a. El comité fue impresionado por [$_{AP}$ lo [$_Q$ e] inteligente] que era la
candidata
'The committee was impressed by how intelligent the candidate
was'

        b. Gustavo sólo hablaba sobre [$_{AP}$ lo] [$_Q$ e] inteligente] que eran sus
hijos
'Gustavo spoke only of how intelligent his children were'

        c. [$_{AP}$ lo [$_Q$ e] diligente] que es Luisa y las buenas notas que ha sacado
siempre parecen garantizar que conseguirá un buen puesto
'How intelligent Luisa is and the good grades she has always
earned seem to guarantee that she will get a good position'

        d. De ser [$_{AP}$ lo [$_Q$ e] delgado] que está el niño síntoma de algo grave,
lo llevaríamos al médico en seguida

'If how thin the boy is were a symptom of something serious, we would take him to the doctor immediately'

e. El comité considera [$_{AP}$ lo [$_Q$ *e*] flojos] que son los estudiantes indicio de que este programa no es bueno
'The committee considers how weak the students are an indication that this program is not good'

In contrast, a quantified clause in which PP appears in COMP cannot occur in these same positions:[13]

(19) a. * Rafael fue asombrado por [$_{PP}$ de los [$_Q$ *e*] extravíos] que es capaz una imaginación exaltada
'Rafael was surprised by of the extravagances that is capable an exalted imagination'

   b. * No me hables sobre [$_{PP}$ en las [$_Q$ muchas] ocasiones] que yo le he prestado ayuda
'Don't talk to me about on the many occasions that I have given him assistance'

   c. * Mi interés en la muchacha y [$_{PP}$ con la [$_Q$ *e*] insistencia] que yo la miraba revelaban mis verdaderas intenciones hacia ella
'My interest in the girl and with the intentness that I was looking at her revealed my true intentions towards her'

   d. * De ser [$_{PP}$ en las [$_Q$ muchas] ocasiones] que yo le he prestado ayuda un tema de interés general, lo habría mencionado mucho antes
Of to-be on the many occasions that I have given him assistance a topic of general interest, (I) would have mentioned it long ago
'If the many occasions on which I have given him assistance were a topic of general interest, I would have mentioned it long ago'

   e. * Luisa considera [$_{PP}$ de la [$_Q$ *e*] manera] que se hila un copo de lana en un torno muy interesante
'Luisa considers the way that one spins a bunch of wool on a spinning wheel very interesting'

Essential for the explanation of these data is the claim that COMP is the head of S' (see Bresnan 1972, Stowell 1981). Stowell (1981) argues, furthermore, that Case is assigned to the head of the phrase. Consequently, when a category to which Case can be assigned is in COMP, Case may be assigned to S' via the phrase in COMP. This means that if a category that receives Case is in COMP, the quantified clause may appear in positions to which Case is assigned. This fact accounts for the grammaticality of (17), (18), in which the respective Case-bearing categories NP and AP occur in COMP. But if PP, which is not a Case-bearing category, occurs in COMP, Case cannot be assigned to S', which explains the ungrammaticality of (19). Returning now to (16), in which a substantive phrase is in COMP, we have seen that such quantified clauses may appear in positions to which Case is assigned. This must be because Case can be assigned to substantives. This difference between the syntactic distribution of quantified clauses headed by SP, NP, and AP, on the one hand, and those headed by PP, on the other, reveals once again that substantives resemble both nouns and adjectives, while differing crucially from prepositions. More specifically, it reveals that the former categories can bear Case, unlike the latter, which cannot.

The Case Criterion of Manzini and Sportiche[14] provides us with yet another reason for believing that substantives, like nouns and adjectives but unlike prepositions, may bear Case. According to Manzini and Sportiche, the Case Criterion may be stated as follows:[15]

(20)   Case Criterion
    a. If β is a lexical nominal phrase, there exists an α such that α is a Case assigner and α Case-marks β.
    b. If α is a Case assigner, there exists a β such that β is a nominal phrase and α Case-marks β.

Part (a) of the Case Criterion is the familiar Case Filter: lexical NP must be Case-marked. Part (b) says in effect that a Case assigner must assign Case. This latter claim is of special interest for our purposes, for I shall take it to mean that in Spanish, all prepositions must assign Case.[16] If this is correct, we must conclude once again that substantives can bear Case since they can be the complement of prepositions. In (21) the preposition assigns Case to its SP complement, but a PP complement is disallowed, since PP cannot bear Case:

(21)   a. Manolo pasó la mano [$_P$ por] [$_{SP}$ encima de la mesa]/*[$_{PP}$ sobre la mesa]
        Manolo passed the hand over on-top of the table/on the table
        'Manolo ran his hand over the top of the table'
    b. El perro salió [$_P$ desde] [$_{SP}$ detrás de la casa]/*[$_{PP}$ tras la casa][17]
        the dog came-out from behind of the house/behind the house
        'The dog came out from behind the house'

This, then, is another piece of evidence in support of the claim that substantives, like nouns and adjectives but unlike prepositions, can be assigned Case.

Another difference between nouns, adjectives, and substantives, on the one hand, and prepositions, on the other, has to do with transitivity. Apparently there are no intransitive prepositions in Spanish, that is, prepositions must have a complement:

(22)   a. El libro estaba [$_P$ sobre/bajo] *(la mesa)
        'The book was on/under the table'
      b. El niño corría [$_P$ tras] *(el perro)
        'The boy was-running after the dog'

This fact may be attributed to the Case Criterion: Without the complement in parentheses, the examples of (22) would be ungrammatical because they would violate part (b) of the Case Criterion. Since these prepositions are Case assigners, they must assign Case, but if there is no complement to which to assign Case, part (b) of the Case Criterion is violated. In contrast, substantives, like nouns and adjectives, can be intransitive. Thus, the complement in parentheses is optional in (23)-(25):

(23)   a. El libro estaba [$_S$ encima/debajo] (de la mesa)
        'The book was on-top/under of the table'
      b. El niño corría [$_S$ detrás] (del perro)
        'The boy was-running after the dog'

(24)   a. Juanita presentó su [$_N$ análisis] (de las construcciones causativas)
        'Juanita presented her analysis of the causative constructions'
      b. Esteban no participó en el [$_N$ robo] (del banco)
        'Esteban did not participate in the robbery of the bank'

(25)   a. Elena estaba [$_A$ contenta] (de su nuevo trabajo)
        'Elena was happy with her new job'
      b. Tomás estaba [$_A$ ansioso] (de un cambio de aires)
        'Tomás was anxious for a change of air'

Since S, N, and A are not Case assigners, part (b) of the Case Criterion does not apply, and nothing impedes their occurring without a complement.

    I shall mention one last respect in which substantives resemble nouns and adjectives and differ from prepositions, namely, their ability to modify an unrealized head noun.[18] Prepositional phrases cannot occur as complements to an unrealized head noun in examples such as (26):

(26)   a. la charla sobre matemáticas y la *∅/charla sobre historia
        'the talk about mathematics and the *∅/talk about history'
      b. el ataque contra Alaska y el *∅/ataque contra Hawaii
        'the attack against Alaska and the *∅/attack against Hawaii'

In contrast, phrases of the form *de + substantive phrase* can modify an unrealized head noun (27), just as can phrases of the form *de + noun phrase* (28):[19]

(27)   a. los problemas de dentro del país y los Ø/problemas de fuera
'the problems of inside of-the country and the Ø/problems of
outside'
b. el coche de delante y el Ø/coche de detrás
'the car of in-front and the Ø/car of behind'

(28)   a. la charla del matemático y la Ø/charla del historiador
'the talk of-the mathematician and the Ø/talk of-the historian'
b. el ataque de Grenada y el Ø/ataque de Hawaii
'the attack of Grenada and the Ø/attack of Hawaii'

Adjective phrases, too, can modify an unrealized head noun (29):[20]

(29)   a. los estudiantes alegres y los Ø/estudiantes tristes
the students cheerful and the Ø/students sad
'the cheerful students and the sad ones/students'
b. los pueblos ricos y los Ø/pueblos pobres
the towns rich and the Ø/towns poor
'the rich towns and the poor ones/towns'

However these facts are to be accounted for, this much is clear: With respect
to the ability to modify an unrealized head noun, substantive phrases preceded by *de* behave like NP and AP and unlike PP.

Summarizing thus far, we have seen that substantives resemble the [+N]
categories N and A and differ from the [–N] category P in various ways.
Substantives do not assign Case, and thus they require *de* before a following
NP complement (5)-(7). Substantives may bear Case, since they are preceded
by *de* when they occur as complement to a noun (10), a quantified clause
whose head is a substantive phrase can occur in positions of Case assignment
(16), and substantives may occur as the complement of prepositions (21).
Substantives may be intransitive (23). And finally, when preceded by *de*,
substantive phrases can be the complement of an unrealized head noun (27).
For all these reasons (as well as others to be discussed subsequently), it seems
we must reject the traditional analysis in which substantives phrases like
encima, debajo, cerca, lejos are classified as prepositions.

We have seen thus far that while substantives differ considerably from
prepositions, they resemble both nouns and adjectives in various ways. But
substantives also differ in certain respects from nouns and in other respects
from adjectives. First consider how substantives resemble nouns and differ
from adjectives. Like nouns but unlike adjectives, substantives can be the
object of preposition, as is shown in the examples of (30) (as well as those of
(21)):

(30) a. El gato me espiaba [p desde] [sp debajo de la mesa]
'The cat was spying on me from under the table'
b. El viejo se paseaba [p por] [sp delante de la casa]
'The old man was strolling around in-front of the house'

(31) a. El gato me espiaba [p desde] [NP la ventana]
'The cat was spying on me from the window'
b. El viejo se paseaba [p por] [NP el parque]
'The old man was strolling through the park'

Turning now to the question of modifiers, certain substantives behave like nouns and unlike adjectives in that they can be modified by possessive adjectives:[21]

(32) a. Venía un hombre detrás [ADJ mío]
was-coming a man behind mine
'A man was coming behind me'
(Cf. Venía un hombre detrás de mí
was-coming a man behind of me
same as (32a))
b. Había un coche delante [ADJ nuestro]
there-was a car in-front our
'There was a car in front of us'
(Cf. Había un coche delante de nosotros
there-was a car in-front of us
same as (32b))

Adjectives, of course, are modified by adverbs, but not by adjectives.
   Now consider how substantives resemble adjectives and differ from nouns. Substantives can be modified by adverbs, like adjectives but unlike nouns:

(33) a. No estamos [ADV exactamente] cerca de resolver el problema
'We are not exactly close to solving the problem'
b. José estaba [ADV lamentablemente] lejos de saber la verdad
'José was lamentably far from finding out the truth'

This is so even with those substantives that can be modified by adjectives:

(34) Venía un camión [ADV justamente] detrás [ADJ nuestro]
was-coming a truck exactly behind our
'A truck was coming close behind us'

Moreover, some substantives occur with the quantifier *muy*, just as do adjectives:

(35)   a. José estaba muy lejos de terminar el proyecto
        'José was very far from finishing the project'
        b. En realidad no vives muy cerca
        'In reality you don't live very near'

With regard to certain aspects of their syntactic distribution, substantives also resemble adjectives and differ from nouns. For example, while both substantive phrases and adjective phrases can occur as the complement of *estar*, noun phrases cannot:

(36)   a. José estaba [$_{AP}$ molesto]
        'José was bothered'
        b. José estaba [$_{SP}$ detrás del profesor]
        'José was behind the professor'
        c. * José estaba [$_{NP}$ el profesor]
        'José was the professor'

Small clause substantive phrases can also occur after *poner*, which may subcategorize either a substantive phrase or an adjective phrase small clause (albeit with a slight difference in meaning), but not a noun phrase:

(37)   a. Samuel puso [$_{AP}$ al bebito [$_{AP}$ contento]]
        'Samuel made the baby happy'
        b. Samuel puso [$_{SP}$ al bebito [$_{SP}$ encima de la cama]]
        'Samuel put the baby on the bed'
        c. * Samuel puso [$_{NP}$ al bebito [$_{NP}$ la cama]]
        'Samuel put the baby the bed'

(38)   a. En su reseña, Samuel puso [$_{AP}$ ese libro [$_{AP}$ muy mal]]
        in his review, Samuel put that book very bad
        'In his review, Samuel really criticized that book'
        b. Samuel puso [$_{SP}$ ese libro [$_{SP}$ cerca del fuego]]
        'Samuel put that book near the fire'
        c. * Samuel puso [$_{NP}$ ese libro [$_{NP}$ el fuego]]
        'Samuel put that book the fire'

The possibility of examples like (37b), (38b) reveals another way in which substantives resemble adjectives and differ from nouns. Recall that while adjective phrases *may* be Case marked (see note 8), noun phrases (according to part (a) of the Case Criterion) *must* be Case marked. It seems that the substantive phrase of (37b), (38b) cannot be Case marked. SP here is not preceded by *de*; neither could it be Case marked by the verb, since according to the Adjacency Condition of Chomsky (1981), V and P assign Case to an adjacent category, but in (37b), (38b), the category adjacent to the verb is the direct object, that is, the subject of the small clause, and not the substantive phrase. (Note that the impossibility of Case marking this position could account for the ungrammaticality of the (c) examples of (37), (38), since the NP following the direct object will not be Case marked, thus violating part (a) of the Case Criterion.[22] Thus, if SP receives Case or not will depend on the syntactic position in which it occurs. The same is true of AP (see the reference of note 9). This situation, of course, contrasts sharply with that of NP, which must always be Case marked, as has been noted.

Having examined various properties of substantives, I turn now to the question of their categorial status. Recall that substantives resemble nouns and adjectives and differ from prepositions in that they do not assign Case, and they may be marked for Case. These two properties are characteristic of the [+N] categories. Thus, it is reasonable to conclude that substantives must be [+N], and that they share this feature in common with nouns, [+N −V], and with adjectives, [+N +V]. The feature [+N] distinguishes substantives from prepositions, which are [−N −V]. (Recall that the [−N] categories assign Case and cannot be Case marked.) Furthermore, we have seen that substantives differ in important ways from both nouns and adjectives. On the one hand, substantives resemble nouns and differ from adjectives in that they can be the object of a preposition (30). Moreover, certain substantives can be modified by possessive adjectives (32). Substantives differ from nouns and resemble adjectives, on the other hand, in that they can be modified by adverbs (33), some substantives can be modified by *muy* (34), and they can occur after verbs like *estar* and *poner* in positions in which an adjective phrase but not a noun phrase may occur (36)-(38). Finally, while Case marking of NP is always obligatory, Case marking of SP/AP is not. Whether these categories receive Case or not depends on the syntactic position in which they occur.

Hence, it seems reasonable to surmise that substantives represent a neutralized category that is "between" N and A. Like both nouns and adjectives, they are [+N]. But unlike nouns and adjectives, they do not contain the feature [V]: While nouns are [−V] and adjectives are [+V], substantives lack this feature entirely. In this way we may capture the fact that although they systematically resemble both nouns and adjectives, at the same time they systematically differ from both categories.

The idea of neutralized syntactic categories is, of course, not new. Chomsky (1981) argues that the syntactic passive participle is a neutralized syntactic category that shares the feature [+V] with both verbs, which are [−N +V], and adjectives, which are [+N +V], but lacks the feature [N], the value of which distinguishes verbs and adjectives. The analysis presented here reveals that, along side of the neutralized category [+V], in Spanish there also exists a neutralized category [+N].[23]

There is a further advantage to the analysis of substantives as simply [+N], namely, this analysis allows an elegant statement of the rule of *de* insertion. Recall that *de* is inserted before NP complements to S (39), N (40), and A (41), as well as before SP complements to N (42):

(39)   a. [$_S$ dentro] *(de) [$_{NP}$ la caja]
           inside of the box
       b. [$_S$ fuera] *(de) [$_{NP}$ la casa]
           outside of the house

(40)   a. la [$_N$ conferencia] *(de) [$_{NP}$ los filósofos]
           the conference of the philosophers
       b. la [$_N$ presentación] *(de) [$_{NP}$ la nueva teoría]
           the presentation of the new theory

(41)   a. [$_A$ contento] *(de) [$_{NP}$ su estación en la vida]
           content of his station in life
       b. [$_A$ desilusionado] *(de) [$_{NP}$ sus estudios]
           disillusioned of his studies

(42)   a. los [$_N$ libros] *(de) [$_{SP}$ encima del escritorio]
           the books of on-top of-the desk
       b. la [$_N$ carta] *(de) [$_{SP}$ dentro del cajón]
           the letter of inside of-the drawer

The rule of *de* insertion will thus have to apply before NP and SP complements to N, S, and A. A first approximation of the rule is given in (43):[24]

(43)   *de* Insertion (preliminary version):

$$
\emptyset \rightarrow de / \quad \left[\ \begin{Bmatrix} N \\ S \\ A \\ N' \\ S' \\ A' \end{Bmatrix} \underline{\hspace{2em}} \begin{Bmatrix} NP \\ SP \end{Bmatrix} \ .\quad . \quad \right]
$$

But if nouns are [+N −V], adjectives are [+N +V], and substantives are simply [+N], we may simplify the statement of the rule to (44):

(44)   *de* Insertion (revised version):

$$0 \rightarrow de \ / \ [_{+N'} \ +N \ \underline{\hspace{1.5cm}} \ +N^{max} \ . \ . \ .]$$

Although I have formulated (44) in a maximally general form, not all possibilities will be realized. For example, $+N^{max}$ will never be an adjective phrase, that is, *de* is never inserted before AP, even though adjectives are [+N]. This can be attributed to independent causes, however, namely, the fact that N, S, and A do not subcategorize AP complements. In particular, general principles prevent generation of AP modifiers at the [+N'] level, and the environment for *de* insertion is never met. It seems likely that similar considerations may account for the impossibility of other unrealizable combinations. If so, rule (44) may stand as formulated.

Note that when formulated in terms of the feature [+N], the rule of *de* insertion predicts that *de* will occur before any $+N^{max}$ category that may occur as a [+N'] complement to a [+N] head. This prediction is borne out, since following a [+N] head, *de* also occurs before sentential complements, which, as in Stowell (1981), we may take to be [+N −V]:[25]

(45)   a. la [$_N$ seguridad] *(de) [$_{S'}$ que Ana va a hacerlo bien]
            the certainty of that Ana is-going to do-it well
        b. el [$_N$ temor] *(de) [$_{S'}$ que Pedro no llegue]
            the fear of that Pedro NEG arrive

(46)   a. [$_A$ seguro] *(de) [$_{S'}$ que Ana va a hacerlo bien]
            sure of that Ana is-going to do-it well
        b. [$_A$ temeroso] *(de) [$_{S'}$ que Pedro no llegue]
            fearful of that Pedro NEG arrive

(47)   a. [$_S$ cerca] *(de) [$_{S'}$ alcanzar mis metas]
            near of to-reach my goals
        b. [$_S$ lejos] *(de) [$_{S'}$ comprender la teoría]
            far of to-comprehend the theory

Thus, the formulation of (44) is further confirmed.

Having stated the rule of *de* insertion in terms of the feature [+N], let us now briefly examine the implications for the claim that substantives are prepositions. I have already argued that, in view of their behavior with respect to Case marking, substantives cannot be classified as prepositions (conventional wisdom notwithstanding). The rule of *de* insertion provides further evidence in favor of my position. Consider the possible complements in the *de* insertion rule: *de* insertion applies before substantive phrases (10), (42) (as well as other [+N] categories), but it never applies before prepositional phrases (11). Thus, it would be erroneous to include the category PP as a possible complement before which *de* is inserted. Were it maintained that substantive phrases are actually PPs, it would be necessary to claim that the rule of *de* insertion is lexically governed, applying before phrases headed by certain "prepositions" (*encima, debajo, detrás, ...*), but not before others (*sobre, bajo, tras,...*). This situation would be especially surprising since *de* insertion applies before NP and S′ without exception. Such a statement of *de* insertion is obviously considerably more complicated than the rule provided here, which states simply that the rule applies before [+N] phrases, a category which in my analysis includes SP but not PP.

A similar problem arises for the claim that substantives are prepositions when we consider the possible heads after which *de* insertion applies. We have seen that the rule applies if the head is a substantive (7), (39), but not if it is a preposition (8). This fact is captured in rule (44) by the claim that the head must be [+N], a category which in my analysis includes substantives but not prepositions. This same fact cannot be systematically captured if it is maintained that substantives are prepositions, however. Once again, *de* insertion would have to be lexically governed, applying after some prepositions but not others. This situation would be quite different from that of nouns and adjectives, after which the rule applies without exception. As before, we are led to conclude that it would be an error to classify substantives as prepositions.

In conclusion, my analysis reveals that the grammar of Spanish contains a neutralized syntactic category, [+N], to which belong substantives such as *encima, debajo, cerca, lejos*. Substantives resemble both nouns and adjectives but also differ crucially from both categories. The analysis of substantives as simply [+N] permits an elegant formulation of the rule of *de* insertion, which would not be possible were these phrases analyzed as PPs.

NOTES

1. A more complete list would include *alrededor, dentro, fuera, enfrente, delante*, and *detrás*.
   In the text below I distinguish between substantives, on the one hand, and prepositions, on the other. Not discussed here but worthy of note is the fact that Spanish also has a class of postpositions, including *arriba, abajo, adentro, afuera, adelante*, and *atrás*. Postpositions assign Case to an NP to the left of the head:

(i)   mar afuera
        sea out
        'out to sea'
(ii)   cuesta arriba
        hill up
        'up hill'

Postpositions cannot be followed by an NP complement, as can prepositions, nor by the phrase *de* + *NP*, as can substantives:

(iii)   * atrás de la casa
          behind of the house
          (Cf. tras la casa, detrás de la casa)

(iv)   * abajo de la mesa
          under of the house
          (Cf. bajo la mesa, debajo de la mesa)

Curiously, although postpositions are Case assigners, postpositional phrases can nevertheless bear Case. For example, they are preceded by *de* when they function as complements to a noun:

(v)   las costumbres *(de) muchos años atrás
          the customs of many years before
(vi)   el cuarto *(de) arriba
          the room of above

Antes and *después* seem to exhibit properties of both postpositions and substantives. Thus, they can assign Case to an NP to the left of the head, but they can also be followed by the phrase *de* + *NP*:

(vii)   [$_{NP}$ muchos años] antes de [$_{NP}$ la guerra]
          many years before of the war
(viii)   [$_{NP}$ varios días] después de [$_{NP}$ la fiesta]
          several days after of the party

Summarizing, as evidenced by their distinct syntactic properties, Spanish appears to have prepositions (e.g., *bajo, tras*), postpositions (e.g. *abajo, atrás*), and substantives (e.g. *debajo, detrás*).
2. For example, Bello (1847) classifies them as adverbs, while Ramsey (1956) classifies them as adverbs when used intransitively and as compound prepositions when used transitively.
3. On Case Theory, see Rouveret and Vergnaud (1980), Chomsky (1981), and the references cited therein.
4. See for instance the discussion of Ramsey (1956), which assigns a wide variety of phrases to the category of adverb. The criteria for classification, although never articulated, seem to be semantic and not syntactic. For example, phrases like *con ligereza, en el acto*, which would doubtlessly be analyzed as prepositional phrases today, are for Ramsey simply "adverbial phrases".
5. See Corominas (1980, Vol. 1:76, Vol. 2:954).
6. The spelling of most substantives provides us with a hint that they are structurally different from prepositional phrases, however, and suggests that the former preposition plus complement structure has "fossilized" into a single unit. An apparent exception to this generalization is *al lado*, which must be a substantive since it is preceded by *de* in examples such as (i), unlike what occurs with prepositional phrases (ii):

(i)   la casa *(de) [$_{SP}$ al lado]
          the house of at-the side
(ii)   los argumentos (*de) [$_{PP}$ en contra]
          the arguments of against

(This and other differences between substantives and prepositions are discussed in the text below.) A plausible motive for writing *al lado* instead of *alado* is the possible ambiguity of the latter: Would it mean *a* + *lado* or *al* + *lado*?

Also calling for a special remark is the "compound preposition" *acerca de*, since the last syllable of its lexical entry (*de*) could be confused with the *de* provided by rule (45) discussed in the text below. When *acerca de* occurs as complement to a noun, it is not preceded by *de*, which means that it does not receive Case:

(iii)   tu charla (*de) acerca del feminismo
          your talk of about of-the feminism

As is to be expected, it cannot be intransitive:

(iv)   *tu charla acerca

Moreover, like prepositions and unlike substantives, it cannot modify an unrealized head noun:

(v)   la charla acerca del feminismo y la *Ø/charla acerca del sexismo
         the talk about of-the feminism and the *Ø/talk about of-the sexism

According to the criteria discussed in the text below, it must be concluded that *acerca de* is a preposition (cf. *cerca de*, a substantive).
7. Although Corominas (1980, Vol. 3:626) believes that *lejos*, first documented in 1236, derives from Latin LAXIUS 'más ampliamente, más libremente, más separadamente', comparative adverb from LAXUS 'amplio, suelto', he notes that other authorities (e.g. F. Diez, *Etymologisches Wörterbuch der romanischen Sprachen*, Bonn, 1853) would derive *lejos* from the adjective LAXUS. In spite of the diversity of their historical origins, however, I believe I demonstrate conclusively in this study that in the synchronic grammar of Spanish, all the phrases under consideration here are instances of substantives.
8. See, for example, Stowell (1981, 4.1) for discussion of Case marked adjectives in German and Russian.
9. Not all the phrases classified in the text and in note 1 as substantives can occur in quantified clauses, however. This is because the obligatory quantifier of this construction (see note 10) is not compatible with all substantives. Compare:

(i)   La casa estaba [$_Q$ muy] cerca/lejos
         the house was very close/far
(ii)   lo [$_Q$ muy *e*] cerca/lejos que estaba la casa
         the very/*e* close/far that was the house
(iii)   * El libro estaba [muy] debajo/detrás/encima
         the book was very under/behind/on-top
(iv)   * lo [$_Q$ muy/*e*] debajo/detrás/encima que estaba el libro
         the very under/behind/on-top that was the book
10. For reasons discussed in Plann (1984b), it is necessary to postulate that the phrase moved to COMP in a quantified clause contains a quantifier. In (13) the quantifier, represented as [$_Q$ e], is not overtly realized. Compare (13) with (i), in which an overt quantifier occurs:

(i)   lo [$_Q$ muy] lejos que vive Tomás
         the very far that lives Tomás
         'how far away Tomás lives'

I assume here the analysis of Torrego (1984), in which movement of a *wh* phrase to COMP triggers V fronting. In (13) application of *wh* movement to the substantive phrase has triggered fronting of the verb, *vive*; '-e_j' represents the trace of the verb and '-e_i', that of the substantive phrase.

11. On small clauses, see, for example, Chomsky (1981), Stowell (1981).

12. Note that a clause whose COMP dominates only -WH at S-structure cannot occur in these same positions:

(i)   * José fue impresionado por *que todos llegaran a tiempo*
          José was impressed by that everyone arrived on time
          (Cf. *Que todos llegaran a tiempo* impresionó a José
              'That everyone arrived on time impressed José')

(ii)   * Gustavo hablaba sobre *que los niños eran inteligentes*
          Gustavo was-talking about that the children were intelligent

(iii)   * La inteligencia de esta mujer y *que haya publicado tanto* hace pensar que es la mejor candidata para el puesto
          'The intelligence of this woman and that (she) has published so much makes (one) think that (she) is the best candidate for the job'

(iv)   * De no representar *que los niños bailen mal* un obstáculo para su futura carrera, no les mandaríamos a clase de ballet
          of NEG to-represent that the children dance badly an obstacle for their future career, NEG them would-send-I-pl to class of ballet
          'If that the children dance badly did not represent an obstacle for their future careers, we would not send them to ballet class'
          (Cf. *Que los niños bailen mal* representa un obstáculo para su futura carrera
              that the children dance badly represents an obstacle for their future careers)

In (i)-(v) COMP dominates simply -WH, and S' cannot receive Case. This does not mean, however, that an S' whose COMP dominates only -WH never receives Case: see, for instance, (46)-(48) in the text. For a discussion of Case marking S' in Spanish, see Plann (1984a).

13. Observe that these same quantified clauses are perfectly acceptable in other contexts. Example (i) occurs in Bello (1847, #1165), and in Ramsey (1956, #5.64), (ii) and (iii) are from Ramsey (1956, #5.64), and (iv) is from Cuervo's notes on Bello (n. 138):

(i)   *De los extravíos que es capaz una imaginación exaltada!*
       'The extravagances of which an exalted imagination is capable!'

(ii)   No quiero referir *en las muchas ocasiones que le he prestado ayuda*
       'I don't want to relate the many occasions on which I have given him assistance'

(iii)   La joven echó de ver *con la insistencia que yo la miraba*
       'The young woman noticed the intentness with which I was looking at her'

(iv)   Mira *de la manera que se hila un copo de lana en un torno*
       'Look at the way in which one spins a bunch of wool on a spinning wheel'

14. The following discussion is based on notes from a graduate seminar presented by Rita Manzini at UCLA during the spring of 1984.

15. Compare the Case Criterion with the Theta (θ) Criterion:

(i) θ Criterion:
       a. If β is an argument, there exists an α such that α is a θ role assigner and α θ-role assigns β.
       b. If α is a θ role assigner, there exists β such that β is an argument and α θ-role assigns β.

(For a discussion of the θ Criterion, see Chomsky 1981.) Manzini and Sportiche seek to establish a parallelism between the respective parts of the θ Criterion and the Case Criterion.

16. There may appear to be an occasional exception to this claim, for example:

(i)   Me miraba [$_{PP}$ [$_P$ desde] [$_{PP}$ entre los árboles]]
'He was looking at me from among the trees'

If the structure of (i) is correct, we might suppose that *desde* does not assign Case here, since its complement, a PP, cannot receive Case. Note, however, that other PPs cannot occur as complement to *desde*:

(ii)   * Me miraba desde [$_{PP}$ tras los árboles]
        (Cf. Me miraba desde [$_{SP}$ detrás de los árboles]
        'He was looking at me from behind the trees')

Moreover, *desde* cannot be intransitive:

(iii)   * Me miraba desde

(See the discussion of transitivity in the text below.) I take the impossibility of (ii) and (iii) to mean that *desde* must assign Case.

If so, the apparent exceptionality of (i) may be due to properties of *entre*, and not to properties of *desde*. Note that unlike (other?) prepositions and like substantives, *entre* is preceded by *de* in examples like the following (cf. (10), (11)):

(iv)   la casa de entre los árboles
        the house of among the trees

But like prepositions and unlike substantives, an NP complement of *entre* is not preceded by *de* (cf. (6), (7)):

(v)   entre (*de) los árboles

Furthermore, *entre* cannot be intransitive:

(vi)   *la casa de entre

Although it is generally classified as a preposition, *entre* (along with a handful of similar lexical items) is also exceptional because its NP complement requires Nominative Case:

(vii)   entre (tú y yo/*ti y mi)
         between (you(Nom) and I(Nom)/*you(Ob) and me(Ob))

Thus, in spite of the acceptability of (i), it seems safe to maintain that all prepositions in Spanish must assign Case, as is stated in the text. How to account for *entre*, which appears to both bear Case (i), (iv) and assign Case (v), (vi), is not clear to me, however. (Carlos Otero suggests (p.c.) that it may be that *entre* is somehow "drifting" or "unsettled" between the categories [+N] and [−N +V].)

17. It has been called to my attention by K. Zagona and H. Contreras that for some speakers, both versions of (21a) are actually acceptable.

18. This phenomenon was first discussed in Plann (1980).

19. Note that when *de* is not provided by rule, the phrase [$_{PP}$ de NP] is not acceptable with an unrealized head noun:

(i)   la huida de la cárcel y la *∅/huida de la prisión
       the flight from the jail and the ∅/flight from the prison

Compare (ii), which reveals that *huir* subcategorizes for [P NP] and P = *de*:

(ii)   Huyeron *de* la cárcel y *de* la prisión
         (they) fled from the jail and from the prison

Moreover, substantive phrases not preceded by *de* cannot occur as complement to an unrealized head noun. Such constructions arise when substantive phrases are relativized:

(iii)   el cajón dentro del que estaban los guantes y el *Ø/cajón dentro del que estaban los calcetines
         'the drawer inside of which were the gloves and the one/drawer inside of which were the socks'
(iv)   la puerta detrás de la que estaba el maestro y la *Ø/puerta detrás de la que estaba el cura
         'the door behind which was the teacher and the one/door behind which was the priest'

In this respect, relative clauses beginning with substantive phrases not preceded by *de* behave exactly like relative clauses beginning with prepositional phrases:

(v)   los motivos por los que se han casado y los *Ø/motivos por los que se han divorciado
         'the motives for which they have married and the ones/motives for which they have divorced'
(vi)   las pastillas sin las que no puede dormirse y las *Ø/pastillas sin las que no puede despertarse
         'the pills without which he cannot fall asleep and the ones/pills without which he cannot wake up'

20. As can relative clauses beginning with *que*:

(i)   los motivos que le he explicado y los Ø/motivos que le he ocultado
         'the motives I have explained to him and the ones/motives I have hidden from him'
(ii)   las pastillas que la duermen y las Ø/pastillas que la despiertan
         'the pills that put her to sleep and the ones/pills that awaken her'

Note that unlike what occurs with SP (27) and with NP (28), *de* is not inserted before AP (29), nor before relative clauses (i), (ii). I return to the topic of *de* insertion in the text below.
21. This occurs in peninsular Spanish, although apparently in some dialects of American Spanish it is not possible.
22. θ roles may only be assigned to A-positions associated with PRO or Case. Thus, the NP following the direct object in (37c), (38c) would not be assigned a θ role, and would also run afoul of the Theta Criterion (see note 15).
23. Another instance of a neutralized category may be the English gerund. Stowell (1981) cites a study by van Riemsdijk ("On the Case of German Adjectives", mimeographed, University of Amsterdam, 1980) that argues that the English gerund is a neutralized category with properties of both the noun phrase and the clause. While noun phrases are [+N, –V, –TENSE], clauses are [+N, –V, +TENSE], and gerunds are simply [+N –V].
24. "S'" in (43) is to be read "substantive-bar", and "S" and "SP" are to be read "substantive" and "substantive phrase", respectively.
     In the formulation of (43) (and also in the revision of (44)) I assume that *de* insertion must be limited to the X' level. This analysis differs from those of Borer (1981) and Stowell (1981), where it is assumed that insertion occurs freely at all structural levels. Since *de* is inserted in Spanish before certain clauses but not before others, it seems necessary to restrict *de* insertion to the X'

level. Crucially, *de* is inserted before clauses immediately dominated by X′, but not before clauses immediately dominated by X″. That is, *de* is inserted before clauses subcategorized by a noun, an adjective, or a substantive (as in (45)-(47), respectively), but not before restrictive relative clauses (as in (iii)-(vi) of note 18 and (i), (ii) of note 19). Assuming, as in Jackendoff (1977), that subcategorized complements occur at the X′ level while restrictive modifiers occur at the X″ level (or alternatively, that restrictive modifiers are adjoined at the X′ level), it will be necessary to limit *de* insertion to the X′ level. Note that this assumption also explains why *de* never occurs before AP complements to nouns, e.g. *la mujer (*de) [AP alta]*, even though such complements are [+N]. (See the text below.)

Stowell's (1981) analysis of all clauses as [+N, −V, +TENSE] (see note 22) differs from that of Picallo (1984a), where it is argued that only indicative clauses have the [+TENSE] feature. Regardless of which analysis one adopts, however, it seems safe to assume that S′ is [+N −V], an assumption crucial to my formulation of *de* insertion.

Some remarks on the nature of strong pronouns in null-subject languages*

Gemma Rigau, *Universitat Autònoma de Barcelona*

It is a well-known fact that Catalan and Spanish are two very similar Romance languages. Both are null-subject languages with a double paradigm of personal pronouns: (*a*) strong lexical pronouns and (*b*) clitic and empty pronouns, exemplified in (1) and (2), respectively.[1]

(1)   a. *Tú* le quieres a *él*
            you him love to him
            'You love him'
      b. *Ell* t'estima a *tu*
            he you loves to you
            'He loves you'

(2)   a. *pro le* quieres *pro*[2]
            pro him love pro
            'You love him'
      b. *pro t*'estima *pro*
            pro you loves pro
            'He loves you'

In (2) the null-subject is locally determined by AGR in INFL, whereas the object *pro* is locally determined by the clitic.[3] In the Oblique Case (i.e., neither Accusative nor Dative), a clitic-doubling structure is not possible.[4] Observe the sentences in (3).

(3)   a. Pepe piensa en ella
            Pepe thinks in her
            'Pepe thinks about her'
      b. En Pere parla de tu
            Pere speaks of you
            'Pere speaks about you'

In Catalan, the only clitic that may appear in (3b) is a clitic standing for a PP, as shown in (4).

(4)   En Pere *en* parla
       Pere it speaks
       'Pere speaks about it'

In Spanish (unlike Catalan, French, or Italian) there are no clitics that may appear in place of a PP.

The objective of this paper is to characterize the similarities and differences in behavior of the strong pronouns in these two languages (Spanish and Catalan). We believe that a comparative study will facilitate both the examination of the pronouns as well as the discovery of factors playing an important role in the acquisition of these languages.

Both phonetically null pronouns as well as overt pronouns may represent a referring expression, an individual constant, and may be coreferential with an NP.[5] The coreferentiality is expressed in terms of coindexing and follows Principle B of the Theory of Binding (Chomsky 1981, 1982).

(5)   Principle B: A pronominal is free in its governing category.

The governing category for α is the minimal S or NP containing α and a governor of α and a SUBJECT accessible to α (Chomsky 1981, 220).[6] Principle B accounts for the grammaticality in (6) and the non-grammaticality of the sentences in (7).

(6)   a. Yo_i ayudo a Pepe y María me_i ayuda a $mí_i$
             I help to Pepe and María me helps to me
             'I help Pepe and María helps me'
       b. $Juan_i$ dice que $\left\{ \frac{\text{pro}}{\text{él}} \right\}_i$ conoce el camino
             Juan says that {pro, he} knows the way
             'Juan says he knows the way'

(7)   a.   *$Juan\ le_i$ dice que $Pepe_i$ conoce el camino
             Juan him says that Pepe knows the way
             '$Juan_i$ tells him_i $Pepe_i$ knows the way.
       b.   *Las $chicas_i$ las_i persiguieron
             the girls them chased
             'The $girls_i$ chased $them_i$'

In addition, in Catalan and Spanish – as in English (see Evans 1980) – pronouns may act as variables in the scope of a quantifier. When functioning as variables, strong pronouns in Catalan and Spanish differ in their behavior, as pointed out by Montalbetti (1984, 189f). We will deal with this question in section two. In section one we will characterize the overt pronouns when they are used as referential expressions.

1.

Given the opportunity offered by Catalan and Spanish to obtain sentences in which a pronominal Subject, Direct Object, and Indirect Object can be phonetically empty or lexically specified, we should ask ourselves the reason for the existence of full pronouns and empty or clitic pronouns in these languages. Traditional grammarians have insisted on the emphatic character of strong pronouns in contexts such as (6b).[7] But, an overt pronoun in normal intonation pattern, such as in (8b), is not emphatic in the same way as the same pronoun in (8c). There is a gradation in (8).

(8)   a. *pro* hablará
        'He will speak'
    b. Él hablará
        'He will speak'
    c. ÉL hablará
        'HE will speak'

While in (8a) there is no emphasis on the subject, in (8c) the subject receives strong emphasis: there is contrastive focus on the pronoun *él*. However, in (8b) the emphasis on the subject is not contrastive: it is a weak emphasis. We can therefore say that the strong pronoun in (8b) acts as a distinctive pronoun in the sense of Ronat (1979). The pronoun *él* in (8b) can thus be compared to the colloquial use of the French pronoun *lui* in (9a), but not to the same pronoun in (9b), where *lui* acts as a topic or contrastive pronoun. Furthermore, *pro* in (8a) will be comparable to *il* in (9c).[8]

(9)   a. Il parlera lui
    b. Il parlera, lui
    c. Il parlera

In constructions like (9a) there is no real contrast. According to Ronat (1979), the real contrast entails the negation of the whole proposition with respect to another subject. Sentence (9a) doesn't imply that another person won't speak, but rather that someone else related through the discourse with *lui* will do something else. Ronat paraphrases the implications of a sentence with a distinctive pronoun like (9a) as follows: A proposition concerning X entails another proposition concerning Y, just in case X and Y are included in the same set (formed, for example, by a common predicate).

We have noted two types of emphasis for languages like Catalan or Spanish: contrastive focus and distinctive interpretation. According to Chomsky (1977, 1981), the contrastively focused element has a quantifier-like character at the level of Logical Form. Therefore, the S-structure (10a) will be represented as (10b) at Logical Form.

(10)   a. [$_s$ÉL viajó a Roma]
        'HE travelled to Rome'
    b. [[$_{Comp}$ for x, x = he] [$_s$ x travelled to Rome]]

ÉL 'HE' is moved to COMP, an $\overline{A}$-position, from where it will bind a variable (Cf. Chomsky 1981, Huang 1982a). Nevertheless, strong pronouns in Catalan and Spanish are interpreted as quantified expressions not involving movement at LF. In short, strong pronouns do not form operator-variable structures. According to Hornstein (1984), the semantics of natural languages requires distinguishing two axes not differentiated in previous work: an interpretative axis and a logical syntax axis. Following the line of this author, we accept that an NP element has two axes relevant to predicting its semantic behavior: it can be [±operator] and [±quantifier]. So then, we may obtain different types of NPs:

(a) [+quantifier, +operator] NPs: *operators* – quantifiers moved to the LF having operator-variable form
(b) [+quantifier, -operator] NPs: *quantified terms* – quantifiers not moved
(c) [-quantifier, -operator] NPs: *names* – elements not having quantificational interpretative properties

According to Hornstein (1984), quantifiers that do not form operator-variable structures are generally interpreted as having wide scope. Their interpretation is functionally independent of the interpretation of moved-quantifier NPs, and involves branching interpretation procedures (see Hornstein 1984, 33f and sect. 2.3). Hornstein (1984, 42) writes:

> 'This typology of quantifiers is an aspect of U.G., an innate feature of language faculty. There is simply not enough evidence to presuppose that the typology itself could be acquired on the basis of primary data. However, there is not a priori basis for expecting in general that a quantifier will fall into one or another class. Which element falls into which class is clearly a parameter set by the primary linguistic data. In short, the parameter [±operator] is innate. The specific value accorded a particular expression is a function of the linguistic environment.'

Pronouns are not descriptions. Deictic pronouns designate but do not describe. In spite of that, the overt pronouns are closer to definite descriptions – terms, according to Hornstein – than are clitic or empty pronouns. Because of their lexical characteristics and the logical feature of uniqueness – i.e., because of their inherent semantic content – strong pronouns may be dealt with as terms (in other words, as elements characterized by the [+quantifier, -operator] features).[9] On the other hand, the [+pronominal] feature means that the pronoun is not a description and, consequently, that if it is not used deictically, it needs to be supported by an antecedent. Principle B of the

Theory of Binding insures that NPs may be antecedents of a pronoun. Therefore, what differentiates a strong pronoun from an empty or clitic pronoun is the [+quantifier] feature. An empty or clitic pronoun, due to its characteristics, cannot behave as a quantified term. This explains why, in some contexts, strong pronouns behave like definite descriptions and not like empty or clitic pronouns.[10]

The characterization of overt pronouns as terms implies that there is no case where ambiguity between the two kinds of emphasis – contrastive focus and distinctive interpretation – may arise. Consider the sentences in (8b) and (8c) repeated here:

(8)   b. Él hablará (distinctive interpretation)
        c. Él hablará (constrastive focus)

The overt pronoun *él* receives either distinctive interpretation or contrastive interpretation, an overlapping between them being impossible.

Moreover, distinctive interpretation occurs in the positions in which a contrastively focused element cannot appear, as shown in (11).

(11)   a.   Qué dice él?
          what says he?
          'What does he say?'
      b.   *Qué dice PEPE?
          what says Pepe?
          'What does PEPE say?'
      c.   El coche que él compró es alemán
          the car that he bought is German
          'The car he bought is German'
      d.   *El coche que PEPE compró es alemán
          the car that Pepe bought is German
          'The car PEPE bought is German'

According to Huang (1982a, 1982b), (11b) and (11d) are not well-formed because the application of contrastive focus is blocked by the presence of a Wh-element in COMP. In other words, application of Wh-movement blocks the application of movement of the contrastively focused element to COMP at LF, with the resulting structure badly formed since neither operator c-commands its variable. To summarize, no contrastively focused element may appear within the scope of elements constituting an island, but a distinctive interpretation element may appear within an island.[11] The complementary distribution of two kinds of emphatic elements observed in (11) is due to the different nature of the emphatic operator and of the overt pronoun.

We will now compare the referential possibilities of strong pronouns with those of empty pronouns. Normally, both types of pronouns may be used referentially and may denote an object of the universe of discourse or a number of objects. On the other hand, according to Principle B of the Binding Theory, they may be coreferential with an NP not found in their governing category. Consider (12):

(12)   a. Pepe dice que $\left\{ {él \atop pro} \right\}$ telefoneará a María
            Pepe says that {he, pro} will-telephone to María
            'Pepe says he'll phone María'

ÉL 'he' as well as *pro* may be coreferential to *Pepe*. It there is a preferred reading, it is due to the discourse context in which the sentence appears, rather than to the presence of a full/empty pronoun. In short, it is due to the discourse grammar.[12] However, there are some constructions where the alternation between *pro* and overt pronouns is not possible for one reason or another. Let us examine some of these cases in (13).

(13)   a.   **pro* hizo la cena y él preparó un cóctel
                    pro made the supper and he prepared a cocktail
                    'He made the supper and he prepared a cocktail'
        b.   ??Porque *pro* quería ser actor, él ingresó en el Instituto del Teatro
                    because pro wanted to-be actor, he joined in the Institute of-the Theater
                    'Because he wanted to be an actor, he joined the Theater Institute'
        c.   ??Si *pro* corre, él llegaiá a tiempo
                    if pro runs he will-arrive at time
                    'If he runs, he will arrive on time'

In (13a), the pronouns cannot be coreferential. Nevertheless, Principle B does not prevent it. Consequently, there must be other reasons for its being ill-formed in comparison with the grammaticality of (14).

(14)   Hizo la cena y preparó un cóctel
            (he)-made the supper and prepared a cocktail
            'He made supper and prepared a cocktail'

Actually, we can adduce the non-grammaticality of (13a) to the fact that in (14) we do not have a coordination of sentences, but a coordination of VPs. Since in (13a) and (14) the two VPs predicate something about the same subject, the sentence must have a single subject and a VP of a coordinated structure.[13] Some principle of grammar will prevent the coordination of Ss in the cases considered in (13) and (14), probably the Avoid Pronoun Principle

(Chomsky 1981, 65)[14] and some extension of the Coordination Restriction Principle postulated by Brucart (1984, 429f), a principle which avoids the proliferation of empty categories in coordinate constructions.[15] Therefore, the structure of (14) will not be (15b), but rather (15a).

(15)   a. [$_S$ *pro* [$_{VP}$ [$_{VP}$ hizo la cena] y [$_{VP}$ preparó un cóctel]]]
         b. [$_S$ [$_S$ *pro* hizo la cena] y [$_S$ *pro* preparó un cóctel]]

Sentences (13b) and (13c) can be seen to have a pattern similar to (13a). According to Haegeman (1984), though they may look like subordinate clauses, they are 'hybrids' of subordination and coordination. Subordinate clauses in these sentences are not embedded in S; they are attached to E-node (= S''). 'It seems preferable' writes Haegeman, 'to treat E as a separate projection of a different type, which falls outside sentence grammar proper and establishes a transition between Sentence and Discourse.' So then, the principles which govern the correct formation of the discourse will show that an overt pronoun cannot possibly appear in (13b) or in (13c).

2.

Until now, we have dealt with the relationships of coreference between an NP and a pronoun in a normal intonation pattern. Nonetheless, sometimes coreference between a pronoun and an NP is impossible. Then, we may have the case where the pronoun is bound by the QP. Hence, the pronoun acts as a variable, as shown in (16).

(16)   Todo el mundo dice que *pro* tiene prisa
         all the world says that pro (he) has haste
         'Everyone says he's in a hurry'

The pronoun *pro* cannot establish a relationship of coreference with the NP *todo el mundo* 'everyone' because the latter is a universal quantifier. The pronoun acts as a bound variable, as a function of the QP; therefore, it does not receive a single value, as shown in (17).

(17)   ((Every x, x: a person) x says that x is in a hurry)

There are two factors which may play a role in the establishment of the relationship of coreference between a quantified NP and a pronoun (aside from Principle B): (a) the nature of the NP antecedent and (b) the type of pronoun.

As far as (a) is concerned, there are some NPs that do not allow coreference, because they cannot be used as referential expressions. They do not denote any object of the domain of discourse. Haïk (1984) calls them 'inherent quantifiers'. Therefore, *todo el mundo* 'everyone', as well as negative quantifiers like *nadie* 'nobody' *nada* 'nothing', *ningún* 'none', etc., are inherent quantifiers.[16] Consider (18):

(18)   a. Nadie sabía que *pro* había aprobado
           nobody knew that pro(he) had passed
           'Nobody knew he'd passed
        b. No he visto a nadie ni le he asustado
           not have seen to nobody nor him have frightened
           'I haven't seen or frightened anyone'

It is usual to assume that c-command at S-structure is the condition that governs bound readings (cf. Reinhart 1976, Higginbotham 1983, and Haïk 1984). In (18a) the empty pronoun may be free or bound, because it is c-commanded by *nadie*. However, *pro* is not coreferential with *nadie*, an inherent quantifier. In (18b), the clitic *le* is not a bound pronoun because *nadie* does not c-command it. The coreferential reading is not possible either, due to the characteristics of this QP. So, the only available interpretation is that in which *le* is free.

As noted by Haïk (1984), coreference is also impossible in certain circumstances with NPs that can be used referentially, when they are NPs referentially dependent on other NPs. Consider (19):

(19)   Tres estudiantes han visitado a un novelista
        three students have visited to a novelist
        'Three students have visited a novelist'

Sentence (16) is ambiguous, depending on the relationship established between the two QPs. If *un novelista* 'a novelist' is interpreted as 'un determinado novelista' (a certain novelist), then it is interpreted as having wide scope – and, according to Hornstein (1984), it acts as a term, without an operator-variable reading. In this case, *un novelista* may be able to establish a relationship of coreference with a pronoun of the discourse, as shown in (20).

(20)   Tres estudiantes han visitado a un novelista y le han hecho una
        entrevista
        three students have visited to a novelist and him have made an
        interview
        'Three students have visited a novelist and interviewed him'

On the other hand, if wide scope is not assigned to *un novelista*, then the NP is in the scope of *tres estudiantes* 'three students'. In this case, *un novelista* will behave as if it were an inherent quantifier and the coreference with *le* in (20) will not be possible.[17] Whether or not *un novelista* is interpreted in the scope of *tres estudiantes*, the latter QP may establish a relationship of coreference with a pronoun:

(21)   Tres estudiantes han visitado a un novelista y dice María que *pro* quieren repetir la experiencia
three students have visited to a novelist and says María that pro(they) want to-repeat the experience
'Three students have visited a novelist and María says they want to repeat the experience'

Should both QPs be operators, the one within the scope of the other will not be able to establish relationships of coreference with a pronoun throughout the discourse.[18] In (22) the NP *dos chicas* 'two girls' will be coreferential with *las* 'them' when it receives wide scope:

(22)   Algunos oficinistas están enamorados de dos chicas. Pepe las conoce bien.
some office-workers are enamored of two girls. Pepe them knows well.
'Some office workers are in love with two girls. Pepe knows them well.'

2.1

Previously we have asserted that the pronoun, depending on its nature, may help establish a non-coreferential relationship with a quantified NP. Indeed, as Montalbetti (1984) has pointed out, Spanish pronouns do not behave in the same way when they are found in the scope of a QP. Let us examine this in (23):

(23)   a. Tres físicos han confirmado que *pro* participarán en el coloquio
three physicists have confirmed that pro(they) will-participate in the colloquium
'Three physicists have confirmed they'll participate in the colloquium'
   b. Tres físicos han confirmado que ellos participarán en el coloquio
three physicists have confirmed that they will-participate in the colloquium
'Three physicists have confirmed that they will participate in the colloquium'
   c. Tres estudiantes aseguran que María les ha escrito *pro*

three students assert that María them has written pro(them)
'Three students assert that María has written them'
d. Tres estudiantes aseguran que María les ha escrito a ellos
three students assert that María them has written to (them) they
'Three students assert that María has written to them'

The empty pronoun in subject position in (23a) may be interpreted as free, as coreferential with *tres físicos* 'three physicists', and, finally, as a function of *tres físicos* (i.e., as a bound variable).[19] Here the coreferential reading can be identified with the group reading; the bound reading, however, can consist of the distributive reading. Montalbetti (1984) has noted that the pronoun *ellos* 'they' in (23b) is not susceptible to being interpreted as a bound pronoun. It can be only either free or coreferential with the subject of the main clause. The same diversity of behavior can be seen in (23c) and in (23d). If a clitic-doubling structure does not occur, as in (23c), *les-pro* 'them' may be interpreted as free, coreferential, or bound. The presence of the strong pronoun *ellos* 'they' in (23d) makes the bound reading impossible.

Now let us observe how no strong pronoun may take as its antecedent a quantified NP in the scope of another quantified NP because – as Haïk (1984) pointed out – the NP lying in the scope of the other NP would lose its referential capacity. Let us consider the sentence in (24).

(24)   Muchos profesores han dicho a algún estudiante que $\left\{ \begin{smallmatrix} él \\ pro \end{smallmatrix} \right\}$ era el mejor
many professors have said to some student that {he,pro} was the best
'Many professors have told a student he was the best'

If it is not free, *él* 'he' may only appear in (24) if its antecedent, *algún estudiante* 'some student', takes wide scope; i.e., if the sentence is interpreted as meaning that there is some student such that many professors have said that he was the best. In this case, *algún estudiante* maintains its referential value and may, therefore, establish a coreferential relationship with the pronoun *él*. The presence of *pro* allows, on the other hand, for the two readings: coreferential and bound. So then, *algún estudiante* may have in its scope the QP *muchos profesores* 'many professors' and establish, the same as with *él*, a coreferential relationship with *pro*. On the other hand, *algún estudiante* may be in the scope of the other QP. In that case, it loses its referential capacity and *pro* is interpreted as a bound variable, thereby acquiring plural value.

2.2

The differences in behavior observed in Spanish between strong pronouns, on the one hand, and empty pronouns and clitics, on the other, appear also in Catalan, as shown in (25).

(25) a. Dos periodistes diuen que $\left\{\frac{pro}{ells}\right\}$ han rebut el premi
      two journalists say that {pro, they} have received the prize
      'Two journalists say they have received the prize'
   b. Alguns periodistes asseguren que els han premiat $\left\{\frac{pro}{a\ ells}\right\}$
      some journalists assert that them have awarded {pro, to them}
      'Some journalists assert that they have been awarded the prize'

Overt and empty pronouns may be interpreted as free and coreferential with the element in the subject position of the main clause. But *pro* and *els-pro* may also be bound by the element in the subject position of the main clause, because it is a QP and c-commands them.

   Nevertheless, when we are dealing with structures more complex than those analyzed until now, Catalan and Spanish pronouns do not behave the same way. Montalbetti (1984, 189f) points out that Catalan overt pronouns cannot be bound by a QP in any context, whereas overt pronouns in Spanish – at least in some of its dialects – may behave like bound variables in certain circumstances. We can see this in (26):

(26) a. Dos periodistes diuen [que *pro* creuen [que $\left\{\frac{pro}{ells}\right\}$ rebran el premi]]
      two journalists say that pro (they) believe that {pro, they} will-receive the prize
      'Two journalists say that they believe that they will receive the prize
   b. Alguns periodistes diuen [que *pro* creuen [que els premiaran $\left\{\substack{a\ ells \\ pro}\right\}$]]
      some journalists say that pro (they) believe that them will-award {to them, pro}
      'Some journalists say that they believe that they will be awarded the prize'

Unlike what we observed in (25), now *ells* 'they' and *els-a ells* 'them' are located in the scope of *pro* of the first subordinate. This pronoun, in turn, lies in the scope of the QP; therefore, it may act as a bound variable. If this is the case and if *pro* is a bound pronoun, then the overt pronoun *ells/els-a ells* may not enter into a relationship with it. The only interpretation for the overt pronoun will be the free reading. In Catalan, an overt pronoun cannot be a function of a QP – not even indirectly (i.e., by way of *pro*). Where we can see clearly that a Catalan overt pronoun cannot be bound, even by way of *pro*, is in those cases where the QP is an inherent quantifier, as in (27).

(27)   Tothom diu que *pro* considera que $\begin{Bmatrix} \text{pro} \\ \text{ell} \end{Bmatrix}$ aprovarà
everyone says that pro(he) considers that {pro, he} will-pass
'Everyone says that he thinks that he will pass'

Ell 'he' may only be free. The strong pronoun is not capable of losing its singular value and of being connected to *tothom* 'everyone' – not even by means of an empty pronoun.

Let us examine at this time the behavior of Spanish pronouns. It has been claimed that Spanish overt pronouns are not bound. However, Montalbetti (1984) has noted that in the following sentences, overt pronouns may be bound.[20]

(28)   a.   Muchos estudiantes dijeron [que *pro* piensan [que ellos son inteligentes]]
many students said that pro (they) think that they are intelligent
'Many students said that they think they are intelligent'
b.   ¿Quiénes dijeron [que *pro* creen [que ellos fueron al cine]]?
who (pl.) said that pro (they) believe that they went to-the cinema?
'Who said they believe that they went to the cinema?'
c.   ¿A quiénes convenció de [que *pro dijeran* [que ellos son tontos]]?
to whom (pl.) convinced of that pro (they) should-say that they are stupid?
'Who did he talk into saying that they are stupid'
d.   Nadie quiere [PRO creer [que él es inteligente]]
nobody wants PRO to-believe that he is intelligent
'Nobody wants to believe that he is intelligent'

In all of these sentences, the overt pronoun can be bound. According to Montalbetti (1984), bound empty pronouns – *pro* and PRO – license the binding of an overt one linked to them.[21]

In order to show the divergences between overt and empty pronouns in Spanish as well as in other languages, Montalbetti (1984) postulates a constraint on LF – the Overt Pronoun Constraint (OPC) – which in Catalan grammar will appear in its strong version (OPC-2); whereas in Spanish grammar, the weak version of this principle (OPC-1) will be what governs the presence of strong pronouns.

> *Overt Pronoun Constraint*:
> OPC-1:   Overt pronouns cannot link to formal variables iff the alternation overt/empty obtains (Montalbetti 1984, 182)
> OPC-2:   Overt pronouns cannot have formal variables as antecedents (Montalbetti 1984, 187)

In Montalbetti (1984, 31f), *antecedent* is defined in terms of linking. Linking is a directional relation that relates only two positions. Linking is not transitive.

The notion of *formal variable* is defined as follows: *v* is a formal variable iff (i) *v* is an empty category in an argument position; and (ii) *v* is linked to a lexical operator in a non-argument position (Montalbetti 1984, 49). The following is one example cited by Montalbetti (1984, 49), in which the trace is a formal variable.:

(29)   [Who] [t] loves Mary

Observe that OPC-1 allows overt pronouns to link to a bound pronoun (not a formal variable).[22]

A series of questions arises: Why OPC? To what is this condition due? Why is it that pronouns in Spanish and Catalan obey OPC, while those in English do not? Besides their coexistence with empty pronouns, what else character-izes the behavior of overt pronouns in Spanish and Catalan? We believe that the answer may lie precisely in the nature of overt pronouns, in their lexical features [+quantifier, -operator] – features which convert them into quanti-fied terms and which give them distinctive interpretation or weak emphasis. We believe that our analysis of strong pronouns as quantified terms gives meaning to the OPC of Montalbetti (1984).

2.3

Let us focus our attention first on overt pronouns in Catalan. Why is it that these pronouns cannot be bound by a QP (or a formal variable)? It is simply because they are not in the scope of the variable. Though strong pronouns are not moved at LF, they take wide scope because they are interpreted in a branching manner. According to Hornstein (1984), a certain kind of interpre-tation rule is associated with unmoved NPs. This interpretation rule has effects of branching quantification in the sense of Hinttika. However, Horn-stein's treatment involves branching interpretation procedures, but not a branching syntactic form at LF.[23] Following Hornstein (1984, ch. 2), we accept that there is a principle of Universal Grammar which holds that unmoved elements are interpretively independent and that moved elements are interpretively dependent. So then, strong pronouns, owing to their cha-racteristic of being unmoved quantifiers, are interpreted independently of other quantifiers; that is, they cannot be a function of a QP. Like definite descriptions, they are freely permutable with respect to all other operators. It is precisely this independence with respect to the QP that frees them from becoming bound variables and allows them to establish coreferential relationships.

Let us now return to Spanish. We have seen that, at least in some dialects, the diversity of behavior between empty and strong pronouns is not as radical as it is in Catalan; this does not mean, however, that the boundaries between the empty and strong pronouns are blurry. But, what causes overt pronouns in Spanish to be closer to empty pronouns than are overt pronouns in Catalan? In other words: How do native speakers deduce that in Spanish, overt pronouns may be bound by an operator (if certain circumstances are present), and that this, in turn, is impossible in Catalan? We will attempt to respond to these questions.[24] It will consequently be necessary to first take into account (*a*) that we are dealing with languages which are typologically and geographically very close to one another, and (*b*) that this behavioral difference between the strong pronouns in these languages cannot be directly observed. It would not be reasonable to think that children have necessarily had direct contact with sentences as infrequent as those cited in (28). On the other hand, we cannot believe that children have direct evidence of ungrammatical sentences (e.g., Catalan sentences with a bound strong pronoun in subject position). We are obliged to search for the reason for this diversity of behavior in the differential characteristics presented by these languages. Actually, the pronominal paradigm of Spanish does not coincide exactly with that of Catalan. We thereby deduce that the role and use of the pronouns do not totally coincide.

In section 1 we have stated that Catalan has two pronouns which have no correlation in Spanish: *en* and *hi*. These clitics may represent verbal objects with Oblique Case. A verbal object introduced by the preposition *de* 'of, about' will be pronominalized by *en*. The clitic *hi*, in turn, will appear in those cases where the introductory preposition is one other than *de*. We may observe this in (30).

(30)   a. En Pere parla de la Maria
           Pere speaks of the Maria
           'Pere speaks about Maria
        b. En Pere en parla
           Pere (of)-her speaks
           'Pere speaks about her'
        c. En Pere pensa en la Maria
           Pere thinks in the Maria
           'Pere thinks about Maria'
        d. En Pere hi pensa
           Pere (in)-her thinks
           'Pere thinks about her'
        e. En Pere s'interessa per la Maria
           Pere himself interests for the Maria
           'Pere is interested in Maria'

    f. En Pere s'hi interessa
       Pere himself (for)-her interests
       'Pere is interested in her'

The NP *la Maria*, because it is an animate NP, may be represented by a strong pronoun, in this case the pronoun *ella* 'she'.[25]

(31)   a. En Pere parla d'ella
          Pere speaks of her (she)
          'Pere speaks about her'
    b. En Pere pensa en ella
          Pere thinks in her (she)
          'Pere thinks about her'
    c. En Pere s'interessa par ella
          Pere himself interests for her (she)
          'Pere is interested in her'

Spanish cannot communicate (30a), (30c), and (30d) in the form of (30b), (30d), and (30f), respectively. Nevertheless, it has the same capability of representing the NP of the PP with a strong pronoun (observed in (31) for Catalan).

    The clitics *en/hi* have traditionally been considered as non-referential, perhaps because they do not permit clitic-doubling and because they represent a PP. In any case, comparison of the sentences in (32) and (33) shows that *en* and *hi*, like Accusative and Dative clitics, cannot represent a PP with a non-referential NP.

(32)   a. La Maria no veu ningú
          the Maria not sees nobody
          'Maria doesn't see anybody'
    b. La Maria no el veu
          the Maria not him sees
          'Maria doesn't see him'
    c. La Maria no ha regalat el llibre a cap amic
          the Maria not has given the book to none friend
          'Maria hasn't given the book to any friend'
    d. La Maria no li ha regalat el llibre
          the Maria not him has given the book
          'Maria hasn't given him the book'

(33)   a. La Maria no pensa en ningú
          the Maria not thinks in nobody
          'Maria doesn't think about anybody'

    b. La Maria no hi pensa
       the Maria not (in)-him thinks
       'Maria doesn't think about him'
    c. La Maria no parla de ningú
       the Maria not speaks of nobody
       'Maria doesn't speak about anybody'
    d. La Maria no en parla
       the Maria not (of)-him speaks
       'Maria doesn't speak about him'

The sentences (32a), (32c), (33a), and (33c) cannot be paraphrased by (32b), (32d), (33b), and (33d), respectively. In the same way, no clitic – whatever its syntactic function may be – can appear in a Right Dislocation construction if the dislocated constituent contains a non-referential NP.

(34)   a. *La Maria no la veu, cap noia
           the Maria not her sees none girl
           'Maria doesn't see her, any girl'
        b. *La Maria no hi pensa, en cap noia
           the Maria not (in)-her thinks in none girl
           'Maria doesn't think about her, any girl'

Thus, the clitics *en* and *hi* respect Principle B of the Binding Theory (as do other clitics). The Case Theory will explain why these clitics – unlike Accusative and Dative clitics – do not allow clitic-doubling constructions.

Spanish, because it does not have clitics such as *en* and *hi*, turns to strong pronouns – even in those cases where Catalan cannot, as shown in (35). The sentence (35b) is the Catalan equivalent of the Spanish sentence (35a).

(35)   a. Este es el Palacio de Oriente. En él vivía antiguamente la familia real.
           this is the Palacio de Oriente. In it lived formerly the family royal
           'This is the Palacio de Oriente. The royal family used to live there.'
        b. Aquest és el Palau d'Orient. Antigament hi vivia la família reial.
           this is the Palau d'Orient. Formerly (in)-it lived the family royal.
           'This is the Palau d'Orient. The royal family used to live there.'

We will now see how the clitics *en/hi*, as other clitics, may behave like bound pronouns, whereas the strong pronouns may not.

(36)   a. Cap company no pot dir que la Maria se n'hagi enamorat
           none classmate not can say that the Maria herself (of)-him has enamored

'No classmate can say that Maria has fallen in love with him'
b. Cap company no pot dir que la Maria s'hagi enamorat d'ell
   none classmate not can say that the Maria herself has enamored of
   him(he)
   'No classmate can say that Maria has fallen in love with him'
c. Quins nois diuen que el professor hi parla sovint?
   what boys say that the professor (with)-them speaks often?
   'Which boys say that the professor often speaks with them?'
d. Quins nois diuen que el professor parla sovint amb ells?
   what boys say that the professor speaks often with them(they)?
   'Which boys say that the professor often speaks with them?'

The clitic *en* (*n'*) in (36a) may be interpreted as free or bound, while *ell* 'he' in (36b) may only be interpreted as free. On the other hand, in (36c) *hi* may receive free reading, bound reading, or coreferential reading, but in (36c) *ells* 'they' may only receive free or coreferential reading.[26]

In Spanish, the possibilities of (36) are reduced to the following two:

(37) a. Ningún compañero puede decir que María se haya enamorado de
          él.
          none classmate can say that María herself has enamored of him
          'No classmate can say that María has fallen in love with him'
      b. ¿Qué chicos dicen que el profesor habla a menudo con ellos?
          what boys say that the professor speaks often with them?
          'Which boys say that the professor often speaks with them?'

In (37a), *él* 'he' receives free or bound reading. In (37b), on the other hand, *ellos* 'they' may be free, bound, or coreferential.

From hearing sentences like those in (30) through (37), children discover that in Catalan a strong pronoun may not be bound by a QP. They deduce that strong pronouns share the features [+quantifier, –operator] with definite descriptions, and therefore may not be bound by a QP. However, strong pronouns (because they are [+ pronominal]) obey Principle B of the Theory of Binding; definite descriptions, on the other hand, obey Principle C: they are R-expressions, they are free. In the same way, from the absence of clitics (such as *en/hi*) in Catalan), as well as from other facts – such as those outlined in note 24 (in addition to others not yet discovered) – children conclude that strong pronouns in Spanish are more distant from definite descriptions than are those in Catalan.

In sum, the data presented here allow us to conclude that when a language has a double pronominal paradigm – lexically full pronouns and clitic/empty pronouns – strong pronouns behave like quantifiers. Thus, they have emphatic value (exhaustive listing interpretation) – a value which, evidently, other pronouns do not possess (not even pronouns in languages that do not have double pronominal paradigm, such as English). It is this quantifier characteristic which is the reason that strong pronouns behave in some instances like definite descriptions (e.g., they cannot be used as variables). However, if the double pronominal paradigm is not complete – as in Spanish – then strong pronouns play a double role: (*1*) of emphatic pronoun and (*2*) of pronoun which in some peculiar circumstances acts like an empty pronoun (i.e., bound pronoun or non-emphatic pronoun).

NOTES

* I would like to thank J.M. Brucart, G. Cinque, M.L. Hernanz, J. Mascaró, and C. Picallo for helpful comments on a draft of this article. I also wish to express my thankfulness to the editors of this volume, in particular to H. Contreras and K. Zagona. The research reported here was supported by Grant 2545/83 from the Comisión Asesora de Investigación Científica y Técnica, Ministerio de Educación y Ciencia of Spain.

1. Catalan strong pronouns are as follows: *jo* (I, sing.); *tu* (II, sing.); *ell* (III, sing. masc.); *ella* (III, sing. fem.); *nosaltres* (I, pl.); *vosaltres* (II, pl.); *ells* (III, pl. masc.); *elles* (III, pl. fem.); *mi* (I, sing., non-Nominative Case). The definite clitics, pure pronominals, are as follows: *em* (I, sing.); *et* (II, sing.); *el* (III, sing. masc., Accusative); *la* (III, sing. fem., Accusative); *els* (III, pl. masc., Accusative); *les* (III, pl. fem., Accusative); *li* (III, sing., Dative); *els* (III, pl., Dative). Other Catalan clitic pronouns are: *ho*, *en*, and *hi*.

Spanish strong pronouns are as follows: *yo* (I, sing.); *tú* (II, sing.); *él* (III, sing. masc.); *ella* (III, sing. fem.); *ello* (III, sing., never); *mi* (I, sing., non-Nominative); *ti* (II, sing., non-Nominative). The definite clitics, pure pronominals, are as follows: *me* (I, sing.); *te* (II, sing.); *lo/le* (III, sing. masc., Accusative); *la* (III, sing. fem., Accusative); *le* (III, sing., Dative); *les* (III, pl., Dative).

2. We will assume without much discussion that the empty element in an argument chain headed by a clitic is *pro*, a non-anaphoric pronominal without lexical specification. See, however, Jaeggli (1982) and Borer (1984).

3. Cf. Rizzi (1982), Chomsky (1982), and the references cited therein.

4. Following Kayne (1975, 153f), we assume that the Catalan and Spanish Indirect Object does not behave like a PP, but instead like an NP. The preposition *a*, appearing with the Indirect Object, in Accusative clitic-doubling, and with the Spanish human Direct Object, must be attributed to an insertion rule. However, see Jaeggli (1982, 1.3.2).

5. In this article we do not discuss reflexive and reciprocal pronouns, which also may have both full and empty versions.

6. We assume the following definitions:
Government: α governs γ in $[_\beta \ldots \gamma \ldots \alpha \ldots \gamma \ldots]$, where a) $\alpha = x^0$; b) where φ is a maximal projection, if φ dominates γ, then φ dominates α; and c) α c-commands γ. (Chomsky 1981, 165)
C-command: α c-commands β if: a) α does not contain β; b) the first maximal projection that dominates α also dominates β. (Aoun and Sportiche 1983).

7. Cf. Gili Gaya (1973, 172f); RAE (1974, 3.10); Badia (1962, 105).

8. Kuno (1972) distinguishes two types of emphatic elements: those of contrastive focus and those of exhaustive listing interpretation. According to Kuno (1972, 270), Japanese has two types of emphatic markers: the particles *wa* and *ga*. *Wa* marks the contrasted element of the sentence, while *ga* stands for the distinctive interpretation or weak emphasis. Spanish and Catalan do not have markers which are as explicit as those of Japanese, but a similar distinction is present in (8c) and (8b).

9. For a different proposal, in which strong pronouns are considered as elements forming an operator-variable structure at LF, see Rigau (1982).

10. See sections 2.2 and 2.3.

11. Contrastive focus elements create an island, a Focus Island (Huang, 1982b), as shown in (i). Nevertheless, distinctive interpretation elements do not create an island, as shown in (ii).

(i)   *PEPE telefonea A MARÍA
       'Pepe phones María'
(ii)   Él te telefoneará a ti
       'He'll phone you'

12. For the principles of discourse that govern the presence of an overt pronoun, see Rigau (1984).

13. Observe that cases of sentence coordination that share the same subject are cases of emphatic environment:

(i)   a. Tú lo prometiste y tú lo cumplirás
          'You promised it and you'll keep your word'
       b. Pepe lo prometió y Pepe lo cumplirá
          'Pepe promised it and Pepe will keep his word'

14. We can restate the Avoid Pronoun Principle as (i):

(i)   Avoid full pronoun.

15. Coordination Restriction Principle (Brucart 1984, 429):
a. Only constituents of the same category and hierarchy may be coordinated.
b. When the structural analysis of a sequence allows different levels of coordination, take as uniquely well-formed the coordination that involves a smaller quantity of empty categories.

16. So-called negative quantifiers are inherent quantifiers if they are in the scope of the operator of negative modality *no*; in some cases *no* may not appear at the level of phonological representation (see Picallo 1984a). However, if negative quantifiers are in the scope of an operator of non-negative modality, then the negative reading disappears, as shown in (ia), a sentence synonymous with (ib).

(i)   a. ¿Viste nada parecido?
          saw-(you) nothing similar?
          'Did you see something similar?'
       b. ¿Viste algo parecido?
          saw-(you) something similar?
          'Did you see something similar?'

17. If the NP *un novelista* 'a novelist' were to appear in (20) in plural form (*unos novelistas*), the only assigned interpretation would be that of wide scope. Haïk (1984) observes that all NPs that denote pluralities may take scope over other NPs if they can be interpreted distributively. According to Haïk (1984), it is presumed that they allow for a quantifier-variable reading. So then, plurality converts NPs – pronouns and definite descriptions – into QPs with wide scope. Consider (i):

(i)   a. ¿Qué día nacieron los hermanos de Marta?

what day were-born the brothers of Marta?
'On which day were Marta's brothers born?'
b. ¿Qué día nacieron ellos?
what day were-born they?
'On which day were they born?'
c. ¿Qué día nacieron *pro*?
what day were-born pro (they)?
'On which day were they born?'

The plural defined NP makes *qué día* 'what day' capable of being distributively interpreted. Therefore, a possible response to (i) may be (ii):

(ii)   María nació el 20 de mayo de 1968 y Pepe nació el 3 de enero de 1972
María was-born the 20 of May of 1968 and Pepe was-born the 3 of January of 1972
'María was born May 20, 1968 and Pepe was born January 3, 1972'

18. For cases of Indirect Binding, see Haïk (1984, 4.3.1).
19. The LF of (23a) when *pro* is coreferential with *tres físicos* 'three physicists' will be (i), while the LF of (23a) when *pro* is bound by *tres físicos* is (ii):

(i)   [[Three x: a physicist [x have confirmed that they will participate in the colloquium]]]
(ii)   [[Three x: x a physicist [x have confirmed that x will participate in the colloquium]]]

20. The sentences of (28) belong to Montalbetti (1984, ch. 5).
21. Observe that in the following contexts strong pronouns may not be bound by QP, but must be free.

(i)   a. Nadie dice que *pro* cree que ÉL está loco
nobody says that pro(he) believes that HE is crazy
'Nobody says he thinks that he is crazy'
b. Nadie dice que *pro* cree que sólo él está loco
nobody says that pro(he) believes that only he is crazy
'Nobody says he believes that only he is crazy'
c. Nadie dice que *pro* cree que está loco él
nobody says that pro(he) believes that is crazy he
'Nobody says that he believes that he is crazy'

In (ia) and (ib) contrastive focus or strong emphasis and the quantifier *sólo* 'only' mean that the Quantifier Rule applies to the pronoun. In (ic) *él* holds a position from which it cannot be bound and which favors distinctive interpretation. The impossibility for a subject pronoun in postverbal position to be interpreted as a bound pronoun was observed by Montalbetti (1984, 3.8).
22. According to Montalbetti (1984, 49), a pronoun P is a bound pronoun iff (i) P is in the scope of a formal variable v and (ii) P is linked to v.
23. In Hinttika's treatment, terms move. However, the positions to which they move branch with respect to the other linearly ordered elements (Cf. Hornstein 1984, ch. 2). The structure (i) shows roughly a case of branching quantification. Different arms of the branching syntactic form are interpreted independently of one another.

(i)   a. Qx
        $\searrow$
        $\qquad$ [x .....y]
        $\nearrow$
        Qy

24. The OPC of Montalbetti (1984) does not explain why *pro* and PRO allow a strong pronoun to be bound. Although this fact is outside the range of this article, we will simply point out some factors that could help to explain it. Actually, the bound interpretation of a Spanish overt pronoun by way of *pro*/PRO depends on the type of complementizer of the subordinate clause, as well as on the type of verbs that are involved, and on the sentence mood. If COMP is occupied by a Wh-element, then it is not easy to interpret the strong pronoun as bound. Let us look at this in (i).

(i)   a.   *Nadie preguntó cuándo sabría cómo él había hecho el examen.
           'Nobody asked when he would know how he had done on the test.'
      b.   Nadie preguntó cuándo *pro* sabría cómo había hecho el examen él.
           (same as (ia))
      c.   ¿Cuántos estudiantes preguntaron cómo sabrían si ellos estaban admitidos?
           'How many students asked how they could find out if they had been admitted?'

Sentence (ia) is ungrammatical because, according to Torrego (1984), the presence of certain Wh-elements in the Comp position of an interrogative sentence in Spanish causes obligatory inversion between subject and verb. In (ib), which is well formed, *él* cannot be interpreted as bound to *nadie* 'nobody'. The postverbal position reinforces the distinctive interpretation of the pronoun. Unlike other Wh-words, the interrogative element *si* does not require obligatory inversion. In spite of this, the bound reading of *ellos* 'they' in (ic) is hard to get. The presence of the conjunction *que* in COMP, on the one hand, and the "bridge verbs" (e.g., *decir, rogar*), on the other, favor the bound interpretation of a strong pronoun by way of *pro*/PRO (cf. Erteschik 1973, Guéron 1981). Nonetheless, not all verbs of saying are "bridge verbs", verbs which (among other traits) have the characteristic of allowing the elision of the complementizer. So, *informar*, *murmurar*, and *decir en francés* are not bridge verbs. Observe (ii):

(ii) a.   ¿Cuántos chicos han dicho en francés que creen que ellos son madrileños?
           'How many boys have said in French that they believe they are from Madrid?'
      b.   Muchos chicos murmuran que creen que ellos son inteligentes.
           'Many boys murmur that they believe they are intelligent.'

The sentence (iia) is unlikely to be interpreted as a question relating to the boys who have said "I am from Madrid" and not "We are from Madrid." In the same way, the verb *murmurar* 'to murmur' blocks any bound interpretation of the overt pronoun in (iib).

On the other hand, an empty or strong pronoun in subject position of a subjunctive sentence cannot be bound with the subject of the main clause:

(iii) Nadie dice que *pro* evitará que {él, *pro*} vaya a la cárcel
       nobody says that pro(he) will-prevent that {he, pro} goes to the prison
       'Nobody says he'll prevent him from going to prison'

This agrees with Picallo (1984b), who treats the subjunctive forms which have a "defective" tense specification like a transparent domain for binding. Therefore, it requires a disjoint interpretation – not a bound one – of its subject.

25. If the NP in PP were not a [+human] NP, it could not be represented by a strong pronoun.

(i)   Parla de política = Parla d'ella
       speak of politics = speak of her(it)
       'He speaks about politics' = 'He speaks about her'

26. Some speakers admit the bound interpretation of the strong pronoun in (36b) and (36d).

Binding in NPs*

María-Luisa Rivero, *University of Ottawa*

In this paper, an account is provided for the binding properties of reflexives, non-reflexive pronouns, and possessives within NP-structures in Spanish.

The analysis is based on two ideas. First, NPs have no syntactic subject position, thus they are head-initial with respect to thematic material, and the arguments specified in the lexical structure of a given N are realized as right-sisters within the NP. Under this hypothesis, possessives such as *su* in *su foto* 'his/her picture' do not occupy the A(rgument)-position traditionally identified as subject-of-NP ([NP,NP]), since such a node is not syntactically available at any level of representation. Rather, the possessive is an element in non-A(rgument) position, and it is coindexed either with a postnominal E(mpty) C(ategory), or with a category containing lexical material. In this sense, a possessive is parallel but not identical to a clitic in the Spanish VP, as discussed in section 2 of the paper.

Second, the thematic frame associated with the head N of an NP contributes to define the domain of application of the Binding Theory. Two classes of Ns must be distinguished in this respect: *1)* Ns which are monadic or assign one unique θ-role, and *2)* Ns which take two (or more) arguments and assign two or more θ-roles. The binding properties of reflexives, non reflexives, and possessives inside NPs are determined differently in these two cases. The first class systematically disallows reflexives. In section 3, I propose that the Binding Theory is sensitive to the notion of Complete Thematic Domain.

1. BINDING AND SUBJECTs

I assume familiarity with the Government and Binding framework (Chomsky 1981, and later work). I adopt the Binding Theory in (1), and do not discuss R-expressions (Principle C in Chomsky 1981, 1982), except for some

* This article is based on work first presented in a syntax course taught at the Universidad Autónoma of Madrid, Spain, in 1983-84. I would like to thank the students in the course, as well as Violeta Demonte and Carlos Piera. I am grateful to the Social Sciences and Humanities Research Council of Canada for financial support under Leave Fellowship 451-83-2864 and Research Grant 410-84-0370.

incidental remarks when comparing some possessive and clitic doubling constructions.

(1)   A. Anaphors are A-bound in their governing category
       B. Pronominals are A-free in their governing category. α A-binds β if α and β are coindexed, α is in an A-position, and c-commands β.

Government is defined in (2) (Aoun and Sportiche 1983):

(2) α governs γ in $[\ldots\gamma\ldots\alpha\ldots\gamma\ldots]$, where
       (i) $\alpha = X^0$
       (ii) where φ is a maximal projection, φ dominates α iff φ dominates γ

Of the two definitions for governing category in (3), I will adopt (3a) in a preliminary way when discussing possessives, until I turn to thematic domains in section 3. This definition is too restrictive for anaphors, although it is appropriate for Spanish pronominals. This will not affect the conclusions in section 2.

(3)   a. The governing category for α is the minimal category NP or S containing α and a governor for α (Chomsky 1981, 188ff)
       b. The governing category for α is the minimal category containing α, a governor for α, and a SUBJECT accessible to α (Chomsky 1981, 211ff)

In (3b), SUBJECT refers to AGR, or to the subject NP, if there is no AGR. Accessibility is defined in terms of c-command and non-violation of the i-over-i condition (i.e. $*_\alpha[\ldots\gamma\ldots]$ where α and γ bear the same index).

The notion of accessible SUBJECT in (3b) eliminates certain earlier conceptual problems, as pointed out by Chomsky. However, it also raises new ones; for example, the identification of AGR and ordinary subjects does not seem to be based on a natural connection. In this paper I propose that NPs are subjectless. If this is correct, it is to be expected that no statement in the Binding Theory should crucially be based on the notion *subject*, since this syntactic position lacks transcategorial validity. Rather, the principles which determine the properties of anaphors and pronominals should relate to aspects which all syntactic categories share.

It is well known that NPs may be opaque or transparent domains for the Binding Theory; however, I argue that their opacity or transparency is not correlated with the presence or absence of a subject-of-NP, since such syntactic position is unavailable in a uniform way. Because of this difference in approach, it is important to examine the Binding Theory in (1)-(3b), and its relevance to Spanish before we proceed. In the discussion which follows, no reference is made to prenominal possessives; those are treated in section 2.

It is not difficult to ascertain that (3b) is empirically inadequate for binding properties in Spanish. In this respect, consider the difference in grammaticality between the English (4a), and the parallel Spanish structure in (4b).

(4)   a.   They$_i$ expected that pictures of each other$_i$ would be on sale

        b. *Los actores$_i$ creían que unas/las fotos de sí mismos$_i$ estaban a la venta

           'The actors$_i$ thought that some/the pictures of themselves$_i$ were on sale'

Spanish anaphors must be A-bound in some local domain but the notion of accessible SUBJECT plays no role in the determination of locality for this purpose. Under definition (3b), the accessible SUBJECT in (4a-b) is the AGR in the matrix. In view of the ungrammaticality of (4b), *accessible SUBJECT* does not define the appropriate binding domain for the reflexive, and a more stringent locality condition is required, as we shall see. Similar comments apply to (5), whose accessible SUBJECT is the AGR in the matrix as well.

(5)   a.   They$_i$ think it is a pity that pictures of each other$_i$ are hanging on the wall

        b. *Los actores$_i$ creen que es verdad que unas/las fotos de sí mismos$_i$ están ya en el museo

           'The actors$_i$ think that it-is true that some/the pictures of themselves$_i$ are already in the museum'

Then, we can assume that the deviance of (6b), parallel to (6a) in the relevant respects, does not result from the fact that the reflexive is not bound in the domain of the accessible SUBJECT (i.e. the AGR on *dijo* 'said'), since such a notion plays no role in (4b) and (5b). Rather, (4b), (5b), and (6b) all fail to meet locality conditions on Spanish anaphors which are defined in terms of complete thematic or propositional domains, not in view of SUBJECTs, as we shall see in section 3.

(6)   a. *They$_i$ think he said that pictures of each other$_i$ are hanging on the wall

        b. *Los actores$_i$ creen que Juan dijo que unas/las fotos de sí mismos$_i$ están ya en el museo

           'The actors$_i$ think that John said that some/the pictures of themselves$_i$ are already in the museum'

Huang has proposed that anaphors and pronominals have different binding domains. He defines governing category as in (7) (1983, 557), and extends the notion of SUBJECT to include the subject NP, AGR, and the head N of NP.

(7) α is the governing category for β if and only if α is the minimal category containing β, a governor of β, and a SUBJECT that, if β is an anaphor, is accessible to β.

The conceptual problems mentioned before in connection with definition (3b) reappear in (7). From an empirical point of view, the predictions are the same for examples (4b) and (5b); these should be grammatical, contrary to fact. Again, definition (7) draws an unwarranted distinction between (4b) and (5b) on the one hand, and (6b) on the other.

   The binding of the anaphor in the English (4a) and (5a) applies across several of the nodes which are considered bounding by other subtheories in the model, and appears to go against locality principles usually associated with core grammar. Suppose that these "long distance" anaphors require auxiliary hypotheses associated with the Binding Theory. Then, it could be proposed that binding domains are defined in view of accessible subjects, as in (3b) or (7), but meet stricter locality requirements in the unmarked case. Huang's proposal is attractive under this perspective, because it accounts for the sentences in (8), with the interpretation as indicated.

(8)   a. $[_S$ Juan$_i$ vio $[_{NP}$ una/la foto   de él$_i$] en la revista]
         John$_i$ saw   a/the picture of he$_i$ in the magazine
         'John$_i$ saw a picture of his$_i$ in the magazine'
       b. $[_S$Juan$_i$ vio $[_{NP}$ una/la foto   de sí mismo$_i$] en la revista]
         'John$_i$ saw   a/the picture of himself$_i$ in the magazine'

Under the approach in (7), the pronominal *él* 'he' in (8a) has the NP-node as governing category, and is free in this domain. The anaphor *sí mismo* 'himself' in (8b) has S as governing category, since the lower NP-node lacks an accessible SUBJECT. The reflexive is bound by *Juan* in the more encompassing domain.

   However, not every NP lacking an accessible SUBJECT allows anaphors to be bound in the immediately superior category. Compare (8) and (9) in this respect.

(9)   a. Juan$_i$ vió $[_{NP}$ una casa de él$_i$] en la revista
         John$_i$ saw   a house   of he$_i$ in the magazine
         'John$_i$ saw a house of is$_i$ in the magazine'
       b. *Juan$_i$ vió $[_{NP}$ una casa de sí mismo$_i$]   en la revista
         John$_i$ saw   a house   of himself$_i$ in the magazine

Following definition (7), the NPs in (8b) and (9b) lack accessible SUBJECTs;

their respective reflexives should exhibit parallel binding characteristics. To claim that the N *casa* 'house' is an accessible SUBJECT in (9), while the N *foto* in (8) is not, goes against the i-over-i condition. Later on, I show that the thematic frames associated with head Ns play a role in the difference seen in (8b) and (9b), and in other binding phenomena in NPs.

I will retain the idea that an anaphor may have as governing category a more encompassing domain than a pronominal, and discuss this aspect in section 3. For the moment, I conclude that the notion of accessible SUBJECT plays no role in the determination of long distance or local binding domain.[1] This result is consistent with the hypothesis that NPs are subjectless in general, but may, nevertheless, function as binding domains (i.e. they may be opaque).

2. POSSESSIVES

The aim of this section is twofold: *a*) to motivate the proposal that Spanish NPs are subjectless, and *b*) to account for the referential characteristics of pronominal possessives under such an approach.

The fact that clauses must have subjects has been the source of much recent discussion. For example, Chomsky (1981) adds a stipulation to the Projection Principle ensuring this obligatoriness. Williams (1980) and Rothstein (1983) use principles connected with the rule(s) of predication to the same end. On the other hand, the fact that NPs contain no obligatory subject position is seen as unproblematic, and requires no special stipulation, although proposals for the internal structure of NP differ.

From a typological perspective, it is quite clear that in Spanish and other Romance languages, the head is initial in the NP-phrase, in the sense that the arguments specified in the lexical frame of a given Noun must appear in post-head position, as in (10a), where the first PP is the Experiencer, and the second the Theme.

(10) a. La admiración de Juan por Europa
         'the admiration of John for Europe'
      b. Juan admira Europa
         'John admires Europe'

The head-initial/head-final parameter has been related to the directionality of Case and θ-role assignment in some recent proposals (Koopman 1983, Travis 1984). Following this approach, it can be assumed that Ns in Spanish assign θ-roles to the right exclusively, excluding θ-positions which precede the head.

Spanish lacks constructions such as the English *the city's destruction*. These are often analyzed as instances of NP-movement into subject-position, as in the corresponding clause *The city was destroyed*.[2] Thus, in Spanish, there is no positive evidence for a non-thematic prenominal A-position in NP.

Based on these typological remarks, I assume that Spanish NPs are subject-less; i.e. they lack the A-position usually identified as [NP, NP]. Under Williams's (1982) approach, typological variation in this respect is not expected, since the subjectless nature of NPs is a consequence of general aspects of the theory, but I will not discuss this issue here. In any case, if the [NP, NP] position is not syntactically available in Spanish, it cannot be filled by thematic material in the base, nor can it be the landing site for NP-movement; the evidence in Spanish is quite clear on both counts.

As is well known, non-pronominal possessors must always be postnominal, and appear with the preposition *de* 'of', while a pronominal possessor may occur prenominally in the form of a possessive pronoun. In most dialects, but not all, this possessive seems to occupy the determiner position: *mi vaso* 'my glass' vs. *el mi vaso* 'the my glass'. If the syntactic structure of NPs is subjectless, a prenominal possessive cannot be treated as a pronominal NP in A-position receiving Genitive Case, as in (11b). Rather, if the possessive is seen as a non-A identifier of an Empty NP category in posthead position, (11c), the structure complies with the syntactic characteristics of Spanish NPs. McCloskey and Hale (1983) have proposed a similar analysis for possessives in Modern Irish.

(11)   a. su casa   'his house'
        b. $[_{NP} [_{NP}$ su] [casa]]
        c. $[_{NP}$ su$_i$ $[_N$ casa] $[_{NP}$ $e]_i]$

Empirical support for (11c) comes from NPs I label *possessive doubling constructions*, with a prenominal possessive and a postnominal possessor which are compatible and must be coindexed obligatorily, as in (12).

(12)   a. Su$_i$ casa de él$_i$
           his$_i$ house of he$_i$ 'His house'
        b. Su$_i$ casa de Vd$_i$
           your$_i$ house of you$_i$ 'Your house'

If the definition for *governing category* is as in (3a), (3b), or (7), and if *su* in (12a-b) is a pronominal in subject position, then Principle B of the Binding Theory is violated. The pronominal *él/Vd* is A-bound in its governing category. Under my proposal, in (12a-b) the coindexation between the non-A *su* and the pronominals *él/Vd* is not subject to the Binding Theory. In (12), the preposition *de* assigns case to the lexical phrase; it is required in view of the Case filter (*NP is lexical and not case-marked), since Ns are not case-assigners in Spanish. Later on, I will show that Spanish *de* can be treated as a semantically unrestricted dummy case-marker, or as a semantically restricted preposition connected with the θ-role Theme.

The treatment of possessives I have outlined has obvious parallelisms with recent analyses of clitic constructions (see, for example, Jaeggli 1982, among others). In these analyses, a clitic is treated as an element in non-A position which does not satisfy the frame of the V. An EC in postverbal position satifies lexical requirements, as in (13a). A common treatment for clitic doubling constructions analyzes the lexical phrase coindexed with the clitic as the complement in A-position, as in (13b); the preposition *a* is considered a dummy case-marker.

(13)   a. $[_{VP}$ lo$_i$ $[_V$ vieron] $[_{NP}$ $e]_i]$
        b. $[_{VP}$ lo$_i$ $[_V$ vieron] a $[_{NP}$ él]$_i]$

It is clear that the possessive functions as a syntactic constituent; the status of clitics vis à vis the morphology/syntax boundary is less clear. Aside from this, many of the issues recently discussed for clitic constructions arise for possessive constructions as well. However, there is an interesting difference in relation to the Binding Theory between the two constructions. In clitic doubling, the lexical phrase coindexed with a non-reflexive clitic may be an R-expression or a pronominal. The sequence *lo$_i$...R-expression$_i$* counts as an R-expression vis à vis the Binding Theory, as we see in (14a), while the sequence *lo$_i$...pronominal$_i$* counts as a pronominal in (14b).

(14)   a. Juan$_i$ dice que lo$_j$ vieron a Juan$_j$
           John$_i$ says that him$_j$ they-saw John$_j$
           'John$_i$ says that they saw John$_j$'
        b. Juan$_i$ dice que lo$_i$ vieron a él$_i$
           John$_i$ says that him$_i$ they-saw him$_i$
           'John$_i$ says that they saw him$_i$'

Then, the lexical properties of the non-clitic phrase appear to determine which principle of the Binding Theory is relevant, and the clitic makes no contribution in this respect. In the analysis that treats *Juan* and *él* in (14a-b) as NPs in A-position, this seems a natural conclusion. When there is no doubling, the situation is less clear, as the discussion in the cited bibliography indicates.

In possessive doubling, on the other hand, the lexical phrase coindexed with the possessive must be a pronominal, as in (12). It cannot be an R-expression at present,[3] as in the deviant (15).

(15)   *Su$_i$ casa de Juan$_i$
         his$_i$ house of John$_i$ 'John's house'

Obviously, there are no restrictions on the type of lexical NP which functions as a possessor, if there is no doubling; *la casa de Juan* 'John's house' and *la casa de él* 'his house' are both well-formed. Then, the ungrammaticality of (15) could be taken as an indication that the possessive is an identifier of a [+pronominal, –anaphor] category exclusively. Furthermore, the sequence su_i...$él_i$ in (12a) functions as a pronominal, and is equivalent in this respect to a non-doubled postnominal pronominal Possessor. Thus, it can be assumed that the phrase in A-position contains the lexical characteristics relevant for the Binding Theory. If this approach is correct, we may assume tentatively that in the usual NP with no doubling, the possessive is coindexed obligatorily with a null pronominal (i.e. little *pro*, [+pronominal, –anaphor]); otherwise, it could not "double" the EC. In brief, *su* 'his' functions as a local identifier of an empty pronominal, and encodes its person feature. Then, we expect prenominal possessives, postnominal pronominal possessors, and possessive doubling sequences to fall uniformly under Principle B of the Binding Theory, and the properties of the EC to mirror those of the lexical category in all respects.[4]

(16) a. Juan$_i$ visitó [$_{NP}$ su$_i$ casa e_i]
          John$_i$ visited   his$_i$ house
      b. Juan$_i$ visitó [$_{NP}$ la casa de él$_i$]
          John$_i$ visited   the house of he$_i$
      c. Juan$_i$ visitó [$_{NP}$ su$_i$ casa de él$_i$]
          John$_i$ visited   his$_i$ house of he$_i$
          'John$_i$ visited his$_i$ house'

In each case in (16), the lexical or null pronominal is free in the NP. Disjoint reference with *Juan* is possible too.

If the above proposal is correct, two consequences follow. First, it is not the case that the prenominal possessive represents a neutralized form that can serve as a pronominal or an anaphor, as sometimes suggested (see Harbert 1982, 1983). Second, NPs such as *su foto de sí mismo* 'his picture of himself' do not constitute cases of doubling; in this sense they differ from clitic doubling constructions such as *se fotografió a sí mismo* 'he photographed himself'. I return to this aspect later.

As already pointed out, *su* and *él* in (12a) and (16c) must be coindexed obligatorily. This is not the case for all NPs. The NP in (17a) has two readings, the doubling interpretation discussed up to now, (17b), and one where *su* and *él* are not coindexed, (17c).

(17) a. Su foto de él
      b. Su$_i$ foto de él$_i$ 'His picture'
      c. Su$_i$ foto de él$_j$ 'His$_i$ picture of him$_j$'

As a result, a sentence such as (18) has five possible interpretations. It combines the two readings of the English *John$_i$ saw his$_{i/j}$ picture.* which depend on the possibility of referring to one individual (*John*) or two, with the three interpretations of *John saw his picture of him*, including three separate individuals, or John and somebody else (*his* is Agent/Possessor, and *him* is Theme).

(18)   Juan vió su foto de él

Sentence (19), on the other hand, has only the two interpretations found in the English *John saw his house* (or the Spanish *Juan vió su casa*), with *his* normally a possessor.

(19)   Juan vió su casa de él

NP-structures with the doubling interpretation as one of two possible readings, such as (17) and (18), allow reflexives. This phenomenon is independent of the presence or absence of a pronominal possessive, as seen in (8b = 20a) and (20b). In these cases, the reflexive NP is the Theme, an aspect I discuss later on. Example (20b) shares the two interpretations of its English counterpart, which depend on the coreference or disjoint reference of *John* and *his*.

(20)   a. Juan$_i$ vió   la/una foto   de sí mismo$_i$
           John$_i$ saw   the/a   picture of himself$_i$
        b. Juan$_{i/j}$ vió   su$_i$ foto   de sí mismo$_i$
           John$_{i/j}$ saw   his$_i$ picture of himself$_i$

NP-structures with the doubling interpretation as the only option, as in (12a) and (16c), disallow reflexives. Again, this factor is independent of the presence or absence of a prenominal possessive, as seen in (9b = 21a) and (21b).

(21)   a. *Juan$_i$ vió   la/una casa   de sí mismo$_i$
           John$_i$ saw   the/a   house of himself$_i$
        b. *Juan$_i$ vió   su$_i$ casa   de sí mismo$_i$
           John$_i$ saw   his$_i$ house of himself$_i$

The properties of *su* as a non-A identifier of a null pronominal, or as a doubling item for a lexical pronominal, and the thematic properties of the head N of the NP combine to create this situation, as we see in the next section.

3. THEMATIC STRUCTURE IN NPs, AND BINDING

The lexical frame of a Noun specifies the number of arguments it takes, the syntactic form of each argument, and the thematic role each of them bears. The arguments are optional, and may be syntactically present or absent. An important difference between the two classes of Ns discussed up to now is the number of arguments specified in the lexical frame of each. Nouns such as *foto* 'picture', *historia* 'story', *cuento* 'fairy tale' (i.e. the class normally used in discussions of the Binding Theory) take at least two arguments. I assume that Concrete Nouns such as *casa* 'house' or Nouns related to the traditional intransitive Verbs such as *llegada* 'arrival' or *vida* 'life' take one argument. I return to this distinction later on.

Under the assumption that *foto* 'picture', *carta* 'letter', *gusto* 'liking' are dyadic, and that *petición* 'request' takes three arguments, we may say that the NPs in (22) are syntactically saturated, because all the arguments specified in the lexical frames of the respective head Ns are present.

(22)   a. La foto   de Juan   de Londres
            the picture of John   of London
            'John's picture of London'
       b. La carta de Juan   a María
            the letter of John   to Mary
            'John's letter to Mary'
       c. El gusto de Juan   por la ropa   cara
            the liking of John   for the clothes   expensive
            'John's liking of expensive clothes'
       d. La petición de Juan a María de que el niño   se callara
            the request of John to Mary of that the child would-quiet-down
            'John's request to Mary for the child to quiet down'

The *de* 'of' in the above examples must be analyzed in two ways. First, it can be a dummy case-marker, assigning Case to a bare NP-argument in order to satisfy the Case filter; in such a situation, the NP-argument receives a θ-role as determined by the properties of the head N. Examples of this first role are the *de*-form preceding the Agent/Possessor *Juan* in (22a,b,d), or the Experiencer *Juan* in (22c). Second, the form *de* can also be a preposition which is not semantically empty, but associates with the assignment of the θ-role Theme by the head N. In this second use, *de* assigns case to the NP as well, allowing the argument to satisfy the Case filter. However, the preposition appears under circumstances where the filter is not relevant–for example, before a tensed clausal complement. Examples of this second *de* appear with the Theme *Londres* in (22a), or preceding the clausal complement which is the Theme in (22d). In this last sentence, *de* identifies the θ-role; under the assumption that clauses need not be case-marked, the preposition plays no case-marking role. In view of this dual treatment of *de*, I assign the syntactic structures in (23a,b) to the NPs in (22a,b), respectively. The constituent with the dummy marker counts as NP.

23   a.

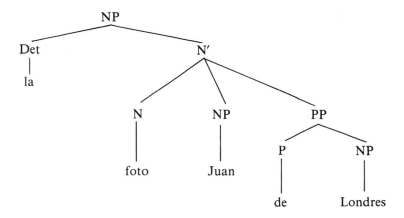

   b.

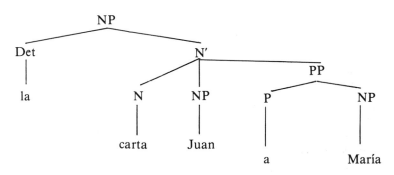

Thus I assume that in Spanish NPs, one thematic role inside the N′ is assigned by N to a bare NP-argument, while other thematic role(s) are assigned through prepositions. This hypothesis plays an important role in explaining the behavior of anaphors inside NPs, as we shall see.[5]

The order among the different arguments of N is free. Next to (22a), *La foto de Londres de Juan* is grammatical as well, and has an identical interpretation; the syntactic structure of this last case is as in (23a), except for the order of the two arguments. Together with (22b), *La carta a María de Juan* is possible too, although it offers a less common sequence. This freedom of order is behind the ambiguity of the examples in (24), which share the two interpretations indicated in the English glosses. Because both NPs are animate, either one of them can be interpreted as Agent/Possessor. In (22a) on the other hand, the usual reading is for the inanimate *Londres* to be the Theme, not the Agent/ Possessor.

(24)   a. La foto de Juan de María
           'John's picture of Mary'
        b. La foto de María de Juan
           'Mary's picture of John'

As in the previous cases, I assume that the syntactic structures in (24) contain a bare NP-argument (Agent/Possessor) and a PP-argument (Theme), without any specific order.

Consider the following examples and the behavior of anaphors, as arguments of a Noun. Sentences (25a-b) are grammatical, with the first one presenting the preferred order; examples (25c-d) are ungrammatical.

(25)   a.   La carta   de Juan$_i$ a sí mismo$_i$
             the letter of John$_i$ to himself$_i$
             'John's letter to himself'
        b.   La carta   a sí mismo$_i$ de Juan$_i$
             the letter to himself$_i$ of John$_i$
        c.   *La carta de sí mismo$_i$ a Juan$_i$
             the letter of himself$_i$ to John$_i$
        d.   *La carta a Juan$_i$ de sí mismo$_i$

In my proposal, the NP *Juan* in (25a-b) c-commands the reflexive, and binds it. This is because the Agent/Possessor phrase has a bare NP-structure, as in (23), while the reflexive is contained in the PP associated with the thematic role Goal. In (25c-d), on the other hand, the NP *Juan* is contained in the PP, does not c-command the anaphor, and cannot bind it. As expected, in NPs such as *La carta de Juan$_i$ a él$_j$* 'John's letter to him', the pronominal cannot be coindexed with the non-pronoun.

Consider the examples in (26).

(26)   a. La foto de $\left\{ \begin{matrix} \text{Juan}_i \\ \text{él}_i \end{matrix} \right\}$ de sí mismo$_i$

        b. La foto de sí mismo$_i$ de $\left\{ \begin{matrix} \text{Juan}_i \\ \text{él}_i \end{matrix} \right\}$
           $\left\{ \begin{matrix} \text{'John's}_i \\ \text{his}_i \end{matrix} \right\}$ picture of himself$_i$'

As in (25a-b), order is irrelevant and the anaphor must be bound to a c-commanding antecedent. Then, the anaphor is contained in the PP with the Theme θ-role, i.e. it is preceded by the "true" preposition; while the R-expression *Juan* or the pronominal *él* represents the bare NP-argument and is preceded by the dummy case marker.

In accordance with these proposals and the treatment of *su* in the previous section, the NPs in (27a) and (20b = 27b) contain a null pronominal NP identified by *su*, and this NP c-commands the anaphor and binds it. Order is irrelevant.

(27)   a. Su$_i$ carta [$_{NP}$ e_i] [$_{PP}$ a sí mismo$_i$]
            'his letter to himself'
       b. Su$_i$ foto [$_{NP}$ e_i] [$_{PP}$ de sí mismo$_i$]
            'his picture of himself'

Corresponding to (27), the possessive doubling constructions are *Su$_i$ carta de él$_i$ a sí mismo$_i$*, and *Su$_i$ foto de él$_i$ de sí mismo$_i$*, with the readings given in (27). Although many of these examples are seldom heard, I have found widespread agreement on their grammaticality and possible interpretations.

We are now in a position to return to the two readings in (17) (i.e. *Su foto de él* 'his picture' vs. 'his$_i$ picture of him$_j$'). In the first case, *su* doubles a lexical pronominal, as discussed in the previous section. However, the lexical frame of the N is dyadic. Since *su* can double lexical material or a null pronominal, it is possible to consider that the possessive identifies a bare NP-argument containing an empty category, and that *de él* is the other argument specified in the lexical frame of the N. Then, given that the EC c-commands the lexical pronominal, the two must be disjoint in reference in view of Principle B. The two possible analyses are indicated in (28).

(28)   a. [$_{NP}$ su$_i$ [$_{N'}$ foto de [$_{NP}$ él$_i$]]]
       b. [$_{NP}$ su$_i$ [$_{N'}$ foto $_{NP}$ e_i] [$_{PP}$ [$_P$ de] [$_{NP}$ él$_j$]]]

The lack of ambiguity in (12a) or (16c) (i.e. *su casa de él* 'his house') correlates with the monadic nature of the head N. *Su* 'his' must be coindexed with the only postnominal position which is syntactically available; this node contains the feature [+pronominal, −anaphor], as I argued before, but can be lexically filled, or empty.[6]

I attribute the ungrammaticality of anaphors in NPs like those in (9b) (**una casa de sí mismo*) and the possibility to bind an anaphor from outside the NP in cases like (8b) (*Juan vió una foto de sí mismo*) to the monadic vs. dyadic nature of their respective head Nouns. Informally, an anaphor inside an NP whose head is monadic occupies the only available argument position, and saturates the thematic frame associated with that N. The complete thematic complex is the governing category for the anaphor, which fails to be bound in this domain in violation of Principle A; therefore, (9b) is ungrammatical. On the other hand, an anaphor in a dyadic NP such as (8b), in which one argument is syntactically absent, is contained in an incomplete thematic domain. Such a complex is not a governing category for the anaphor; rather, the anaphor is bound in a complete thematic domain which functions as its governing category, the S-node. In brief, an NP with a monadic head is a complete thematic domain or argument complex if it contains one argument, while a dyadic head requires two arguments in its syntactic structure for its maximal projection to be complete as an argument complex.

This distinction is necessary for anaphors, but it is not applicable to pronominals, as seen in the comparison of (8a) and (9a), among other cases. The binding domains for anaphors and pronominals differ, as Huang has proposed. Inside NPs, Spanish pronominals are free irrespective of the properties of the head N. If the governing category for a pronominal is defined as in (3a), the right results follow not only for NPs, but for the case of arguments within S as well. I have not considered those, but they seem unproblematic. In examples such as (8a) and (9a), among others, *él* has the expected properties; it is free in the minimal NP that contains its governor (the head N, or *de* as a prepositional). Outside of this domain, it is possible for *él* to corefer with no ill effects, as indicated by the readings in (8a,9a).

In this paper, I have concentrated on arguments within NP. In such a domain, syntactic saturation is related to the lexical frame of the head N as a θ-role assigner exclusively. Turning to arguments within the clause, syntactic saturation is determined by the thematic properties of a role assigner such as the Verb, and the properties of INFL connected with TENSE and/or AGR. In this context, to speak of *complete propositional domains* is more appropriate. In both cases, however, it is the notion of complete domain, as determined by the internal properties of the category in question (NP or S), which is relevant for binding of anaphors in Spanish. Consider (4b), (5), and (6) in this respect; the NP which contains the anaphor has a dyadic head and only one argument; this NP is an incomplete thematic domain, and is not the governing category for *sí mismos*. However, the immediately dominating S is a complete propositional domain because the lexical frame of its θ-role assigner is syntactically saturated, and INFL has TENSE and/or AGR. Then, the lower S-node in each structure is the governing category for the anaphor, but the anaphor cannot be bound in this domain. All three sentences are ruled out for the same reason. As expected, if a pronominal is substituted for a reflexive in these cases, the resulting structures are all grammatical (under coreference or disjoint reference between *los actores* and *ellos*): *Los actores$_i$ creían que unas/las fotos de ellos$_{i/j}$ estaban a la venta; Los actores$_i$ creen que es verdad que unas/las fotos de ellos$_{i/j}$ están ya en el museo; Los actores$_i$ creen que Juan dijo que unas/las fotos de ellos$_{i/j}$ están ya en el museo.*

To reflect these different situations, I adopt the definition of governing category in (29).

(29) α is a governing category for β, if α is the minimal category $\{^{NP}_S\}$ containing β, and a governor for β. If β is an anaphor, α must be a complete $\{^{\text{thematic}}_{\text{propositional}}\}$ domain.

Completeness is defined in terms of c-command. A thematic domain is complete for an anaphor if the arguments specified in the frame of the θ-role assigner which c-command the anaphor are syntactically present. Otherwise, the complex is incomplete. Arguments which are part of a lexical frame but do not c-command the anaphor do not enter into the determination of completeness. This approach implies that the bare NP interpreted as Agent/Possessor will be the "missing" argument in a dyadic construction with only one argument containing an anaphor, syntactically present. As I have pointed out before, in sentences such as (8b) or (30), the anaphor is always the Theme, not the Agent/Possessor.

(30)   María tiene [$_{NP}$ una foto   de sí misma]
         'Mary has   a picture of herself'

In view of our previous discussion of the ambiguity of (24), and the fact that a postnominal *de + NP* sequence can be treated as Agent/Possessor, an interpretation along the lines of 'Mary$_i$ has a picture that she$_i$ took' should, in principle, be available in (30), but in fact is not. Given the internal structure of the NP headed by *foto* (see (23a)), the Agent/Possessor NP c-commands the Theme NP. In determining completeness in relation to an anaphor, c-commanding arguments are checked. When the anaphor is correlated with a PP-structure and interpreted as Theme, the NP containing the anaphor in (30) is an incomplete thematic domain. Then, the anaphor is bound in the S as a complete domain.

On the other hand, the Theme NP does not c-command the Agent/Possessor in (23a). When the anaphor is treated as Agent/Possessor and correlated with the bare NP-structure, the thematic domain of *foto* is complete vis à vis the anaphor. Even though the Theme is not present, its absence is irrelevant for the determination of completeness with respect to the anaphor. Under the Agent reading, *sí misma* must be bound within the NP, but there is no potential antecedent in that domain, and the interpretation is ruled out (i.e. the sentence is ungrammatical with that reading). In this respect dyadic NPs containing anaphors treated as Agent/Possessors are similar to monadic NPs containing anaphors, and both are excluded.

Under the same approach, an NP such as *la petición de Juan$_i$ a sí mismo$_i$* 'John's request to himself' is a complete thematic domain for the anaphor, even though the Theme is not expressed. Thus, the salient effects of the "subject" are obtained through the structure of the arguments, even though the NP has no subject position.

Since completeness is not relevant for pronominals, in a sentence such as *María$_i$ tiene una foto de ella$_{i/j}$* 'Mary$_i$ has a picture of hers$_{i/j}$' *ella* 'she' can be interpreted as Agent/Possessor or Theme.

To conclude, I have not adopted the traditional perspective that opacity effects in NP are due to the subject. Instead, I have argued that NPs are subjectless, and have approached the Binding Theory for arguments in NP from the perspective of thematic domains and their complete or incomplete character, in connection with the syntactic structure of those arguments.

NOTES

1. The above discussion gives a partial indication of the problems a theory based on SUBJECTs faces. See Bouchard 1982, Harbert 1982, 1983 for other difficulties.

A theory partially based on *subjects* is presented in Manzini 1983b. Under Manzini's approach, which I do not attempt to summarize, (4) and (5) are excluded from the theory of binding; in her system, an anaphor must be locally bound in the sense that it can never have an antecedent outside the minimal NP or S that contains it, or the immediately superior category. Thus the locality effects we observe in Spanish could be captured correctly under this approach. On the other hand, the distinction between (8) and (9) requires an ad hoc treatment, as far as I can see. For (8b) a PRO controlled by *Juan* would have to be postulated in the determiner position; alternatively the NP could lack a subject. Example (9b) would contain an obligatory PRO with arbitrary reference in the determiner position; arbitrary PRO would not be a possible antecedent for *sí mismo*. As I argue later on, there is no evidence for subjects in NPs; more importantly, there is no evidence that *casa* 'house' takes two arguments, as this treatment would require.

2. But see Williams (1982), who argues that the determiner position is not the subject of the NP in English, and who rejects the movement analysis.

3. Doubling, as in (15), is common in Old Spanish. This may require a different analysis for possessive doubling in the two periods.

4. The final solution to this question depends on factors I cannot examine here, such as the general theory of ECs which is adopted. In this respect, possessive doubling constructions raise many of the questions hotly debated in the bibliography on clitic doubling, and I will not attempt to answer them. Consider (i), a frequent structure in the contemporary Spanish press (*El País* 19-12-83, p. 33)

(i)   Comienza su primera tarea investigadora al lado del profesor B.C., del que$_i$ fue su$_i$ principal colaborador
'He-begins his first research next to professor B.C., of whom$_i$ he-was his$_i$ main collaborator'

Under my approach, the relevant structure in (i) is of the form *del que$_i$...su$_i$...e$_i$*. The parallelism with the hotly debated *A quién$_i$ lo$_i$ vieron e$_i$?* 'Whom did they see?' should be apparent (see Aoun 1982, Borer 1981, Hurtado 1982a,b, Jaeggli 1982, among others). The issues are similar in the two cases: *a*) What is the nature of the EC? *b*) How does it relate to the two lexical items it is coindexed with? *c*) Is the *wh*-phrase base-generated in situ, or does it undergo *Move α*?

5. Rappaport (1983) has proposed that in English, the assignment of θ-roles by N is always

mediated by "true" prepositions. Many of the differences between Spanish and English NPs may be due to this distinction.

6. The same type of ambiguity is seen in clitic doubling. A verb such as *entregar* 'deliver, surrender' is associated with two (internal) arguments. Clitics can be coindexed with empty or lexical categories with the appropriate features ("doubling"). Consider the examples in (i). This clitic *lo* 'him' is coindexed with the lexical phrase *él* in a doubling construction in (ia), or with an empty category in (ib-c). In the last case, the pronominal and the anaphor are the goal(s), and subject to Principle B and Principle A of the Binding Theory, respectively. Finally, in (id), the two argument positions are lexically filled, if doubling is analyzed as in Jaeggli (1982).

(i)   a.   Juan lo$_i$ entregó [$_{NP}$ a él]$_i$ (a María)
           John   delivered   him   (to Mary)

      b.   Juan lo$_i$ entregó [$_{NP}$ e]$_i$ a él$_j$ (*a María)
           John   delivered   him$_i$ to him$_j$ (*to Mary)

      c.   Juan lo$_i$ entregó [$_{NP}$ e]$_i$ a sí mismo$_i$ (*a María)
           John   delivered   him$_i$ to himself$_i$ (*to Mary)

      d.   Juan lo$_i$ entregó [$_{NP}$ a él]$_i$ a sí mismo$_i$
           gloss as in (ic)

Along parallel lines, *Juan se entregó a sí mismo* can be interpreted as a case of doubling–'John surrendered (to no one in particular)'–or as a two (internal) argument structure: 'John surrendered to himself'.

A verb such as *visitar* 'to visit' is similar to *casa* in that it contains only one (internal) argument. Thus *Juan lo$_i$ visitó a él$_i$* is a doubling construction exclusively: 'John visited him'.

On the referential properties of embedded finite clause subjects*

Margarita Suñer, *Cornell University*

Although generative grammar has a long tradition of trying to extricate and explain the referential properties of the subjects of infinitival clauses (see Jackendoff 1972, Manzini 1983a, to name just two), the same cannot be said about the referential properties of the subjects of embedded finite clauses. This may be because the topic was not considered interesting enough. However, the situation has been changing of late. In particular, the strict complementarity between the pronominal anaphor and a pronoun which characterizes the complement subject position of volition verbs in the Romance languages has given rise to speculations about the proper way to capture the facts illustrated in (1) with Spanish.

(1)   a. Paco$_i$ quiere [PRO$_i$ estudiar latín]
          'Paco wants   to study Latin'
      b. Paco$_i$ quiere [que pro$_j$ estudie latín]
          'Paco wants   that 3s   study-SUBJ Latin'

In (1a) the embedded PRO subject of the infinitive clause is controlled by the matrix subject, and as a consequence both subjects can only be interpreted as having the same referent. On the other hand, the pronominal subject of the subjunctive clause in (1b) must be obligatorily disjoint in reference from the matrix subject.

In trying to solve this puzzle, Meireles and Raposo (1984), working with Portuguese data, suggest a modification of the Binding Theory, while Bouchard (1982) resorts to a version of the Avoid Pronoun Principle.

The purpose of this paper is to show first that the complementarity in (1) can neither be taken as an argument for reformulating the Binding Theory, nor explained away as an instance of the Avoid Pronoun strategy; and second, that lexical/semantic properties of some verbs are responsible for the

* My appreciation goes to José Padilla-Rivera for the many hours of productive discussion on this and related topics. Therefore, it should be understood that some portions of the present paper draw heavily from the section on obviation in Suñer and Padilla-Rivera (1984). I have also profited from a conversation with J.C. Milner. As usual, all errors remain my responsibility.

obligatory disjoint reference interpretation of some subjunctive clause subjects with respect to the matrix subject. In addition, a major portion of this study is devoted to explaining the networks of coreference established by verbs of influence.

1. BINDING THEORY

The principles of the Binding Theory (Chomsky 1981, 188) are stated in (2), and the other definitions pertinent to the discussion, from Chomsky (1982), are given in (3).

(2)   A. An anaphor is bound in its governing category.
       B. A pronominal is free in its governing category.
       C. An R-expression is free.

(3)   a. Governing category: β is a governing category for α, iff β is the minimal category containing α, a governor of α, and a SUBJECT accessible to α.
       b. SUBJECT: [+AGR], or [NP, S]
       c. Accessible: α is accessible to β iff β is in the c-command domain of α and assignment of the index of α would not violate *$[_\gamma \ldots \delta \ldots]$ (where γ and δ bear the same index).
       d. α binds β iff
          (i) α and β are coindexed, and
          (ii) α c-commands β.

1.1. *Meireles and Raposo (1984)*

These linguists interpret coreference facts like those illustrated in (1b) as an exception to Principle B of the Binding Theory (BT) in (2), which states that a pronominal must be free (i.e. not coindexed) in its governing category (GC). The GC for the embedded *pro* is the subordinate S, since it contains α ($= pro$) and a governor of α ($=$ AGR), and a SUBJECT accessible to α. From this, it has been assumed–mistakenly, I think–that BT predicts that *pro* in (1b) should be able to corefer freely *outside* of its governing category. Note that strictly speaking BT remains silent about what could happen outside the pronoun's governing category.
    Taking into account examples like those in (4), where the reference of the subject of the subordinate indicative clause (4a) as well as the subjects embedded under factive predicates (4b) is free, M & R offer the hypothesis that in Portuguese the crucial element in determining opacity for the subject position is a semantic operator-like element TENSE, and not AGR.[1]

(4) a. Bri$_i$ dijo que *pro*$_{i/j}$ iba (indic.) al cine
      'Bri said that *pro* was-going to-the movies'
   b. Drei$_i$ sentía que *pro*$_{i/j}$ no pudiera (sub.) ir al cine
      'Drei$_i$ was-sorry that *pro* could not go to-the movies'

Since their claim is that TENSE is selected for by the main verb, *decir* 'to say' and *sentir* 'to be sorry' would select for it while *querer*-type verbs would not. In the latter case, the time-frame features would depend on the time reference of the main clause. In this way, they arrive at the alleged generalization in (5), which is offered as a possible reformulation of BT. Note that under this proposal, the GC for *pro* in (1b) would not be the main clause.

(5) A pronoun in clausal subject position is free within the domain of a TENSE operator.

Unfortunately, some major problems arise when trying to establish the correlation [−TENSE] → [+DR] for Spanish. In the first place, as Suñer and Padilla (1984) have shown, although volition predicates observe rather strict requirements concerning sequences of tenses, it is still possible to find examples of unlike sequences of tenses.

(6) a. Yo he querido (−pa) que mantuviese (+pa) siempre viva la memoria de lo que pasó   (Farley 1965, 550)
      'I have wanted that 3s kept always alive the memory of what happened'
   b. **Pregunto por qué ha querido (−pa)** usted que se los cambiara (+pa)   (Farley 1970, 472)
      'I wonder why you have wanted that I exchange them for you'
   c. ...las voces de mis "guaguas" que deseaban (+pa) que mande (−pa) a comprar pan, llenaron mi cabeza   (Kany 1969, 182)
      '...the voices of my children who wished that I send for bread, filled my head'

The examples in (6) cast doubt on the tenselessness of subjunctive clauses.
   Second, (5) runs into problems with the other major semantic verb class which requires subject-to-subject obviation. Verbs of influence, such as *animar* 'to encourage', *exhortar* 'to exhort', *obligar* 'to oblige', *invitar* 'to invite', *pedir* 'to ask for', *ordenar* 'to order', obligatorily require the subjunctive mood whenever their embedded clause is finite, but they cannot be said to select for tenseless subjunctive (7) (see Suñer and Padilla (1984) for details).[2]

(7)   a. ...exhortó (+pa) a los visitantes a que aquilaten (–pa) los produc-
        tos   (Obaid 1967, 114)
        '...3s exhorted the visitors that they evaluate the products'
        b. La invitamos (+pa) a que defienda (–pa) su hipótesis
        'We invited her that she defend her hypothesis'
        c. El presidente ordenó (+pa) también al Departamento de la Defen-
        sa que incremente (–pa) en todo el país el adiestramiento...
                                                               (Obaid 1967, 113)
        'the president ordered also the Defense Department that it in-
        crease in the whole country the training...'

In essence, (5) fails for at least two reasons: first, because even within volition
predicates one can find unlike sequences of tenses, and second, because
influence verbs are [+TENSE] but [+DR]. Hence (5) cannot explain the
complementarity in (1) in a straightforward way. This conclusion seems to
indicate that the answer is not to be found by reformulating BT.

2. THE AVOID PRONOUN STRATEGY

Bouchard (1982) also remarks on the obligatory disjoint reference facts of the
type found in (1) and their correlation with the subjunctive in French. After
presenting the Elsewhere Principle (8), he explains the examples with French
vouloir 'to want' (9) in the following manner.

(8)   Don't put a pronoun in a position where an anaphor is possible, i.e. in
        a position where the pronoun will be interpreted as corefential with
        an NP that can bind it.

(9)   a. *Je veux que j'aille voir ce film
        b. Je veux [PRO aller voir ce film]

"Like-pronouns" are not possible in a subjunctive clause (9a) if the corresponding infinitival clause has a controlled PRO (9b).[3] Although the behavior
of Spanish volition Vs could be explained in this manner, Bouchard's reasoning does not generalize to the Spanish Vs of influence examined in (7). In
these, the subjunctive clause alternates with an infinitival one. Compare the
(a) and (b) versions of (10).

(10)   José$_i$ lo$_j$ animó/exhortó/persuadió a...
        'Jose encouraged/exhorted/persuaded him...'
        a. ... [PRO$_j$ apagar la TV]
                 'to-turn-off the TV'

    b. ... [que pro$_j$ apagara la TV]
          that 3s turn-off the TV

Moreover, there are other semantic V classes for which (8) fails: denial (11), factive (12), doubt (13), and lack of knowledge (14) are among them.

(11)   a. Pedro negó [PRO saber la verdad]
        b.   [que pro$_{i/j}$ supiera la verdad]
        'Pedro denied knowing the truth/that 3s knew the truth'

(12)   a. [yo]$_i$ sentí mucho [PRO$_i$ no haberlo visto cuando...]
        b.   [que pro$_{i/j}$ no lo haya visto...]
                                    (Obaid 1967, 117)
        'I deeply regretted not having seen him when.../ that 1s/3s have not seen him when...'

(13)   a. Dudo$_i$ [PRO$_i$ haberlos pagado]
        b.   [que pro$_{i/j}$ lo hubiera pagado]
        'I doubt having paid them/ that 1s/3s had paid them'

(14)   a. X$_i$ ignoraba [PRO$_i$ haber firmado ese papel]
        b.   [que pro$_{i/j}$ hubiera firmado ese papel]
        (¡En qué estaría pensando!)
        'X was not aware of having signed that paper/ that 3s had signed that paper. (What could he have been thinking about!)

Thus, for Spanish the hypothesis fails both ways: (*a*) because despite having controlled PRO in the infinitival clause, the corresponding subjunctive one may still have a pronominal subject with the same referent as a matrix argument ((11)-(14)), and (*b*) because in (10) the "like-pronouns" reading between the direct object and the lower subject is in fact the only one available.

3. THE EXPLANATION

Since, as was demonstrated above, neither a proposal which appeals to a modified version of Binding Theory nor one which resorts to the Avoid Pronoun strategy proves to be satisfactory, the explanation must necessarily lie elsewhere.

    What I have to offer is based on a semantic feature which forms part of the lexical make-up of the predicates we have been examining, i.e., of volition and influence Vs. The feature WILL [W] is the one responsible for the obviation requirement (see Suñer and Padilla 1984 for detailed discussion). But first let me make the following clarifications.

First, the [± coreferent] readings imposed by volition Vs on the one hand, and by influence Vs on the other, are not related to principle B of BT. As noted above, in every instance the embedded pronominal subject is free in its governing category (the lower S). Thus no violation of this principle ensues. The Binding Theory is seen as a structural/configurational theory (so that the c-command condition is met) of A-binding which applies at S-structure (Chomsky 1981). This theory is blind to semantic factors.

Second, the facts under examination cannot be explained by Control Theory (CT) either. Note that since the embedded S has a filled COMP, a barrier to government from the outside is present, i.e., S′.[4] Hence, neither the matrix subject nor the matrix direct object can bind–in the strict sense of CT–the embedded subject.[5]

Third, I assume the existence of a theory of (free) indexing along the lines of Chomsky (1981), where each NP receives an index. The reading of *pro* as proximate or obviative in (1b), (7), and (10) through (14) should be achieved by checking indices against the semantic content of the relevant predicate. An example to help visualize how the correct interpretation is arrived at is in order. Consider the sentences in (15) where free indexing has operated.

(15)   a. pro_i quiere [que pro_k compre...
                3s   wants   that   3s   buy...
        b. pro_i (le_d) pidió   que pro_k compre...
                3s to 3s   asked   that 3s   buy...

At S-structure BT checks that the pronouns are not coindexed by an antecedent within their GC. Since all the relevant elements in (15) have different referential indices, BT is satisfied. It is at the level of LF that the checking of indices required by the semantics of the main verb must apply for the sentence to receive its grammatical reading. Since volition and influence Vs carry the feature [W], disjoint reference must obtain in (15) so that i ≠ k. This process–induced by the lexical feature–ensures that the embedded subject has a referent distinct from that of the matrix. The reason for this is obviously semantic; notice that the relationship these predicates establish is that one entity (the matrix subject) influences another entity (the embedded subject) to act in the manner specified by the lower verb. Thus, an instigator-instigated relationship can be isolated in all cases. This fact confirms that the disjoint reference reading imposed by these predicates in examples like those in (15) is the result of their lexical make-up.[6] Note that in all the examples discussed thus far, the matrix subject is the instigating Agent. Let us see what happens whenever the matrix subject does not carry the required feature. As seen in (16), where passivization has applied, the matrix subject (a Theme) is co-referent with the embedded *pro*.[7]

(16)   pro$_i$ fue invitado/exhortado a [que pro$_i$ presentara sus ideas con más claridad]
'3s was invited/encouraged that 3s presented his ideas more clearly'

The examples in (16) confirm that the semantic role/features of the main subject are crucial to possible coreference relations. In essence, the feature [W] triggers non-coreferentially of subjects provided the upper subject carries the necessary features (i.e., instigating Agent).

This conclusion is supported by the behavior of adjunct phrases of purpose introduced by *para que* 'so that' and *sin que* 'without'. These Spanish conjunctions also carry the feature [W] (see Suñer and Padilla 1984). However, subject-subject obviation obtains only when the matrix subject has the relevant features, that is, in (17) but not in (18).

(17)   a. Drei$_i$ notificó a José$_j$ para que pro$_j$ se presentara
           'Drei notified Jose so that 3s would come'
        b. María engañó a Juan$_j$ sin que pro$_{j/k}$ se diera(n) cuenta
           'Maria cheated on Juan without 3s(pl) noticing'

(18)   a. José$_j$ fue notificado para que pro$_j$ se presentara
           'Jose was notified so that 3s would come'
        b. Juan$_j$ fue engañado sin que pro$_{j/k}$ se diera(n) cuenta
           'Juan was cheated without 3s(pl) noticing'

The same lack of DR occurs in (19), where the upper subject is a coerced or influenced Agent (Padilla-Rivera 1985).

(19)   pro$_i$ presta atención para que pro$_i$ lo entiendas!
        'pay attention so that you understand it!'

Furthermore, it is possible to demonstrate that what the lexical feature [W] triggers is not exactly subject-subject obviation but rather that it is non-strict coreferentiality. Note that in the examples in (20), one of the conjuncts which forms part of the lower subject may be interpreted as coreferent with the upper one despite [W].

(20)   a. Lola$_i$ quería que José y ella$_{i/j}$ fueran al cine juntos
           'Lola wanted that Jose and she go to movies together'
        b. Ana$_i$ (me) prometió que ella$_{i/j}$ y su$_{i/j}$ mamá pasarían a buscarnos en 15 minutos
           'Ana promised (me) that she and her mother would come for us in 15 minutes'
        c. Paco$_j$ le^i pidió a María$_i^i$ que [ellos dos]$_{i+j/2}$ viajaran juntos al congreso de lingüística

'Paco asked Mary that the two of them travel together to the
linguistics conference'

d. Lía$_j$ animó Julián$_i$ a que pro$_{i+j/2}$ escribieran algo juntos
'Lia encouraged Julian that they write something together'

e. [Que Juan y ella$_{i/j}$ decidan la fecha de casamiento], Drea$_{i/2}$ lo
desea fervientemente
[That John and she set their wedding date], Drea wants it fervently

Thus, given the appropriate environment, the correct generalization of the
requisite imposed by [W] emerges: it mandates non-strict coreferentiality
between subjects, i.e., although the subjects cannot be identical in reference,
they may be "partially" coreferent. This state of affairs seems to have gone
unnoticed because in the majority of instances [+DR] and non-coreferentiality produce the same outcome. The sentences in (20) are crucial to the
discussion, because although BT can clearly refer to [±DR] relationships, it
appears unable to express non-strict coreferentiality directly.

In brief, the import of the above facts is that it is not possible to encompass
the data dealt with by reformulating Principle B of BT. Any attempt at doing
this would not only have to refer to the lexical feature [W] but also to the
θ-role features carried by the matrix subject, and check on the composition of
the lower subject. I see no reason to incorporate all of these lexical semantic
traits into BT.

3.1. *Influence verbs*

Although volition and influence Vs pattern together with respect to the
non-strict coreferentiality facts, there are some differences between these two
classes because of their distinct argument structure: while volition Vs are
two-argument predicates, influence Vs have three. As a consequence, influence Vs exhibit some interesting networks of coreference. To explore these
networks is the aim of this section.

In the first place it becomes necessary to separate influence Vs into two
subclasses: the *le*-type and the *lo*-type. Some Vs which belong to the first
subgroup are *pedir* 'to request', *ordenar* 'to order', *decir* 'to tell', and *rogar* 'to
beg'. *Animar* 'to encourage', *invitar* 'to invite', *exhortar* 'to exhort', *obligar* 'to
oblige', and *forzar* 'to force' belong to the second subset.[8] Both subclasses
subcategorize for an NP and a clause. Whereas in the *lo*-type the NP functions
as direct object (DO), in the *le*-type it works as an indirect object (IO). This
difference gives rise to distinct patterns of coreference.

Consider the examples in (21) with *le*-type Vs.

(21) a. Ella$_j$ le^i pidió $\left\{\begin{matrix}\text{a la secretaria}^i_i \\ \text{pro}^i_i\end{matrix}\right\}$ que pro$_{i/k}$ no entre

'She requested $\left\{\begin{matrix}\text{the secretary} \\ \text{her}\end{matrix}\right\}$ that 3s not enter'

   b. (Yo$_j$) le^i sugerí al general^i_i que pro$_{i/k}$ dejara(n) de disparar
       'I suggested to the general that 3s(pl) stop shooting'

In these examples, non-coreferentiality obtains due to [W], thus j = i ≠ k. The IO argument–*le...pro* or *le...*NP–must be DR with respect to its subject because of Principle B if a pronominal, or because of Principle C if it is an R-expression. However, the IO and the embedded *pro* can be [+DR]; in other words, one can either tell X to carry out the action of the lower predicate, or alternatively, this X can in turn influence another entity to execute the action. In short, although the lower *pro* is non-coreferential concerning the matrix subject (cf. 20b-c), it is free regarding the matrix IO.

In contrast, consider the sentences in (22) with *lo*-type Vs.

(22) a. El$_j$ los^i obligó pro^i_i a que pro$_k$ llamaran...
          'He obliged them that 3pl call...'
   b. Bri$_j$ lo^i persuadió pro^i_i a que pro$_k$ ayudara a X
          'Bri persuaded him that 3s help X'

The main DO and the subject are DR (j ≠ i) because of Principle B. The lower subject is free in its GC, the embedded S. Thus, no violation of BT ensues. However, at a late level of LF several checks must be performed for the sentence to receive its correct interpretation. First, the feature [W] causes non-coreferentiality of subjects (in (22): j ≠ k). Second, the matrix DO and the lower *pro* must necessarily be read as coreferent; in other words, i = k obligatorily.

This last point distinguishes the two subgroups of influence Vs: while in the *le*-type the embedded subject is [±DR] regarding the matrix IO, in the *lo*-type the lower subject can only be coreferential with respect to the matrix DO. Once again, I hypothesize that this difference between the two subtypes has nothing to do with BT operating at S-structure; rather this behavior reflects the semantics of the V types which in turn results in distinct networks of coreference. Allow me to clarify this point. The explanation lies at least in part in the θ-roles displayed by the pertinent argument. The DO role seems to be invariably that of patient/theme, i.e., this role is not determined by the specific meaning of the predicate. As a rule, the theme is acted upon directly by the entity representing the Agent. Moreover, in the *lo*-type of influence Vs, the DO is [+animate] and as such capable of performing an action/process. Thus, the matrix subject acts upon/causes the DO to do/react in the particu-

lar way specified by the embedded clause. Jackendoff (1972) already expressed this in a similar way when talking about English:

> A verb can mark an NP in its clause as Agent over the complement
> clause, and restrictions on coreference independent of the network of
> coreference result.

Of course, the Spanish data are slightly more complicated than the English,
because with these Vs there exists the choice between an infinitival and a
subjunctive (i.e. tensed) clause (cf. examples in (10)). Only in the former
instance can we have control proper as established by Control Theory. The
curious fact is that in Spanish, the networks of coreference remain constant
regardless of the [±finite] nature of the subordinate clause.

And how can one explain the coreferent pattern of the *le*-type of influence
Vs? Once again, one has to invoke semantic reasons. Although the IO cannot
be acted upon by the matrix subject *directly*, it still can be influenced so that
its referent either carries the action or can in turn influence somebody else to
act, thus [±DR] with respect to the lower subject. Note that IOs are able to
embody different roles, e.g. goal, source, benefactor, experiencer; these roles
tend to vary according to the meaning of the predicate. The above two
reasons seem to be why in establishing networks of coreference the IO is
interpreted more freely than the DO.

The line of thought outlined above confirms that coreference is a semantic
property and that the selection of a "controller" (used in an informal extended sense to cover *que*-clauses) is based on θ-roles (Jackendoff 1972, Manzini
1983a, Nishigauchi 1984).

There are other differences between the two subgroups of Vs of influence.
First, while the *le*-type may appear in contexts such as (23), which shows that
the IO is optional, the *lo*-type cannot leave the DO argument aside since this
leads to ungrammaticality (24). This seems to provide more weight to the
assertion that the DO, but not the IO, obligatorily "controls" the embedded
subject.[9]

(23)   (Ella) pidió/sugirió/ordenó que *pro* viniera más tarde
        'She requested/suggested/ordered that 3s come later'

(24)   *(Ella) obligó/animó/invitó a que *pro* viniera más tarde
        'She obliged/encouraged/invited that 3s come later'

Second, *le*-Vs may take a name as the embedded subject (25). This is not the
case for the *lo*-type of influence Vs, for which only *pro* seems to be an
acceptable subject (26a). Not even subject postponing makes a difference in
the grammaticality judgments (26b).

(25)   El general le ordenó al sargento que *las tropas* acampen por tres
        semanas
        'The general ordered the sargent that the troops camp out for three
        weeks'

(26)   a. Lo animé a que **Paco/*mi cliente/*él/pro* examinara los docu-
           mentos
           'I encouraged him that Paco/my client/he/3s examine the docu-
           ments'
        b. Lo animé a que examinara los documentos **Paco/*mi cliente/*él/
           pro*

As a matter of fact, it seems that the only way in which a lexically expressed
subject strictly coreferential with the DO may appear is when it carries
contrastive stress or focus. One unequivocal way of focalizing is by adding
the intensifier *mismo* 'self' to a pronoun (RAE 1974, Ramsey 1956). In this
instance, *él mismo* 'he himself' (27) can appear either preverbally or postverbally.

(27)   Lo animé a que ⎰*él mismo* examinara los documentos⎱
                      ⎱examinara los documentos *él mismo*⎰
        'I encouraged him that he himself examine the documents'

To a large extent the data in (25)-(27) fall out directly from the aforementioned differences which characterize the two subgroups under discussion.
Example (25) is grammatical because the embedded subject is free with
respect to the matrix IO (cf. (21)); therefore, a subject which is distinct in
reference from the IO may be lexically expressed. On the other hand, a name
cannot appear as the lower subject in (26) because this name would not be
free–recall that the matrix DO and this subject must have the same referent
(cf. (22))–hence, a clear violation of Principle C (R-expressions must be free)
rejects the examples. As pointed out by Chomsky (1981, 3.2.3), names tend to
be interpreted as disjoint in reference even apart from the c-command
condition. The fact that a non-contrastive lexical pronoun is also barred from
the embedded subject position of *lo*-Vs might appear puzzling at first sight
because this element complies with Principle B. However, when one takes
into account that the version with *él* sounds considerably better than the ones
with names, it might indicate that the sentence is merely unacceptable and not
ungrammatical. In other words, since the sentence sounds awkward, the
assumption is that it is discarded at the level of the discourse because of its
highly redundant nature. This line of reasoning is confirmed by an example
like (28), where a lexical pronoun sounds natural under the interpretation

that *ellos* represents *Julián* plus *Lía* or a third party; in other words, a lexical pronoun is acceptable when sanctioned by split antecedents.

(28)   Lía$_j$ animó a Julián$_i$ a que ellos $_{i+j/2}$ escribieran algo juntos
        'Lia encouraged Julian that they write something together'

In view of the above, why is (27) perfectly grammatical? Two plausible explanations come to mind. One possibility arises if *él mismo* were in basic subject position. In this case all that would be evident in (27) before LF is a pronominal subject free in its GC, thus no BT violation would ensue. At LF, the sentence would be interpreted as in (29) by the rule of Focus.

(29)   for x = he, I encouraged him that x call

The variable must be free by Principle C, but since BT applies at S-structure, (29) escapes violating this principle even though *him* and the variable must be read as having the same referent for the S to be interpreted correctly. Nevertheless, this line of reasoning is at odds with the assertion that *lo*-Vs bar embedded lexical subjects when strictly coreferential with the DO.

The second alternative would be to claim that *él mismo* is in a non-θ-position, linked to the *pro* in basic subject position with which it agrees in reference. In this latter instance, *él mismo* would be an anaphor and not a pronominal, since it would not have independent reference. Evidence of this is found when considering that *él mismo* may also appear in the infinitival clause counterpart of (27), i.e., (30).

(30)   Lo animé a examinar los documentos *él mismo*
        'I encouraged him to examine he himself the documents'

Piera (1982) studies structures similar to (30) and conludes that the *italicized* elements are anaphors which receive nominative Case by (31). They appear in the environment of control verbs.

(31)   An anaphor in a θ-position is nominative when coindexed with a c-commanding subject.

Presumably, the rule of Focus (29) could still operate on (27) even if *él mismo* is in non-θ-position because of the anaphor being coindexed with the subject *pro*. Since this second alternative is consistent with the observation that *lo*-Vs disallow subordinate lexical subjects strictly coreferential with their DO, it is to be preferred. *El mismo* escapes this restriction because it is not in argument position.

One further point deserves consideration before closing the discussion on influence Vs. Note that although the feature [W], proper to volition and influence Vs, is intimately related to the subjunctive mood, the same cannot be maintained for the network of coreference established by the *lo*-type of influence Vs. This pattern is replicated in all details by perception Vs and impersonal *haber*–witness (32) where the relevant coreference network is indicated.[10]

(32)   a. Ella los[i] vio pro[i] que pro[i] llegaban...
          'She saw them that they were arriving...'
       b. Los[i] hay pro[i] que pro[i] nunca trabajan
          them there-exist that 3pl never work
          'There exist those who never work'

Since the Vs in (32) take a clause in the indicative mood, it can safely be assumed that this particular type of coreferent pattern is independent of subjunctive-selecting predicates.

4. CONCLUSION

The referential properties of the subjects of finite embedded clauses have been explored, and although the body of data comes from Spanish, the claims and generalizations made in this study should be valid for other Romance languages, save possibly for language-specific constraints.

The main findings can be summarized as follows: (*a*) Volition and influence Vs carry the feature [WILL] as part of their lexical meaning; this feature is responsible for the non-strict coreferentiality of subjects. In the process of demonstrating the above, it was argued that neither a reformulation of BT which takes advantage of an alleged anaphoricity of tenses, nor the Avoid Pronoun strategy could account for the data. (*b*) While examining the networks of coreference of influence Vs, it was concluded that their subcategorization frame together with the θ-roles displayed by their arguments explained the two distinct patterns which emerged. The principal claim which unifies (*a*) and (*b*) is that lexical/semantic factors play the crucial role in setting the referential properties of embedded subjects.

NOTES

1. Luján (1980), Anderson (1982), and Picallo (1984a) claim that subjunctive clauses are tenseless in Spanish, Icelandic, and Catalan, respectively. See Suñer (1980) and Suñer and Padilla (1984) for arguments to the contrary.
2. Furthermore, even if it were possible to say that influence Vs are [–TENSE], (5) could not account for the facts. Note that (5) claims that the GC for *pro* is the main clause. However, in (i)

the matrix direct object must be coreferent with the embedded *pro*, a possibility barred by (5), which predicts that each of the pronouns must have a distinct reference because they are in the same GC.

(i)   Ella lo^i obligó a él$_i$ a que pro$_i$ se levantara
          'She obliged him that he get up'

3. Bouchard argues for the non-existence of an empty category with the feature [+pronominal +anaphoric]. Instead, he states that PRO is an anaphor if controlled, a pronoun if free. In addition he claims that the distribution of PRO is due to Case theory; Manzini (1983a) agrees with this last point.

4. Belletti and Rizzi (1981) allow for heads of maximal projections to be accessible to an external governor. However, their proposal has no bearing on the discussion because the embedded subject position is not the head of S (or S').

5. In Suñer (1984) I showed that little *pro* could be controlled. The article is misleading in part due to the terminology employed. Little *pro* is "controlled" but this is not accomplished through Control theory but through index checking at LF. Note that in that article I also maintained that BT was not violated because *pro* was free in its GC.

6. There is experimental support for this conclusion. Padilla-Rivera (1985) reports the results of a language acquisition study conducted in Puerto Rico with children ages 3 to 9. He found that children are sensitive to the lexical content of main verbs and that they use this information in establishing binding relations. Thus, the factor *volition* was significant in determining the amount of DR (but restrictions on sequence of tenses did not have an effect on binding relations).

7. Passivization is a restricted process in Spanish, thus it comes as no surprise that not all speakers find (16) equally acceptable. Furthermore, since Spanish only passivizes DOs, the claim can be tested only with a subset of influence Vs.

8. To my knowledge, Bordelois (1974) was the first to discuss these Spanish Vs within generative grammar.

9. It seems that the [±finite] status of the embedded clause makes a difference with respect to the obligatoriness of the DO argument. Thus, although (24)–without the DO–is ungrammatical, some of the infinitival sentences in (i) are judged to be grammatical.

(i)   a.   El jefe obligó a ayudar a los pobres
                'The boss obliged to help the poor'
          b.   La policía exhortó a desalojar los edificios
                'The policemen exhorted to vacate the buildings'
          c.   ?*El presidente persuadió a contribuir dinero para el proyecto
                'The president persuaded to contribute money for the project'
          d.   *Paco animó a abandonar el proyecto
                'Paco encouraged to abandon the project'

This does not necessarily mean that the grammatical examples in (i) lack a DO argument. It could be hypothesized that some *lo*-type influence Vs allow for a non-lexical DO with arb interpretation which in turn controls the embedded PRO$_{arb}$ subject. The control relationship might be condition enough to properly identify the DO *pro* under some circumstances to be determined.

10. For discussion of these Vs, see Suñer (1982a) and (1984).

References

Akmajian, A. 1977. "The Complement Structure of Perception Verbs in an Autonomous Syntax Framework". In Culicover et al. (1977).

Anderson, S. 1982. "Types of Dependency in Anaphora: Icelandic (and Other) Reflexives". To appear in *Journal of Linguistic Research*.

Aoun, J. 1981. *The Formal Nature of Anaphoric Relations*. Doctoral dissertation, MIT, Cambridge, Mass.

Aoun, J., and D. Sportiche. 1983. "On the Formal Theory of Government". *The Linguistic Review* 2, 211–36.

Argente, J. 1976. "Un Exercici d'Anàlisi Transformacional Entorn del Pronom EN". In V. Sánchez de Zavala, ed., *Estudios de Gramática Generativa*. Barcelona: Labor.

Badia, A.M. 1962. *Gramática catalana*. Madrid: Gredos.

Baker, M., and K. Johnson. 1985. "On the Passive". Ms., MIT.

Baltin, M. 1982. "A Landing Site Theory of Movement Rules". *Linguistic Inquiry* 13, 1–38.

Bar-Hillel, Y. 1954. "Indexical Expressions". *Mind* 63, 359–79. Reprinted in Bar-Hillel (1970).

Bar-Hillel, Y. 1970. *Aspects of Language*. Jerusalem: The Magnes Press / The Hebrew University.

Bastos, L.O. 1960. *Do pronome se somo sujeito*. Rio de Janeiro: Ozon.

Belletti, A. 1980. "'Morphological' Passive and Pro-drop: A note on the Impersonal Construction in Italian". Ms., MIT and Scuola Normale Superiore.

Belletti, A. 1982. "'Morphological' Passive and Pro-drop: The Impersonal Construction in Italian". *Journal of Linguistic Research* 2, 1–34.

Belletti, A., and L. Rizzi. 1981. "The Syntax of 'Ne': Some Theoretical Implications". *The Linguistic Review* 1, 117–54.

Bello, A. 1847. *Gramática de la lengua castellana*. With notes by R. Cuervo, prologue and notes by N. Alcalá-Zamora y Torres, 8th ed. Buenos Aires: Editorial Sopena Argentina, 1970.

Bordelois, I. 1974. *The Grammar of Spanish Causative Complements*. Doctoral dissertation, MIT, Cambridge, Mass.

Bordelois, I. 1982. "Transparency". *Linguistic Analysis* 9, 161–203.

Bordelois, I. 1983. "Dependencies Under the Scope of Infinitival Complements in Spanish". To appear in Hurtado (forthcoming).

Borer, H. 1981. *Parametric Variation in Clitic Constructions*. Doctoral dissertation, MIT, Cambridge, Mass.

Borer, H. 1984. *Parametric Syntax: Case Studies in Semitic and Romance Languages*. Dordrecht: Foris.

Borer, H. 1984a. "I-subjects". Ms., University of California, Irvine.

Bouchard, D., 1984. *On the Content of Empty Categories*. Dordrecht: Foris. (Sometimes cited as Bouchard (1982), Doctoral dissertation, MIT.)

Brandi, L., and P. Cordin. 1983. "Dialette e italiano: un confronto sul parametro del soggetto nullo". *Rivista di Grammatica Generativa* 6, 33–87 [dated 1981].

Brody, M. 1984. "On Contextual Definitions and the Role of Theta Chains". *Linguistic Inquiry* 15, 355–80.

Brown, C.B. 1931. "The Disappearance of the Indefinite *hombre* from Spanish". *Language* 7, 265–77.

Brucart, J.M. 1984. *La elipsis: aspectos de la elisión sintáctica en español*. Doctoral dissertation, Universidad Autónoma de Barcelona.

Bull, W. 1968. *Time, Tense, and the Verb*. Berkeley: Univ. of California Press.

Burge, T. 1973. "Reference and Proper Names". *The Journal of Philosophy* 70, 425–39.

Burzio, L. 1981. *Intransitive Verbs and Italian Auxiliaries*. Doctoral dissertation, MIT, Cambridge, Mass. (To be published by Reidel).

Chomsky, N. 1957. *Syntactic Structures*. The Hague: Mouton.

Chomsky, N. 1965. *Aspects of the Theory of Syntax*. Cambridge, Mass.: MIT Press.

Chomsky, N. 1970. "Remarks on Nominalization". In R. Jacobs and P. Rosenbaum, eds., *Readings in English Transformational Grammar*. Ginn-Blaisdell.

Chomsky, N. 1973. "Conditions on Transformations". In S. Anderson and P. Kiparsky, eds., *A Festschrift for Morris Halle*, 232–86. New York: Holt, Rinehart and Winston.

Chomsky, N. 1974. "The Amherst Lectures". Presented at the 1974 Linguistic Institute. *Documents Linguistiques*. Université de Paris VII.

Chomsky, N. 1977a. "On Wh-Movement". In Culicover et al. (1977).

Chomsky, N. 1977b. *Essays on Form and Interpretation*. New York/Amsterdam: North-Holland.

Chomsky, N. 1978. "On Opacity". In Greenbaum et al. (1980), 1–6.

Chomsky, N. 1980. "On Binding". *Linguistic Inquiry* 11.1.

Chomsky, N. 1981. *Lectures on Government and Binding*. Dordrecht: Foris.

Chomsky, N. 1982. *Some Concepts and Consequences of the Theory of Government and Binding*. Cambridge, Mass.: MIT Press.

Chomsky, N. 1984. "Changing Perspectives on Knowledge and Use of Language". Ms., MIT.

Chomsky, N. Forthcoming. *Knowledge of Language: Its Nature, Origin and Use*. Praeger.

Chomsky, N., et al. 1979. *La teoría estándar extendida*. Madrid: Cátedra.

Chomsky, N., and H. Lasnik. 1977. "Filters and Control". *Linguistic Inquiry* 8.3.

Cinque, G. 1976a. "Appropriateness Conditions for the Use of Passives and Impersonals in Italian". *Italian Linguistics* 1, 11–31.

Cinque, G. 1976b. "*Propio* e l'unita del *si*". *Rivista di grammatica generativa* 2, 101–13.

Cinque, G. 1980. "On Extraction from NP in Italian". *Journal of Italian Linguistics* 1.2. (Sometimes cited as Cinque (1979), ms.)

Cinque, G. 1984. "A'-bound *pro* vs. Variable". Ms., Università di Venezia.

Contreras, H. 1976. *A Theory of Word Order with Special Reference to Spanish*. North-Holland Linguistic Series 29. Amsterdam: North-Holland.

Contreras, H. 1982. "Small Clauses in Spanish". To appear in Hurtado (forthcoming).

Contreras, H. 1983. "ECP as an S-structure Principle". Ms., University of Washington.

Contreras, H. 1984a. "Multiple Questions in English and Spanish". In P. Baldi, ed., *Papers from the XIIth Linguistic Symposium on Romance Languages*. Amsterdam: John Benjamins.

Contreras, H. 1984b. "A Note on Parasitic Gaps". *Linguistic Inquiry* 15, 698–701.

Corominas, J., and J. Pascual. 1980. *Diccionario crítico etimológico castellano e hispánico*. Madrid: Gredos.

Culicover, P., T. Wasow, and A. Akmajian, eds. 1977. *Formal Syntax*. New York: Academic Press.

Demonte, V. 1985. "On Adjectival Predication". Ms., Universidad Autónoma de Madrid and MIT.

É. Kiss, K. 1981. "Structural Relations in Hungarian, a 'Free' Word Order Language". *Linguistic Inquiry* 12, 185–213.

Emonds, J. 1976. *A Transformational Approach to English Syntax*. New York: Academic Press.

Emonds, J. 1982. "VP Gerunds, S' Infinitives, and Required Theoretical Modifications". To appear in Hurtado (forthcoming).

Enç, M. 1983. "Anchored Expressions". *Proceedings of the West Coast Conference on Formal Linguistics* 2, 79-88. Stanford Linguistic Association.

Engdahl, E. 1983. "Parasitic Gaps". *Linguistics and Philosophy* 6, 5-34.

Epstein, S.D. 1984. "Quantifier-pro and the LF Representation of PRO-arb". *Linguistic Inquiry* 15, 499-505.

Erteschik, N. 1973. *On the Nature of Island Conditions*. Doctoral dissertation, MIT, Cambridge, Mass.

Evans, G. 1980. "Pronouns". *Linguistic Inquiry* 11, 337-62.

Evans, G. 1982. *The Varieties of Reference*. Edited by J. McDowell. Oxford University Press.

Farley, R. 1965. "Sequence of Tenses: A Useful Principle?" *Hispania* 48, 549-53.

Farley, R. 1970. "Tine and the Subjunctive in Contemporary Spanish". *Hispania* 53, 466-75.

Freidin, R. 1985. *Foundations of Syntactic Theory*. Ms., Princeton University.

Gabriel, J. 1917. "Gramática ideológica: nueva oración activa". *Nosotros* (Buenos Aires) 25, 152-77.

Gee, J.P. 1977. "Comments on the Paper by Akmajian". In Culicover et al. (1977).

George, L., and J. Kornfilt. 1981. "Finiteness and Boundedness in Turkish". In F. Heny (1981), 105-27.

Gili Gaya, S. 1973. *Curso superior de sintaxis española*. (1st ed. 1961). Barcelona: Vox.

Giorgi, A. 1984. "Toward a Theory of Long Distance Anaphors: A GB Approach". To appear in *The Linguistic Review*.

Godard, D. 1983. "Anaphores et relatives en français". To appear in J. Guéron and J.Y. Pollock, eds., *Grammatical Representation*. Dordrecht: Foris.

Goodall, G.T. 1984. *Parallel Structures in Syntax*. Doctoral dissertation, University of California at San Diego.

Greenbaum, S., G. Leech, and J. Svartvik, eds. 1980. *Studies in English Linguistics for Randolph Quirk*. London/New York: Longman.

Greenberg, J.H., ed. 1978. *Universals of Human Language*. 4 vol. Stanford University Press, California.

Guéron, J. 1981. "Logical Operators, Complete Constituents, and Extraction Transformations". In R. May and J. Koster, eds., *Levels of Syntactic Representation*. Dordrecht: Foris.

Haegeman, L. 1984. "Remarks on Adverbial Clauses and Definite NP-Anaphora". *Linguistic Inquiry* 15, 712-15.

Haik, I. 1984. "Indirect Binding". *Linguistic Inquiry* 15, 185-224.

Harbert, W. 1982. "Should Binding Refer to SUBJECT?" *NELS* 12, 116-31, Amherst, Mass.

Harbert, W. 1983. "On the Definition of Binding Domains". *Proceedings of the West Coast Conference on Formal Linguistics* 2, 102-13. Stanford, California.

Hawkins, J.A. 1978. *Definiteness and Indefiniteness*. London: Croom Helm; Atlantic Highlands, N.J.: Humanities Press.

Heim, I.R. 1982. *The Semantics of Definite and Indefinite Noun Phrases*. Doctoral dissertation, University of Massachusetts at Amherst.

Hendrick, R. 1983. "The distribution of the Clitic *En* and the ECP". Paper read at the 13th Linguistic Symposium on Romance Languages, Chapel Hill, North Carolina.

Heny, F., ed. 1981. *Binding and Filtering*. London: Croom Helm; MIT Press.

Higginbotham, J. 1983. "Logical Form, Binding, and Nominals". *Linguistic Inquiry* 14, 395-420.

Higginbotham, J. 1984. "Indefiniteness and Predication". Ms., MIT.

Holmback, H.K. 1982. *The Interpretation of Definite and Indefinite Descriptions*. Doctoral dissertation, University of Southern California.

Horn, G. 1975. "On the Nonsentential Nature of the POSS-ing construction". *Linguistic Analysis* 1, 333-88.

Hornstein, N. 1984. *Logic as Grammar*. Cambridge, Mass.: MIT Press.

Huang, J. 1982a. *Logical Relations in Chinese and the Theory of Grammar*. Doctoral disseration, MIT, Cambridge, Mass.

Huang, J. 1982b. "Move WH in a Language without WH Movement". *The Linguistic Review* 1, 369–416.

Huang, J. 1983. "A note on the Binding Theory". *Linguistic Inquiry* 14, 554–61.

Humboldt, W. von. 1971. *Linguistic Variability and Intellectual Development*. Translated by G.C. Buck and F.A. Raven. Coral Gables, Florida: University of Miami Press. Originally published in 1836 by the Royal Academy of Sciences of Berlin under the title *Über die Verschiedenheit des menschlichen Sprachbaues und ihren Einfluss auf die geitige Entwicklung des Menschengeschlechts*.

Hurtado, A. 1982a. "The Unagreement Hypothesis". To appear in L. King and C. Maley, eds., *Selected Papers from the Thirteenth Linguistic Symposium on Romance Languages*. Amsterdam: John Benjamins.

Hurtado, A. 1982b. "Clitic Chains". To appear in Hurtado (forthcoming).

Hurtado, A. 1983. "On the Properties of LF'". To appear in *Cornell Working Papers in Linguistics*, vol. 5.

Hurtado, A. Forthcoming. *Linguistic Theory and Spanish Syntax*. Dordrecht: Reidel.

Hyams, N. 1983. *The Acquisition of Parameterized Grammars*. Doctoral dissertation, C.U.N.Y.

Ingram, D. 1978. "Typology and Universals of Personal Pronouns". In Greenberg (1978), vol. 3 (Word Structure), 213–47.

Jackendoff, R. 1972. *Semantic Interpretation in Generative Grammar*. Cambridge, Mass.: MIT Press.

Jackendoff, R. 1977. $\overline{X}$ *Syntax: A Study of Phrase Structure*. Linguistic Inquiry Monograph 2. Cambridge, Mass.: MIT Press.

Jaeggli, O. 1982. *Topics in Romance Syntax*. Dordrecht: Foris.

Jaeggli, O. 1984. "Passive". Ms., Univ. of Southern California.

Jespersen, O. 1924. *The Philosophy of Grammar*. London: George Allen & Unwin Ltd.

Kany, C. 1969. *Sintaxis hispanoamericana*. Madrid: Gredos.

Kärde, Sven. 1943. *Quelques manières d'exprimer l'idée d'un sujet indéterminé ou général en espagnol*. Uppsala.

Kayne, R. 1975. *French Syntax*. Cambridge, Mass.: MIT Press.

Kayne, R. 1980. "Extensions of Binding and Case Marking". *Linguistic Inquiry* 11.1.

Kayne, R. 1981a. "ECP Extensions". *Linguistic Inquiry* 12, 93–133.

Kayne, R. 1981b. "On Certain Differences Between French and English". *Linguistic Inquiry* 12, 349–71.

Kayne, R. 1983. "Chains, Categories External to S, and French Complex Inversion". *Natural Language and Linguistic Theory* 1.1.

Keyser, S.J., and T. Roeper. 1984. "On the Middle and Ergative Constructions in English". *Linguistic Inquiry* 15, 381–416.

Koopman, H. 1984. *The Syntax of Verbs*. Dordrecht: Foris.

Koster, J. 1978. "Why Subject Sentences Don't Exist". In S.J. Keyser, ed., *Recent Transformational Studies in European Languages"*. Cambridge, Mass.: MIT Press.

Koster, J. 1984. "On Binding and Control". *Linguistic Inquiry* 15, 417–59.

Kuno, S. 1972. "Functional Sentence Perspective". *Linguistic Inquiry* 3, 269–320.

Kuno, S. 1973. "Constraints on Internal Clauses and Sentential Subjects". *Linguistic Inquiry* 4.3.

Lasnik, H., and R. Freidin, 1981. "Disjoint Reference and the Theory of Trace". *Linguistic Inquiry* 12, 39–53.

Lasnik, H., and M. Saito. 1984. "On the Nature of Proper Government". *Linguistic Inquiry* 15.2.

Lightfoot, D., and N. Hornstein. 1984. "Rethinking Predication". To appear.

Lo Cascio, V. 1974. "Alcune strutture della frase impersonale italiana". In Medici and Sangregorio (1974), vol. I, 167–95.

Lo Cascio, V., ed., 1976a. *Passive and Impersonal Sentences*. Dordrecht: Foris. (= Italian Linguistics 1).

Lo Cascio, V., ed. 1976b. *On Clitic Pronominalization*. Dordrecht: Foris.(= Italian Linguistics 2).

Longobardi, G., 1984. "Some Remarks on Connectedness and C-command". In W. de Geest and Y. Putseys, eds., *Sentential Complementation*, 151-65. Dordrecht: Foris.

Longobardi, G. 1985. "Connectedness, Scope and C-command". *Linguistic Inquiry* 16, 163-92.

Luján, M. 1980. "Clitic Promotion and Mood in Spanish Verbal Complements". *Linguistics* 18, 381-484.

Manzini, R. 1983a. "On Control and Control Theory". *Linguistic Inquiry* 14, 421-46.

Manzini, R. 1983b. *Restructuring and Reanalysis*. Doctoral dissertation, MIT, Cambridge, Mass.

Marantz, A. 1982. "On the Acquisition of Grammatical Relations". *Linguistische Berichte* 80-82, 32-69.

Marantz, A. 1984. *On the Nature of Grammatical Relations*. Cambridge, Mass.: MIT Press.

Martín Zorraquino, M.A. 1979. *Las construcciones pronominales en español: Paradigmas y desviaciones*. Madrid: Gredos.

May, R., and J. Koster, eds. 1981. *Levels of Syntactic Representation*. Dordrecht: Foris.

McCloskey, P., and K. Hale. 1983. "The Syntax of Inflection in Modern Irish". *NELS* 13, 173-90. Amherst, Mass.

Medici, M., and A. Sangregorio, eds. 1974. *Fenomeni morfologici e sintattici nell'italiano contemporaneo*. Roma: Bulzoni.

Meireles, J., and E. Raposo. 1984. "Tense and Binding Theory in Portuguese". Ms.

Milner, J.C., 1975. "A propos des génitifs adnominaux en français". In *Actes du Colloque Franco-Allemand de Linguistique Théorique*, Tübingen.

Monge, F. 1955. "Las frases pronominales de sentido impersonal en español". *Archivo de Filología Aragonesa* 7, 7-102.

Montalbetti, M. 1984. *After Binding. On the Interpretation of Pronouns*. Doctoral dissertation, MIT, Cambridge, Mass.

Napoli, D.J. 1976. "At Least Two *si*'s". In Lo Cascio (1976b), 123-48.

Napoli, D.J. 1981. "Semantic Interpretation vs. Lexical Governance: Clitic Climbing in Italian". *Language* 57, 841-87.

Newmeyer, F.J. 1980. *Linguistic Theory in America: The First Quarter-Century of Transformational Generative Grammar*. New York: Academic Press.

Nishigauchi, T. 1984. "Control and the Thematic Domain". *Language* 60, 215-50.

Obaid, A. 1967. "A Sequence of Tenses? - What Sequence of Tenses? *Hispania* 50, 112-19.

Oca, E. 1914. "El pronombre *se* en nominativo". *Boletín de la Real Academia Española* 1, 573-81.

Otero, C.P. 1968. *Introducción a la lingüística transformacional: Retrospectiva de una confluencia*. 5th edition. México: Siglo XXI, 1977.

Otero, C.P. 1974. "Grammar's Definition vs. Speaker's Judgment: From the Psychology to the Sociology of Language". Ms., UCLA. (French translation in Ronat (1977), 123-51; Spanish translation, enlarged, in Chomsky et al. (1979), 131-75).

Otero, C.P. 1984. *La revolución de Chomsky: Ciencia y Sociedad*. Madrid: Tecnos.

Padilla-Rivera, J. 1985. *On the Definition of Binding Domains in Spanish: The Roles of the Binding Theory Module and the Lexicon*. Doctoral dissertation, Cornell University.

Parisi, D. 1976. "*Lo* sta a *suo* come *si* sta a *propio*". *Rivista di Grammatica Generativa* 1, 99-102.

Perlmutter, D. 1971. *Deep and Surface Structure Constraints in Syntax*. New York: Holt.

Perlmutter, D. 1978. "Impersonal Passives and the Unaccusative Hypothesis". *Proceedings of the 4th Annual Meeting of the Berkeley Linguistic Society*, 157-89.

Pesetsky, D. 1982. *Paths and Categories*. Doctoral dissertation, MIT, Cambridge, Mass.

Picallo, M.C. 1984a. "The Infl Node and the Null Subject Parameter". *Linguistic Inquiry* 15, 75-102.

Picallo, M.C., 1984b. "La interpretació obviativa i la noció 'categoria de règim'". *Estudis Gramaticals 1*, 217–48. *Working Papers in Linguistics*, Universitat Autònoma de Barcelona, Bellaterra.

Picallo, M.C. 1985. *Opaque Domains*. Doctoral dissertation, C.U.N.Y.

Piera, C. 1982. "On the Structure of Infinitival Clauses". To appear in Hurtado (forthcoming).

Plann, S. 1984a. "On Case Marking S' in Spanish". Ms., UCLA.

Plann, S. 1984b. "Cláusulas cuantificadas". To appear in *Verba*.

Postal, P. 1966. "On So-called Pronouns in English". Reprinted in Reibel and Schane 1969, 201–24.

Quicoli, C. 1976. "Conditions on Clitic Movement in Portuguese". *Linguistic Analysis 2*, 192–223.

Ramsey, M. 1956. *A Textbook of Modern Spanish*. Revised by R.K. Spaulding. New York: Holt, Rinehart and Winston.

Randeri, M. 1980. *The Use of Clitics in Spanish Between the Ages of Five and Nine*. Doctoral dissertation, UCLA.

Rappaport, M. 1983. "On the Nature of Derived Nominals". In L. Levin, M. Rappaport, and A. Zaenen, eds., *Papers in Lexical Functional Grammar*. Indiana University Linguistics Club.

Real Academia Española (RAE). 1974. *Esbozo de una nueva gramática de la lengua española*. Madrid: Espasa-Calpe.

Reibel, D.A., and S.A. Schane, eds. 1969. *Modern Studies in English: Readings in Transformational Grammar*. Englewood Cliffs, N.J.: Prentice-Hall.

Reinhart, T. 1976. *The Syntactic Domain of Anaphora*. Doctoral dissertation, MIT, Cambridge, Mass.

Reuland, E. 1981. "On Extraposition of Complement Clauses". In V. Burke and J. Pustejovsky, eds., *Proceedings of the Eleventh Annual Meeting of the N.E.L.S.*

Reuland, E. 1983. "Governing -*ing*". *Linguistic Inquiry* 14, 101–36.

Riemsdijk, H. van. 1980. "On Theories of Case: The Case of German Adjectives". Ms., University of Amsterdam and MIT.

Rigau, G. 1982. "On the Avoid Pronoun Principle and the Emphatic Operator". Ms., Universitat Autònoma de Barcelona and MIT.

Rigau, G. 1984. "Connexity Established by Emphatic Pronouns". In M.E. Conte, J.S. Petöfi, and E. Sözer, eds., *Text and Discourse Connectedness*. Amsterdam.

Rivero, M.L. 1970. "A surface Structure Constraint on Negation in Spanish". *Language* 46, 640–66.

Rizzi, L. 1976. "La *montée du sujet*, le *si* impersonnel et une règle de restructuration dans la syntaxe italienne". *Recherches Linguistiques* 4.

Rizzi, L. 1978. "Violations of the *Wh* Island Constraint in Italian and the Subjacency Condition". In *Montreal Working Papers in Linguistics*, vol. 11, 1980.

Rizzi, L. 1980. "Negation, Wh Movement and the Null-subject Parameter". In Rizzi (1982).

Rizzi, L. 1982. *Issues in Italian Syntax*. Dordrecht: Foris.

Ronat, M., ed. 1977. *Théorie générative étendue*. Paris: Hermann.

Ronat, M. 1979. "Pronoms topiques et pronoms distinctifs". *Langue Française* 44, 106–28.

Rosenbaum, P. 1967. *The Grammar of English Predicate Complement Constructions*. Cambridge, Mass.: MIT Press.

Ross, J. 1967. *Constraints on Variables in Syntax*. Doctoral dissertation, MIT, Cambridge, Mass.

Rothstein, S. 1983. *The Syntactic Forms of Predication*. Doctoral dissertation, MIT, Cambridge, Mass.

Rouveret, A., and J.-R. Vergnaud. 1980. "Specifying Reference to the Subject: French Causatives and Conditions on Representation". *Linguistic Inquiry* 11.1

Ruwet, N. 1972. *Théorie syntaxique et syntaxe du français*. Paris: Seuil.

Safir, K., 1982. *Syntactic Chains and the Definiteness Effect*. Doctoral dissertation, MIT, Cambridge, Mass.

Safir, K. 1983. "On Small Clauses as Constituents". *Linguistic Inquiry* 14, 730–35.

Saito, M., and H. Hoji. 1983. "Weak Crossover and Move alpha in Japanese". *Natural Language and Linguistic Theory* 1, 245–59.

Sandfeld, Kr. 1982. *Syntaxe du français contemporaine: 1. Le pronoms*. Paris: H. Champion.

Schroten, J. 1978. "Marking Rules and the Underlying Order of Constituents in Spanish". *Utrecht Working Papers in Linguistics* 6.

Schroten, J. 1981. "Subject Deletion or Subject Formation: Evidence from Spanish". *Linguistic Analysis* 7, 121–69.

Schwartz, A. 1975. "Verb-Anchoring and Verb-Movement". In C. Li, ed., *Word Order and Word Order Change*. Austin and London: University of Texas Press.

Simpson, J. 1983. *Aspects of Walpiri Morphology and Syntax*. Doctoral dissertation, MIT, Cambridge, Mass.

Sloat, C. 1969. "Proper Nouns in English". *Language* 45, 26–30.

Solan, L. 1984. "Focus and Levels of Representation". *Linguistic Inquiry* 15, 174–78.

Sportiche, D. 1981. "Bounding Nodes in French". *The Linguistic Review* 1, 219–46.

Sportiche, D. 1983. *Structural Invariance and Symmetry*. Doctoral dissertation, MIT, Cambridge, Mass.

Stowell, T. 1981. *Origins of Phrase Structure*. Doctoral dissertation, MIT, Cambridge, Mass.

Stowell, T. 1983. "Subjects Across Categories". *The Linguistic Review* 2, 285–312.

Strozer, J. 1976. *Clitics in Spanish*. Doctoral dissertation, UCLA.

Suñer, M. 1980. "Clitic Promotion in Spanish Revisited". In F. Nuessel, ed., *Contemporary Studies in Romance Languages*. Bloomington: Indiana University Linguistics Club.

Suñer, M. 1982a. *The Syntax and Semantics of Presentational-Type Sentences in Spanish*. Washington, D.C.: Georgetown. University Press.

Suñer, M. 1982b. "Big PRO and Little *pro*". To appear in Hurtado (forthcoming).

Suñer, M. 1983. "*pro*$_{arb}$". *Linguistic Inquiry* 14, 188–91.

Suñer, M. 1984. "Controlled *pro*". In P. Baldi, ed., *Papers from the XIIth Linguistic Symposium on Romance Languages*. Amsterdam/Philadelphia: Benjamins.

Suñer, M., and J. Padilla-Rivera. 1984. "On the Subjunctive and the Role of the Features of INFL: Evidence from a Null Subject Language". Ms., Cornell University.

Torrego, E. 1984. "On Inversion in Spanish and Some of Its Effects". *Linguistic Inquiry* 15, 103–29.

Travis, L. 1984. *Parameters and Effects of Word Order Variation*. Doctoral dissertation, MIT, Cambridge, Mass.

Valesio, P. 1976. "Between Italian and French: The Fine Semantics of Active vs., Passive". In Lo Cascio (1976a), 107–44.

Wahl, A. 1985. "Two Types of Locality". Ms.

Wasow, T., and T. Roeper. 1972. "On the Subject of Gerunds". *Foundations of Language* 8, 44–61.

Westphal, G. 1980. *Subjects and Pseudo-subjects in Spanish: The verb Agreement Question in the Impersonal "se" Construction*. Carbondale: Linguistic Research, Inc.

Williams, E. 1975. "Small Clauses in English". In J.P. Kimball, ed., *Syntax and Semantics*, vol. 4. New York: Seminar Press.

Williams, E. 1980. "Predication". *Linguistic Inquiry* 11, 203–38.

Williams, E. 1981. "Argument Structure and Morphology". *The Linguistic Review* 1, 81–114.

Williams, E. 1982. "The NP Cycle". *Linguistic Inquiry* 13, 277–95.

Williams, E. 1983. "Against Small Clauses". *Linguistic Inquiry* 14, 287–308.

Zagona, K. 1982. *Government and Proper Government of Verbal Projections*. Doctoral dissertation, University of Washington, Seattle.

Zubizarreta, M.L. 1979. "Extraction from NP and Reformulation of Subjacency". Ms., MIT.

Zubizarreta, M.L. 1982. *On the Relationship of the Lexicon to the Syntax*. Doctoral dissertation, MIT, Cambridge, Mass.

Zubizarreta, M.L. 1985. "The Relation between Morpho-phonology and Morpho-syntax: The Case of Romance Causatives". *Linguistic Inquiry* 16, 247–89. (Sometimes cited as Zubizarreta (1983), ms.)

Index

A-binding, 167, 188
A'-binding, 78
A-chain, 61–3, 112–14, 118
A'-chain, 2
A-position, 29, 83, 87, 155, 165, 170–2
A'-position, 1, 5, 11, 146
absolute construction, 72–4
absorber clitic, 85, 90–1, 99
absorption of θ-role, 54, 61
accessible subject, 3, 6, 9–10, 166–7
accusative clitic, 157–8
adjacency, 3–11, 14, 16, 24n12, 42, 132
Adjacency Condition, 132
adjectival predication in passive sentences,
　51–66
adjunction to S, 45, 48n16, 69–71
　Move-alpha in Spanish as rightward
　　adjunction, 75–6, 78
adverb preposing, 40
adverbial clause, 1–8, 11, 14, 19, 23n10, 57
adverbial gap, 11–15, 21
AGR, 86, 93–4, 99, 104n35, 113–14,
　117–18, 143, 166–7, 178
Akmajian, A., 48
anaphor, 1–6, 10, 13–15, 21, 33, 81,
　166–9, 175–80, 183, 194
　long-distance, 168–9
anaphoric chain, 6, 23n4
anaphoric gap, 11–14
anaphoric variable, 1, 15, 20–1
Anderson, S., 195
antecedent, 6–21, 112, 146–7, 152, 155,
　177–80, 194
Aoun, J., 5, 6, 21, 30, 47, 57, 100, 111,
　113, 160, 166, 180
arbitrary *pro*, 58
arbitrary PRO, 6, 82, 196n9
arbitrary subject, 81–109
Argente, J., 116
argument, 54–6, 95, 111–19, 122, 165,

169, 174–80, 190–1
　external, 54–6, 61–4
　see also A-chain; A-position
AS-government, 30–4, 37, 48n10
Avoid Pronoun Principle, 100n4, 148–9,
　183, 186–7

Badia, A.M., 160
Baker, M., 55, 66
Baltin, M., 48n16
Bar-Hillel, Y., 101, 102
bare NP, 25–49, 175–9
Bastos, L.O., 102
Belletti, A., 11, 12, 82, 83, 101, 102, 103,
　104, 197
Bello, A., 45–6, 137, 139
binding, 58, 78, 96, 112, 154, 178
　binding in NPs, 165–81
　binding properties of possessives, 165–73
Binding Theory, 1–2, 5–10, 13–15, 21, 32,
　61–2, 81, 100, 144, 147–8, 158–9,
　165–74, 180, 183–95
Bok-Bennema, R., 23, 108
Bordelois, I., 5, 20, 49, 67, 77, 196
Borer, H., 83, 94, 101, 141, 160, 180
Bouchard, D., 6, 17, 21, 23, 101, 180, 183,
　186, 196
bouding node (*see also* subjacency), 16,
　70–1
Brandi, L., 102
Bresnan, J., 127
Breton, 93
Brown, C.B., 103
Brucart, J.M., 149, 161
Burge, T., 101
Burzio, L., 26, 30, 41, 61, 82, 90, 99, 102,
　103, 104, 106, 109, 113, 119

c-command, 2, 7, 14, 53, 56–7, 63–4,
　112–13, 147, 150, 153, 166, 176–9,
　188